LIFE AT HEA

MEMORIES OF WOR

HEAD WRIGHTSON

THORNABY-ON-TEES

HEAD WRIGHTSON & Co
No 21
TEESDALE IRON WORKS
STOCKTON ON TEES
1870

Editor: Margaret Williamson

Head Wrightson Thornaby (pre-1948)

Head Wrightson Thornaby (post 1948)

Dedicated to the men and women of Head Wrightson

Published by Teesside Industrial Memories Project, April 2013. ©
timp@uncommercial.co.uk

Designed and produced by Ambient Creative Services Ltd. 43 Swinburne Road, Darlington, Co. Durham DL3 7TD. Tel: 01325 364144 www.ambientcreative.com

Printed by Billingham Press Limited, 155 Central Avenue, Billingham TS23 1LF.

ISBN 978 0 9571307 1 5

Contents

	Preface	vii
	Family Tree	viii
	Acknowledgements	ix
	Foreword by Viscount Eccles	xi
	Head Wrightson: a brief history	xiii
Chapter 1	'I got the job, and I'm glad I did': starting work	1
Chapter 2	'It was tremendous work': jobs in Head Wrightson	15
Chapter 3	'Our bread-and-butter': Head Wrightson's products	41
Chapter 4	'Engineers to the World': Organisation of Head Wrightson	57
Chapter 5	'You had to appreciate how things were manufactured': training	85
Chapter 6	'It could get dangerous': health and safety	99
Chapter 7	'The atmosphere was always absolutely A1': relationships in the work place	107
Chapter 8	'The social side was excellent': benefits and facilities	123
Chapter 9	'I felt as if I was doing something for the war effort': Head Wrightson at war	139
Chapter 10	'It came as shock': closure	149
Chapter 11	'I loved it': final thoughts	165
	Contributors	167
	Photographic archives	171
	Colour photographic archives	177

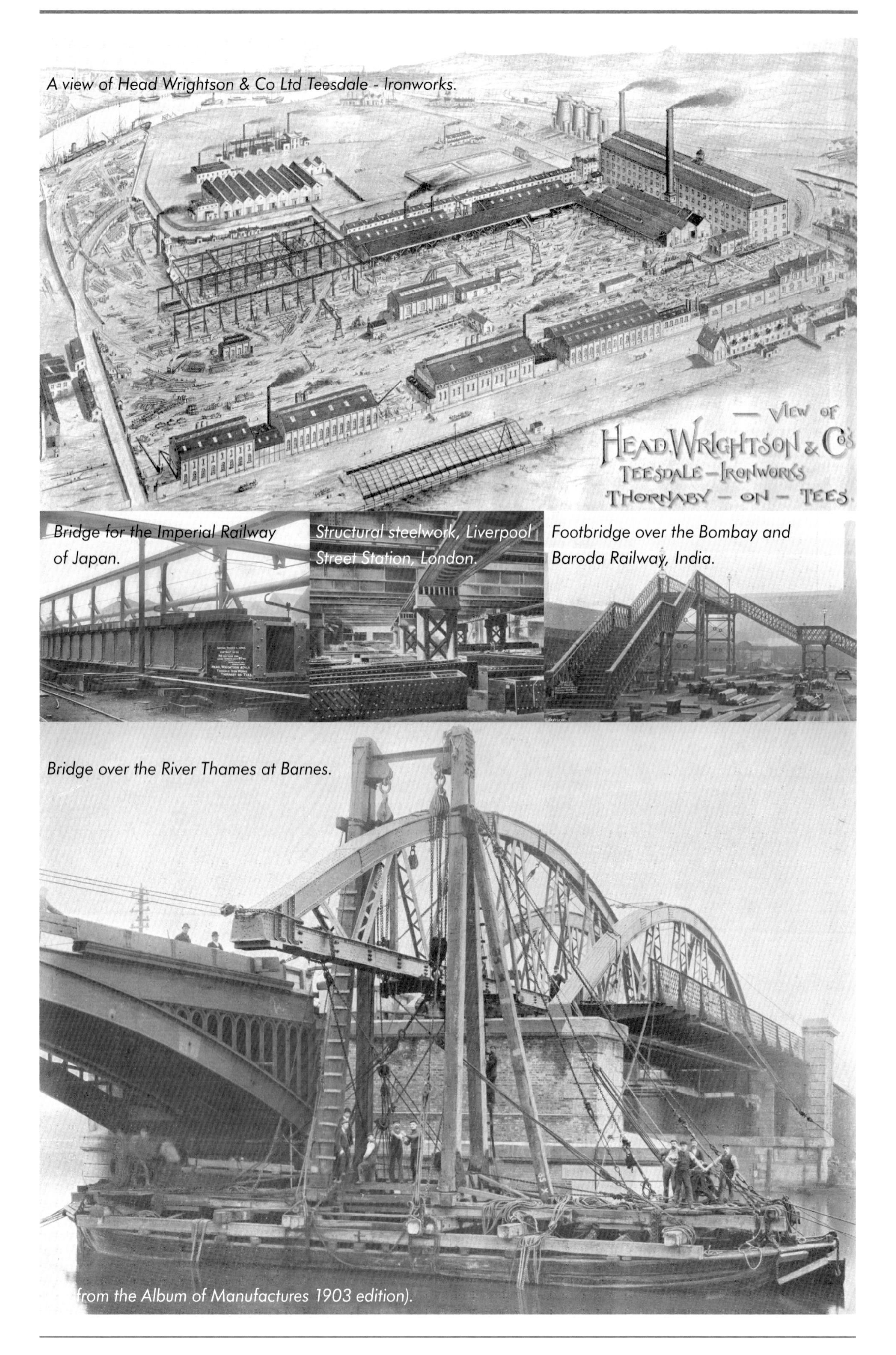

A view of Head Wrightson & Co Ltd Teesdale - Ironworks.

Bridge for the Imperial Railway of Japan.

Structural steelwork, Liverpool Street Station, London.

Footbridge over the Bombay and Baroda Railway, India.

Bridge over the River Thames at Barnes.

(from the Album of Manufactures 1903 edition).

Preface

This is the third book in the series produced by Teesside Industrial Memories Project. Previously we have completed volumes about ICI and Smith's Dock. We have now turned our attention to Teesside's engineering giant, Head Wrightson. This book records the experiences of over 90 former employees who agreed to be interviewed after responding to appeals in the local press, media and libraries.

We have once again talked to men and women who were representative of this large and varied workforce. Editing of the selected extracts from these interviews has been kept to a minimum and only done to improve the clarity of the book. For those who would like to examine the interviews in full, we intend to deposit recordings of the interviews and copies of the interview transcripts at Beamish Museum and Teesside Archives.

We also have included an account of the history of Head Wrightson written by Julian Phillips, the chairman of Teesside Industrial Memories Project. At the start of each chapter I have provided a small amount of relevant background information. We hope this supporting material helps to contextualize the interviews.

I would like to thank the members of Teesside Industrial Memories Project Management Committee for their support whilst compiling this volume; Josie Jones, Julian Phillips, Jean Richards and Albert Roxborough. Albert, in particular, has been instrumental in organizing this project and has always been generous with his extensive knowledge of Head Wrightson. As always, this book could not have been produced without the men and women who agreed to share their memories. It has been a privilege to listen to their experiences.

Margaret Williamson
December 2012

NB Throughout the text there are references to the Egglescliffe Iron Foundry and the Eaglescliffe Iron Foundry. The former is the original name of the site.

Family Tree

Head Wrightson senior staff at Norton Hall, the home of Thomas later Sir Thomas Wrightson, (circled left) and Charles Arthur Head (circled right). Sir Thomas later moved to Neasham Hall which became the family seat.

Charles Arthur Head (1838-1924) lived in the demolished Hartburn Hall now Jesmond Grove. He was the first Chairman.

Thomas Wrightson (1839-1921) was a Conservative MP for Stockton (1892-1889) and later for St. Pancras East (1899-1906). He was created a (1st) Baronet of Neasham Hall and appointed a Deputy Lieutenant of Durham in 1900. On incorporation of the company in 1890 he was appointed a director becoming Vice-Chairman in 1902.

Sir Guy Wrightson, (1871-1950) elder son of Sir Thomas, became a director in 1899 and later served as Chairman and Managing Director to his death in 1950.

His younger brother Wilfred was appointed a director in 1911 and remained so to his retirement in 1945.

Richard Miles was appointed as joint Managing Director in 1932. He succeeded to the Chairmanship on the death of Sir Guy in 1950. Standing down as Chairman in 1960 he remained on the Board to 1966.

Sir John Wrightson (1911-1983) was appointed to the Board in 1937 becoming Chairman and Managing Director of the Main Board in 1966 to his retirement in 1976. (The group was split into subsidiary companies in the 1960s and Sir John and Mr. Peter also held various positions as Chairmen and/or Managing Directors of the subsidiary companies).

His younger brother Peter Wrightson (1914-1995) was appointed a director in 1948, becoming the main Board Vice-Chairman and Managing Director in 1960.

John Eccles was appointed to the board in 1964 becoming company Managing Director in 1968 and from 1976 combined that role with company Chairman to 1977.

Acknowledgements

It is with pride and pleasure in equal measure that TIMP launches its third book of industrial memories in just five years. 'Life at Head's joins 'Life at the ICI' and 'Life at the Yard' not just as a serious industrial social history of a time when the industries of Teesside were buzzing and growing, but perhaps more importantly as a fun read. Anyone who has worked in these companies, or has relatives and friends who knew people in them, should enjoy these tales of life as it really was. The tears, the toil, and the laughter are all here; but, above all, what comes through all three books is the pride and camaraderie of those years.

Like any big project, it was truly a team effort. Firstly, we must thank our funders: the Tees Valley Community Foundation, the Ropner Trust, and Thornaby Town Council whose initial grant enabled us to print the leaflet with which we recruited our interviewees. The prodigious efforts of two people were crucial to our success: Albert Roxborough who brought the idea to the TIMP Committee, and then coordinated and administered the whole project and also undertook most of the interviewing himself; then Margaret Williamson, who retired eighteen months ago from Teesside University, has again worked indefatigably weaving her magic in turning many hours of interviews into a manageable and entertaining book.

But like an arch, each and every brick is needed or it will fall down. So every bit of specialist support was equally key to the project. Albert was joined in his interviewing by Carol Johnson (a practical example of how our numerous links with the History Department of Teesside University have proved so important to us), Josie Jones, Ken Oliver, John Robinson and Margaret Williamson, our editor herself. Margaret Hope digitized many old historical items about the Head Wrightson company as well as editing many of the raw interview transcripts. Derek Proctor compiled the contributors' photographic section and helped with photographic repair and enhancement as did Ken Oliver.

Teesside Archives were again very helpful in providing historical photographs and maps, whilst the Stockton Borough Library Service helped with company history and photographs as did Caparo Forgings. Teesside University, Stockton Borough Council and Stockton Cricket Club helped us with free meeting rooms, whilst our launch in April 2013 was at the Borough's Preston Hall Museum, a very worthy venue indeed. We must also thank Councillor Bob Cook, leader of Stockton Borough Council, for formally launching this book.

Steam tube terephthalic acid dryer for ICI Wilton. (Photograph courtesy Ian Semple)

The vital task of transcribing the interviews was done as before by Carolyn Mumford; whilst the design of the book, unique to Head's but clearly one of our series, was again done by Greg Marshall's Ambient Creative Services. The final stage of production, the painstaking task of proof reading was undertaken once more with his customary care by Sid Field. Meanwhile TIMP as an organization has continued to be run smoothly by Jean Richards, our Secretary, who has continued to inform and entertain us with a flow of newsletters.

Finally, I do hope that that long list is complete; if I have inadvertently left anyone out, please accept my apologies. I can only repeat, this has throughout been a tremendous team effort and TIMP thanks you all.

But perhaps after all that, I've left out the real heroes: you, the interviewees, for without you giving up your time to tell us your stories there would be no industrial memories for our readers to enjoy. So please, reader, do enjoy and do share in the pride of the people whose memories made this book.

'A Pride Job': A Video by Derek Smith

Fairly soon after TIMP got going on 'Life at Head's' we met Derek Smith who had also started an interview video. Derek who has worked for ITV is now a freelance video documentary producer. He was born in Thornaby and Thornaby blood still runs through his veins!

At an early stage we decided to collaborate and not to compete; the book and the video are clearly complementary. So TIMP takes pride in presenting 'A Pride Job' together with 'Life at Head's'.

Congratulations and thank you Derek, you have certainly enhanced our project.

Julian Phillips
Chairman
Teesside Industrial Memories Project
April 2013

Cones and pressings under manufacture at HWT for thick wall reactors. (HW Photographic Section)

Foreword

By Viscount Eccles, CBE, former Head Wrightson MD 1968-77 & Group Chairman 1976-77

Coming down from university and following an interview with Richard Miles I joined HW in 1954 on a Frank Shepherd premium apprenticeship along with two or three others. I was twenty three and had done, as most then did, National Service. I lodged in 195, Durham Road and my landlady worked for the Council distributing coal ration coupons. I started in the Teesdale pattern shop and it was a great day when a pattern of mine went into the foundry. Then for about a year I experienced many of the skilled trades from moulding to turning and horizontal boring. I became a tolerable welder in days when the boilermakers frequented the Bradford Vaults at the bottom of Trafalgar Street. I recall the team at Seaton Carew giving forgings of mine one more blow under the hammer to be sure that they were 'in spec'. I had acquired a second hand bicycle which carried me swiftly from works to works

Viscount Eccles, CBE. (Photograph by Derek Smith)

although some of the smells in the 'wilderness' between Norton, where we lived by then, and the river were pretty nasty.

I went to Sheffield to Colliery Engineering and on to Maerdy Colliery in South Wales where HW were building a coal washing plant. There I remember the landlady's late night hymns at the piano together with thick bread Marmite and raw onion sandwiches. I still put raw onion in a sandwich!

Next I became Progress Chaser for the plates being prepared for the Bradwell boilers and then Clerk of the Works when the Heavy Plate Shop was being erected for HW Teesdale. The slipway used to launch those Bradwell boilers into the Tees for towing to site was under construction and the shipwrights nearby were busy finishing the sealing timbers of dock gates.

It was then that I was sent, arguably, to the most enjoyable job I ever did in my long career – Stockton Steel Foundry in Light Pipe Hall Road, Stockton. I found a superb team there the majority being time served craftsmen. Everybody seemed to know by instinct and from their mates exactly what to do and how to do it safely. I remember the foundry going like a sewing machine on the day when we and the French went into Suez in 1956. I still have a pair of trousers with small burnt holes made when the factory inspector came and we took him onto the casting floor to discourage too many visits.

Later I went on to Stockton Forge where HW designed and built mining and process equipment, our customers being as far apart as ICI and English China Clays in Cornwall, and in Africa, Sierra Leone and Ghana, Ashanti Gold fields being a long standing customer. And, of course, the Coal Board.

Later things became much more complicated, with subsidiary companies in Australia, Chile, India, South Africa, Spain and a joint venture in Brazil. Then, the inflation of the mid seventies and the failure of national planning to deliver a sound economy.

One day I may write about those difficult times but for now my abiding memories are HW's great range of skilled engineering capability and the friendship of all those who worked to deliver to our customers. I often think of the day when the Russian Vice Minister of Steel came to negotiate the Machine Company's bid for an electrolytic tinning line. HW got the contract as we did for so many iron and steel making customers. It is this amazing diversity of customer and product which stays with me today.

I am a frequent London Underground traveller and I often look to see the HW on tunnel segments as equally I remember Egglescliffe when in the Tyne Tunnel on the way to visit my daughter in Wallsend.

We are right to celebrate the history of HW. We have much to celebrate, HW made a great engineering contribution to today's society and we can recall it with pride.

JDE.

OFFICE OF
THE CHAIRMAN AND MANAGING DIRECTOR
HEAD WRIGHTSON & CO. LTD.
THORNABY-ON-TEES
TELEPHONE STOCKTON 6581

May 1952.

This book shows some of the things we make.

It goes out with my thanks to all those who have made its production possible.

Shortly we shall begin our second century as makers of heavy industrial equipment. The last century saw remarkable progress. The pace in future may be faster. At Head Wrightson's we shall try to play our part.

Richard Miles.

Introductory page from an old Head Wrightson product brochure circa 1950s.

Head Wrightson's : A Brief History

Such was the sign, known affectionately as the 'Plum Pudding', that once greeted travellers to the North as they arrived at King's Cross Station in London.

How Head Wrightson in Thornaby on Teesside in North East England grew to justify this proud claim, and how it suddenly declined in the 1970s to a merger in 1977 with Davy that was in reality a takeover, and then to final closure in 1984 is the subject of this brief overview of the company's history.

The First Beginnings – 1866 Purchase of the Teesdale Ironworks in South Stockton

The first works on the main site was the Teesdale Iron Works founded in 1840 on the recently opened extension to Middlesbrough of the Stockton and Darlington Railway – an early example of how the railways drove Victorian industrial expansion. The area was then known as South Stockton but was incorporated as the Borough of Thornaby from 1891. In 1866 the works was bought by Charles Arthur Head and Thomas Wrightson. They each invested £8,000 in the private company which became a public limited company in 1890 when its assets were valued at £310,000.

Over the years the Teesdale site expanded from its original five acres to 73 acres as more foundries, fabrication, welding and assembly shops together with machine and engineering shops, were built, whilst the former independent shipyards on the Tees (Richardson Duck and Craig Taylor's) were taken over as erection yards, offices and launching points for heavy fabricated vessels for the steel, chemical, and nuclear industries.

John W Wardell who wrote an internally circulated history of Head Wrightson & Company Limited from 1859 to 1952 described the growth of the company's activities thus:

> *From making small iron castings and cast-iron columns, girders and bridges at the beginning of the period, the firm progressed through the manufacturing of wrought-iron bridges for home and abroad, cast and wrought-iron blast furnace plant, dock and harbour work, general castings and forgings and mechanical engineering, to the beginning of the steel construction era.*

John Wardell then goes on to describe how the capabilities and product range of the company developed in the first half of the twentieth century.

> *From 1890 to 1952 there have been considerable changes to the layout and equipment of Teesdale Iron Works and in the classes of work manufactured there. The Engineering Division, the largest unit of the Head Wrightson Group, occupies the bulk of the site to the east of Trafalgar Street, which is favourably situated for rail, road, and river access. Loads up to 60 tons can be handled at the wharf and dock gates, caissons and other items can be launched direct into the river from the slipways.*
>
> *The constructional shops of four bays cover an area of 180,000 square feet, and are sub-divided into preparation, wagon, and assembly bays, with welding and press shops. These are served by a stock yard, template shop, and product storage yard. The shops are fitted with heavy modern equipment and lifts up to 60 tons can be made. In connection with the Class I welding shop, X-ray equipment is available. The light and heavy machine shops of three bays cover an area of 52,000 square feet, including assembly area and tool room, and boring up to 18 feet diameter can be accepted. The heat exchanger shop has an area of 16,000 square feet.*
> *The Engineering Division is divided into six sections; the Constructional Department, dealing with buildings, structures and bridge spans; the Dock and Harbour Department, handling floating docks, caissons, dock gates, opening bridges, slipways, pontoons, etc.; the Iron and Steel Plant Department, working in conjunction with the McKee Iron and Steel Division on blast-furnace plant including all accessories; the Process Plant Department, producing heat exchangers, fractionating towers, etc. for Head Wrightson Processes Limited; the Wagon Department dealing with all types of wagons for railways and blast-furnace plants; and the General Engineering Department handling copper converters and many kinds of heavy plate and machine work.*

Early Expansion: The Stockton Forge and Egglescliffe Foundry

In 1897 the company in search of extra capacity bought the Stockton Forge (seven and a half acres) and the Egglescliffe Foundry. Both had complex histories including changes of ownerships, but both became the "senior outside divisions" of the parent company. The Stockton Forge, originally established in 1870s, specialised in supplying equipment to coal mines, and from 1905 this work expanded to mine head frames, steel chimneys, tube mills, and cyanide tanks for South Africa. After the First World War this trade expanded to the copper belt of Northern Rhodesia, and later to many other countries in Africa and Asia. Indeed, a company was set up in Johannesburg, South Africa, in 1905 and in 1930 it started manufacturing on its own 30 acre site.

The Egglescliffe Foundry was originally seven acres, but by 1915 Head Wrightson had bought the worked-out clay pits from the Eaglescliffe Brick Company and the total became ten and a half acres. Until the end of the Second World War it acted as an overflow for the original Iron Foundries at Teesdale and Stockton Forge, but in 1950 it became the main iron foundry centre when the Stockton Forge foundry equipment was moved to Eaglescliffe and an extensive new investment was made in 1952 when John Wardell wrote:

> *The combined output of Egglescliffe and Teesdale iron foundries, which together constitute the Iron Foundries Division, is about 50,000 tons per annum, consisting mainly of haematite ingot moulds and bottoms for the steel industry, ranging from 2 to 30 tons each, cast-iron tunnel and mine tubbing segments, from 5 to 35 feet diameter, cast-iron chairs and base plates for the railways, and haematite and grey-iron castings from a few pounds to 40 tons for general purposes, including slag ladled for blast-furnace plants.*

In 1917 electric arc furnaces were installed at Thornaby enabling the manufacture of steel castings up to 35 tons. In 1927 a second steel foundry was purchased at Light Pipe Hall Road in Stockton and was also fully modernised at the time enabling the production of carbon, manganese and alloy steel castings. Steelcast, previously the Davy United Roll Foundry at Haverton Hill was bought by HW in 1971 when it changed to a more general steel casting role.

Other Subsidiary Companies

By 1976 the group included 22 subsidiaries in the UK and overseas but most of the manufacturing continued to be centred on Teesside. Other major outlying sites bought later by Head Wrightson included the stampings site at Seaton Carew, bought from the Earl of Eldon in 1938 for £800. A further one and a half acres were bought for £300 in 1942 to allow for expansion. Incidentally, Lord Eldon was not amused when he later visited and found that Head Wrightson had used London bricks and not the Lord's own Durham bricks for buildings on the site.

The Stampings operation originally housed on the ground floor of the old factory building at Thornaby was transferred to Seaton over a two year period. This then allowed better access to the steel stockyard and the opportunity to develop the Thornaby site.

By 1952 the output had risen to 12,000 tons/yr from hammers up to five tons producing forgings up to 300 pounds from bars to four inch diameter.

Stampings were transferred to Davy when the two companies merged in 1978, who sold it to Caparo Forgings in 1989. In 2013 it was still in operation with 15 former Head Wrightson employees working here. It was considered to have the hardest of working conditions, very noisy, very smelly, and very hot and was compared with Dante's inferno by interviewees. The Head Wrightson Machine Company in Middlesbrough, specialising in the design and manufacture of finishing equipment for steel and non-ferrous metals, was founded in 1939 and was a world leader in the design and building of plate levellers, sheet and strip processing equipment, galvanising, tinning, powder coating, tube drawing and other equipment. They moved to Middlesbrough in 1945 to extremely fine machine shops where they specialised solely in design, contracting and manufacture, their works being taken over in 1974 by Head Wrightson Teesdale who then had two manufacturing units at Thornaby and Middlesbrough.

The extension of skills and scope was facilitated by a great deal of research. This was brought together into a Research and Development Department in 1956 and became a Division in 1960. It employed 160 graduates and other staff who worked closely with all technical departments. Specialist staff included metallurgists, physicists, chemists, and computer operators. Few other UK companies in engineering devoted so much to development and place such emphasis on it. Examples of Head Wrightson's forward looking approach to engineering are its early use of CNC (Computer Numerically Controlled) machines especially for horizontal boring; the adoption of the CO_2 silicate process for forming casting moulds, and later the use of furan and sand which cut the scrap rate from 23% to just 0.6%.

To put the work of the R&D department into profitable practice there was a technical company HWISWEL (Head Wrightson Iron and Steelworks Engineering Limited) and a nuclear design and manufacturing facility. The design section started life at the Friarage in Yarm, but transferred to Teesdale in 1968. Before the 1977 merger with Davy both had been merged into PEL (Process Engineering Ltd) which became a part of Davy that still operates having been bought first by a Russian company, and then by Johnson Matthey Plc. It still trades under the name of Davy.

In 1957 the company bought the Friarage at Yarm, rebuilt by Edward Meynell (a name still around in Stockton) in the 1770s on the site of a medieval Dominican Friary. It had always been in the hands of Roman Catholic families and during restoration a priest hole was found. It was bought by Head Wrightsons in 1957 and first used as offices for Head Wrightson Processes Ltd. In the 1960s it was restored to its Georgian glory, and in 1966 became the headquarters of the group. It was occupied by the directors and non technical departments including legal, financial, publicity, and personnel. It is now occupied by Yarm School.

From its very beginnings Head Wrightson was a big exporter. By 1976 the Annual Report listed foreign subsidiaries in South Africa, India, Venezuela, and Spain and previously there had been companies in Australia, Canada and Brazil. These, however, were far from being the only countries worldwide where Head Wrightson products found a market. There were also associate companies in Spain, Chile, and Brazil, whilst in the 1930s an agreement had been made with the US company Arthur G. McKee of Cleveland, Ohio, to form a joint Head Wrightson McKee Company. This name persisted after the merger in 1978 as Davy McKee Ltd.

1931-1945: the Slump, the Recovery, and the War

The slump of 1931, which followed the 1929 Wall Street Crash, was savage and sudden. Older interviewees recount how the works was almost devoid of work. To ensure survival Sir Guy Wrightson mortgaged the family seat, Neasham Hall, near Hurworth-on-Tees. A large loan was arranged with Barclays Bank who in 1932 installed Richard Miles as General Manager. Both actions were aimed at long term survival which has often seemed sadly lacking in more recent responses to company problems in the UK.

Richard Miles, working with Sir Guy, is credited with steering Head Wrightson through the depression and taking advantage of rearmament in late 1930s so that the company was again making profits reaching £1 million/yr. He organised Head Wrightson for the demands of war production, many of which, like landing craft, were quite unexpected.

Early in the war the Germans used aerial photography to map and describe most of British industry in surprisingly accurate detail including "Eisenwerk (Ironworks) – Head Wrightson". In spite of this, however, of the 107 recorded bombing raids on Teesside from 1940 to 1943 only one on the night of 15/16 April 1941 seems to have resulted in damage to the Thornaby site. Two parachute mines were dropped; one on derelict buildings nearby, but the other fell on the union foundry and damaged the mine shop which machined bomb casings, the bar shop and the wagon shop. Also, one hundred and forty one houses were damaged. Five people were injured of whom one died later of shock.

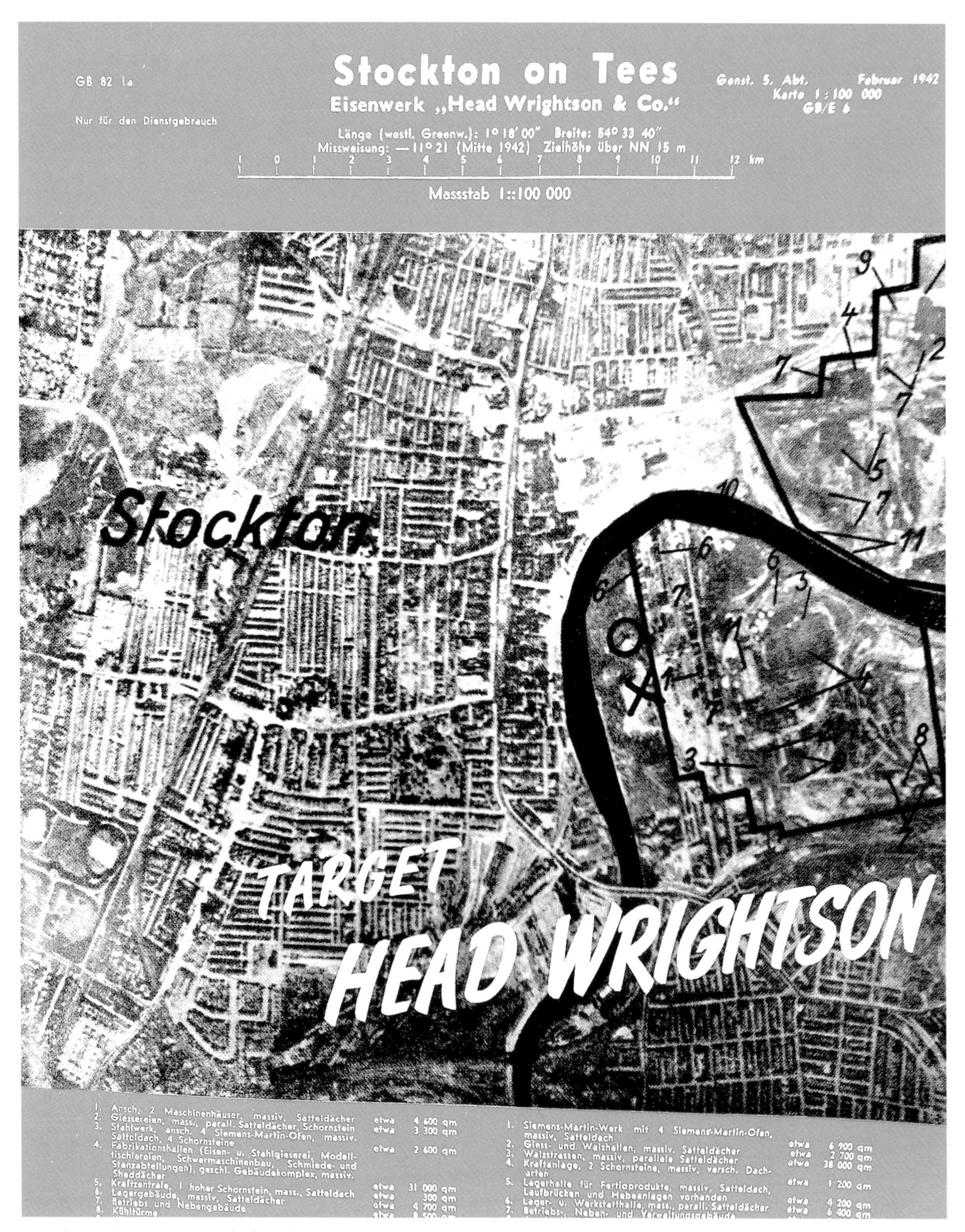

Head Wrightson was singled out by the Germans for a bombing attack. (HW Company brochure)

Modernisation after the War and merger with Davy

The post-war years were similarly successful, The Research Division was created, and there was a concentration on very high quality Apprentice Training (1945), which in turn ensured the high-quality production which justified the company's high reputation. Head Wrightson used its technical strengths to seize the opportunity to participate extensively and profitably in the first Magnox generation of nuclear reactors in the 1960s.

Indeed, the company became a shareholder in British Nuclear Associates Limited which coordinated the export of nuclear reactors. A well-qualified group of lawyers in the Secretary's Department oversaw all the contracts using their knowledge not only of English law, but also of the contract law of the many overseas countries in which the company operated. Again, this use of qualified lawyers to negotiate contracts was not common to all engineering companies, as Head Wrightson staff were to find out after the merger with Davy in 1977. Davy was a larger Sheffield-based engineering competitor with some facilities on Teesside. Paradoxically, less than ten years before, a cash strapped Davy had offered themselves to Head Wrightson for sale although the only outcome at that stage was the purchase of Steelcast, Billingham. Also an agreement was made with Davy that Head Wrightson would not sell directly to the steel industry while Davy would award the company with any subsequent steel industry fabrications.

The important role played by the company in the UK's economy was underlined when the then Prime Minister Harold Macmillan, the former MP for Stockton, visited the Thornaby site on 14th January 1959. At the time Head Wrightson were working on the Durgapur steel plant in India, the Bradwell nuclear power station in Essex and the Ross Spur project of the M5, all key projects for the UK's modernisation programme and for increasing exports. Interestingly, as well as meeting the nine directors and twenty senior staff he was introduced to over a 100 employees drawn from every department and workshop on the site.

Richard Miles stood down from the chairmanship in 1960 after a ten year tenure but remained on the board up to his retirement in 1966 leaving a well organised, technically strong company in the hands of Sir John

TEESDALE HALL

Catering Manager — Mr. V. Spence
Hall Manager — Mr. J. Rickelton
Secretary — Miss E. Thurlwell

Tees-side Colour Film Society	Mr. J. B. Milnes, (Sec.) Works Office.	Tuesday evening — each week
Institute of British Foundrymen	Mr. Frank Shepherd, President & Secretary	Friday evening — monthly
Head Wrightson Dramatic Society	Miss E. O'Hara, (Sec.) McKee Division.	Weekly
Miniature Air Rifle Club	Mr. E. Cooker, (Sec.) Constructional Dept.	Monday and Wednesday evenings
Head Wrightsons' Band	Mr. J. E. Burton, (Sec.) Alloy Shop.	Wednesday evenings and Sundays
Head Wrightson Salon Orchestra	Mr. Richard Blakey, Musical Director, Personnel Dept.	By arrangement.
	Athletic Sub-Committee	
Cricket	Mr. H. Wilson, (Sec.) Stockton Forge	Interdepartmental Matches
Football	Mr. J. H. Dickenson, (Sec.) Maintenance, D.O.	Cup & League Matches — Interdepartmentals
Bowls	Mr. A. Littlewood, (Sec.) Constructional Dept.	Cup & League Matches — Interdepartmentals
Lawn Tennis	Mr. E. Slack, Steel Castings, Mr. K. Proctor, Accounts (Joint Secs.)	Tournaments & Matches
Table Tennis	Mr. J. H. Dickenson, (Sec.) Maintenance D.O.	Cup & League — Interdepartmentals
Swimming	Mr. H. Ayre, (Sec.) Fitting Shop, Stockton Forge	Swimming Gala. Fortnightly Club Night at Stockton Baths.
Darts	Mr. W. E. Bartaby, (Sec.) Stockton Steel Foundry.	Leagues, Tournaments — Interdepartmentals
Entertainment	Mr. T. H. Harper, (Organiser) Constructional Dept.	Concerts, etc., in Club.

Welfare Sub-Committee

This committee is responsible for organising:-
Old Age Pensioners' Outing, Old Age Pensioners' Xmas Gifts, Children's Christmas Pantomime, Annual Fruit and Vegetable Show.

Activities available at Head Wrightson's in 1955 via the company and Works Council. (Wright Ahead)

Wrightson (Chairman 1960-1976) and his brother Peter. There were still good years to come and Peter proved to be an adept salesman across the globe.

The last Company Chairman was John Eccles, a nephew of Sir John. He was fully steeped in Head Wrightson's activities as he had joined in 1954, after National Service and university, as a premium apprentice which meant that he had worked on the shop floor in most departments before moving upwards into the management of the company.

Head Wrightson was, by the standards of post-war Britain, modern in its organisation, equipment and technical staffing. It was perhaps more traditional in its attitudes and ethos which was hierarchical and paternalistic. The hierarchical nature showed itself in the five levels of dining at the Teesdale and Stampings sites, plus another three at the Friarage in Yarm. The paternalism was shown not only by Sir John Wrightson's spoken concern for his staff, but also by the array of sports and social opportunities offered by the company to its employees. Indeed, the brass band survived well after the closure in 1984. Such paternalism is much derided in the twenty-first century, but was it really worse than the present Human

Margaret Thatcher's iconic walk in the HW wilderness in September 1987. It is now totally changed and home to Stockton Technical College, Durham University's Teesside Campus, offices, care homes and housing. There are no references among road or street names to its glorious HW history apart from the name Teesdale still appertaining to the site. (Photograph courtesy of Evening Gazette Media Company (GMC) Middlesbrough)

Resources approach? This seems to treat people as mere costs, as if they were just CNC machines or steam hammers for stamping.

The Final Years

Sadly, however, within twenty years Head Wrightson was to close, almost completely with a brief remission from 1984-1986 when ITM took over part of the site. When ITM closed, Davy sold the site to the Teesside Development Corporation who kept the name Teesdale for their prestigious development of offices, the Stockton Campus of Durham University, and Stockton Riverside College. All very clean, and very impressive, but the never-to-be replaced loss to the UK's manufacturing capacity from Head Wrightson and innumerable other British industrial companies, shows up month by month in the UK's negative balance of payment figures.

It is not possible to understand what happened in those last few years without looking at the economic environment of the times. The 1964 sterling crisis had weakened the UK's economy, although the devaluation of the pound against the dollar did provide a fillip for exports which Head Wrightson was able to take advantage of. The 1970s however, started with the three day week during the miners' strike which again shook the company's home markets. Then the oil crises of 1973 and 1979, and the rampant inflation that followed, made life increasingly difficult for British industry. Public investment tumbled after the government was forced to accept an IMF loan in 1975, and this meant that the previously regular flow of large orders from the big nationalised bodies such as the CEGB, the National Coal Board, British Steel and British Rail dried up. Meanwhile, as well as facing US and European competition, Japan, South Korea, and Taiwan were building new green field state-of-the-art factories using cheaper labour and pricing UK companies out of their traditional overseas markets even in the Commonwealth. The final straw came with the

Thatcher/Howe experiment with Chicagoan monetarism which raised the value of the pound so high as to make profitable exporting very difficult indeed.

Stockton Forge closed in 1969 and manufacturing and design transferred to Teesdale. Around the time of the merger (1978) Lazard's, merchant bankers, were asked by the government to prepare a report on the overcapacity in the UK foundry industry. They recommended the rationalisation of the foundry industry resulting in the closure of foundries throughout the country for recompense. Egglescliffe Iron Foundry was closed by 1982. Other HW foundry sites closed later, including Steelcast Ltd at Billingham in 1983 with the loss of 135 jobs. Middlesbrough Works closed in 1979 but not without a determined fight by the workforce to keep it open.

The intention was to strengthen the core activities, but as so often with root and branch change recommended by outside financial experts it unintentionally had the opposite result. Indeed, some of our interviewees involved in the process at the time described it as asset stripping. The end result was that the newly named Davy McKee closed what was left of Head Wrightson in 1984. However, given the economic background, the merger with Davy had seemed very sensible; a big force to attack the new Far East competition. But academic research has shown that few mergers achieve their original hopes of synergies, cost reductions, and increased sales and profits.

Putting two industrial cultures together is never easy; the changes take much longer to bed-in than expected, whilst the two partners jockey for supremacy. In the event, the external circumstances described above, overtook the Head Wrightson – Davy merger before it had had a real chance of success. And we were just left with Margaret Thatcher's September 1987 *walk in the wilderness*!

Sources

I must thank those former employees of Head Wrightson whose unpublished papers on various aspects of the company's history has made writing this brief overview possible. Sadly, many of the shorter notes on particular departments or sites are anonymous but those named are:

- 'A Brief History of Head, Wrightson & Company Limited from 1859-1952', John W Wardell 12 June 1952.
- 'The Work of Richard Miles', Ronnie Purnell Commercial Director, Head Wrightson Teesdale.
- 'The Friarage', Bob Irwin.
- 'The History of Thornaby', Lawrence Peter O'Harvey, February 1968.
- 'Stampings History', Albert Roxborough June 2012.
- 'A Brief History of Head Wrightson Company Limited 1859-1976', author unknown, supplied by Enid Thurlwell.

For the account of the air raid of 1941 I have consulted

- 'Bombs by the hundred over Stockton' by David Brown.
- 'Air Raid Diary' by Bill Norman.

Also, of course, many of the interviewees themselves, provided historical detail and insights, and I thank them too.

Julian Phillips
TIMP

Chapter 1

'I got the job, and I'm glad I did': starting work

The history of Head Wrightson can be traced back to the early 19th century when Teesdale Ironworks was established. This company was taken over by Thomas Head and Joseph Wright in 1859 and there were a number of name changes before the firm became known as Head Wrightson & Company in 1866.

Head Wrightson established an excellent reputation in the 19th century for building bridges, viaducts, piers, mining equipment and a wide range of iron and steel castings. Throughout the twentieth century the company continued to diversify, designing and manufacturing a range of engineering products such as nuclear plant and equipment, heat exchangers, iron and steel plant and equipment, steel castings and stampings, dock and harbour equipment, and forgings many for automotive parts. Such a successful company was an important source of local employment and at its height more than 5,000 men and women were employed at six sites around Teesside in the extensive range of jobs needed to sustain production.

The following interview extracts demonstrate the status of Head Wrightson in the local community and the high value placed on getting a job there. An apprenticeship at Head Wrightson was especially sought after. Explore below our contributors' feelings about joining and working for Head Wrightson.

DICTATED BY

ALL ORDERS ARE ACCEPTED SUBJECT TO THE USUAL STRIKE AND ACCIDENT CLAUSE.

TELEGRAMS:- "TEESDALE, VIC. LONDON." "TEESDALE, STOCKTON ON TEES."

TELEPHONE Nº 587 (4 LINES)

CODES:- LIEBERS, WESTERN UNION, BENTLEYS, A.B.C. 5TH EDITION.

MSB JT

HEAD, WRIGHTSON & Cº LIMITED.

STOCKTON FORGE, STOCKTON-ON-TEES. TELEPHONE Nº 568.

EGGLESCLIFFE FOUNDRY, STOCKTON ON TEES.

LONDON OFFICE: 5, VICTORIA STREET, WESTMINSTER, S.W.1.

PARIS OFFICE:- 6, BOULEVARD DES CAPUCINES.

SOUTH AFRICAN OFFICE:- P.O. BOX 1034, JOHANNESBURG.

CANADIAN AGENTS:- MACKAY BROTHERS, 14, ROSS BLOCK, SYDNEY, NOVA SCOTIA.

S. A. WILLIAMS, 847, BEATTY STREET, VANCOUVER, B.C.

Registered Office:-
TEESDALE IRON WORKS,
THORNABY ON TEES.

UNDER GOVERNMENT CONTROL.

26th February, 1918.

Mr. Edward Moss,
17, Saint Bernards Road,
STOCKTON/TEES.

Dear Sir,

RE APPRENTICE EXAMINATION

We are pleased to inform you that your work at the above examination has been proved satisfactory.

We therefore wish you to present yourself at the Drawing Office at 8-45 am. on Monday 11th March 1918, to commence work for one month on probation.

We are,

Yours faithfully,
HEAD, WRIGHTSON & Co., LIMITED.
Joseph Thompson
Chief Draughtsman

Successful apprentice examination letter from 1918. Found in a house clearance. (Supplied by D. Proctor)

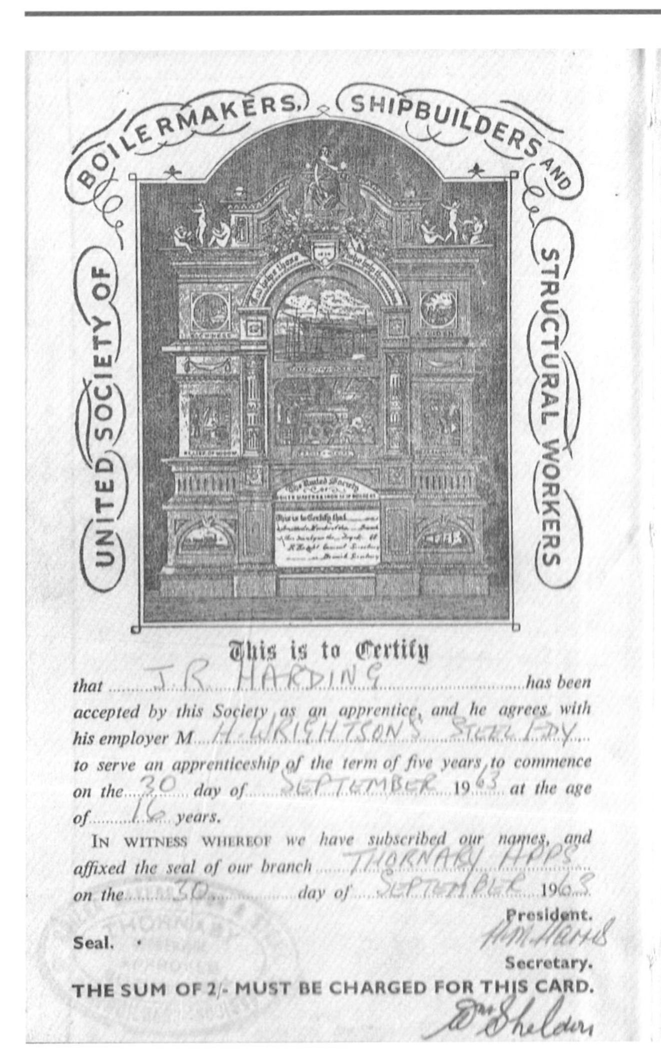

UNITED SOCIETY OF BOILERMAKERS, SHIPBUILDERS AND STRUCTURAL WORKERS

This is to Certify

that J R HARDING has been accepted by this Society as an apprentice, and he agrees with his employer M H WRIGHTSONS STEEL FDY to serve an apprenticeship of the term of five years to commence on the 30 day of SEPTEMBER 1963 at the age of 16 years.

IN WITNESS WHEREOF we have subscribed our names, and affixed the seal of our branch THORNABY APPS on the 30 day of SEPTEMBER 1963

Seal. President.

Secretary.

THE SUM OF 2/- MUST BE CHARGED FOR THIS CARD.

64

This card is for the period of apprenticeship and great care should be taken of same.

This Society will not recognise any young man as a legitimate apprentice, and entitled to become a member of our Society, who has not been supplied with one of these cards by the officers of the branch nearest where he is working.

Apprentices joining this section to be charged the sum of 2s. entrance fee, which will be deducted from the amount of adult entrance fee when they transfer to full membership. Any apprentice having four years' continuous membership of the Society shall be exempt from the payment of entrance fees on transfer to full membership.

This card is to the owner a certificate of the Society's recognition of apprenticeship and a guarantee to him of his admission into the Society at the proper time, if all other conditions are fulfilled according to the Society's rules.

This card must be issued in accordance with Rule 23, and be signed and stamped by the President and Secretary of the branch from which the card is granted, but not by the officers of any other branch unless by a written sanction of the District Committee or Executive Council.

Branch Officers when granting these cards must see to it that the proportion of apprentices where the lad is to serve his time does not exceed one to five.

E. J. HILL,
General Secretary.

John Harding's boilermaker's union card. (Supplied by J Harding)

Choosing Head Wrightson

I joined Head Wrightson's after having served two years National Service in the Royal Engineers. I had worked for a small firm in Middlesbrough and I fancied spreading my wings somewhat with a larger company. Head Wrightson had a very good name and I wrote to them and got a job with the McKee Division of Head Wrightson when I came out of the Army. I didn't write for a specific job, I just wrote and said I was a mechanical draughtsman and I would like to work for a bigger company than the one I had been working for prior to doing National Service. My first interview was with Ossie Bell who was the Chief Draughtsman of Head Wrightson, Teesdale. He was not really taking people on at that time but McKee Division, where Harry Welford was Chief Draughtsman, were looking for draughtsmen so I went down to the McKee Division and Harry Welford gave me a job. *(Eric Brown)*

I started applying for jobs in the spring of 1970. I applied for nine apprenticeships ranging from craft apprenticeships at ICI at Billingham and Wilton and Whessoe. Powergas was a big employer in the town at that time as well. Davy Ashmore's and Head Wrightson and British Steel. I found where the best offer in terms of training were. I could see from speaking to lads that I knew who'd already been there that although Head Wrightson never paid very much money to apprentices or even when you came out of your apprenticeship, the training you'd got was second to none. Quite a lot of other companies used to send their apprentices to Head Wrightson to be trained. We had careers advice at school. People were very complimentary. I suppose it helped that my father worked there but it confirmed that the company had a good reputation in the area. *(Chris Stoddart)*

I always had a fair opinion of Head's as a layman. I was an accountant and there always seemed to be a nice sort of feeling about the way Head Wrightson did things. Their silver and black vehicles travelling round were attractive and I always used to think that they were obviously a good company. I knew a director of one of the companies, a chap called Tom Wilson who was a director of Head Wrightson Process Engineering. I came back from Africa and joined Barrowcliffe's, which was a firm of accountants, and my nephew became an articled clerk at Barrowcliffe's and I suggested that he went to Head Wrightson's to get some commercial experience. So he went to Head Wrightson's and got some commercial experience and came back with an offer for me from the Chief Accountant. Would I go and meet the Chief Accountant with a view to getting a job at Head Wrightson's? I got a job at Head Wrightson's under the Chief Accountant, which wasn't a great success but I eventually got into Pensions and did make a success of that. *(Peter French)*

It was the only choice there was. There was no choice. Because I went to an interview at ICI but I couldn't get in there because there was two busloads of public school lads. You had about as much chance of getting in ICI as kicking my backside. But apparently I found out later on that all lads who went to Stockton Technical College automatically got into Head Wrightson's because the Personnel Manager of it all said, 'All the lads from Stockton Tech get a job here.' That's how I got in Head Wrightson's. *(Thomas Wilson)*

I was sent there by the Youth Employment Office because I decided I didn't want to go on at school any longer and I was nearly fifteen and I wanted a job. So they sent me for an interview and I started in what they called the Labour Department in those days. The war was on, of course. That's where I started with Frank Shepherd in 1942. We were in little cottages facing the main office. They'd been houses at one time but Heads bought all the land along there. There were still a couple living in two of the cottages that worked at Head Wrightson's. They were just looking for young clerical staff because they were starting up a new card system to keep records of the employees and we had to sit and write up all the cards to go on the machine. *(Enid Thurlwell)*

I could see the Coal Board was starting to be shrunk a bit so I looked around for a job and I saw a job advertised through the management consultants and it referred to an engineering company in the North East of England. It didn't say what it was. But I went for an interview in York with their rep and he told me then it was Head Wrightson. I'd heard of the name, of course. I got the job, and I'm glad I did. *(Joe Doran)*

What do you want to do when you leave school? Today it's go to college, get a degree, doesn't matter what the degree's in but get a degree. In our day it was get an apprenticeship. Head Wrightson had got a good reputation. Didn't really know what I wanted to do and that's why I thought the Apprentice School was a great idea. Because it exposed you to all facets of engineering business and you found your level. You found what you had an affinity for. So it was an excellent opportunity for me. *(Charlie Tighe)*

The word on the street, as it were, was that it was a good place to work. They paid well but it was a bit of a sweatshop. So I thought, 'Well, we'll give it a go. I could do with the brass and see how it ticks over.' In those days there wasn't a big worry about employment because you could go from job to job. You could move around so therefore I wasn't particularly worried if it didn't work out but I thought, 'We'll give it a try.' So I moved into what was then known as Head Wrightson's Machine Company and their premises were on Commercial Street.
My work at Smith's Dock where I served my time, it was all to do with marine, with ships engines. This was something new entirely. So I was nervous and a bit unsure to start with as

whether I would be able to fit in. But it was quite interesting. I think we were on three months' probation. So at the end of three months you were viewed, and at the time I think they had some sort of grading system. You went in at Grade Four and then the idea was you could go down or you could go up. And so after six months you were re-appraised and then depending on the sort of work that you'd been doing you either stopped where you were or you were upgraded. *(Stuart Thompson)*

Our family really weren't well off enough for me to stay on and go into the sixth form, which we could have done with the qualifications. So my friend and I from school had an interview for ICI and an interview for Head Wrightson's training schemes. We quite liked both companies but decided that Head Wrightson's seemed a friendlier place to go to in our wisdom. An uncle, Jimmy Hudson, was working there, but he was in the foundry so nothing to do with the office. So it was going there blind really in a way. We were both accepted for the training scheme so we said, 'Alright, we liked Head Wrightson's, we'll go to Head Wrightson's,' which we did and started there before our results came out. *(Wendy Heald)*

I'm indebted to father and one of his friends really because one of father's friends said, 'What's your son thinking of doing when he leaves school? Has he ever thought about engineering? Would he like to have a look round sometime?' This gentleman was a Mr. Mather from one of Head Wrightson's companies and he very kindly took father and I for a walk round Head Wrightson Machine Company before I'd left school. It looked a fascinating place to me. I actually won an Art scholarship when I was at school so I was debating whether to go and become a long-haired artist or I thought perhaps engineering was a more reliable safer profession. So after looking round Head Wrightson Machine Company, Mr. Mather said, 'Well he needs to get five GCSEs including Maths and English and apply,' which I duly did. So I left school at sixteen and finished up joining the Head Wrightson apprentices scheme in September fifty-nine. *(Michael Waring)*

Went to ICI for an interview and Head Wrightson. At Richard Hind School we had the option to learn Pitman shorthand or Gregg shorthand and nobody had heard of Gregg. Pitman we were told was like angles and Gregg was like curves. So we all put our name down on the Pitman side and they just came along and said, 'Right, first lot Pitman, below there Gregg,' so I learnt Gregg. Went to ICI for an interview and they said, 'Oh we only want people that do Pitman,' so that was the end of that. Went to Head Wrightson to start as a commercial trainee. Although it sounds a glorified title it was a case of collecting mail from the building, folding it up, sealing it in the envelope, putting it through the franking machine, delivering post and all this, that and the other. *(Margaret Partridge)*

I was on the dole, I'd just lost my job at George Blair's in Newcastle. I was living at Wallsend. The job came up, probably in the Evening Chronicle I would imagine, and I came down for interview. I was interviewed by a guy called Percy Pugh who I think was Works Director at the time. I came down on a Friday, had the interview, don't remember much about it other than the fact that it was okay I guess. By the end of the interview he said, 'When can you start?' I said, 'Monday,' but I think that got me the job and that was it. Got in touch with him and I came in as what they called their Unit Metallurgist. *(Jim Matthews)*

I was finishing with the RAF and travelling up by train from London and was feeling somewhat pushed about on the third-class carriage so I just went into the first-class carriage and I had plenty of space and sat down. Opposite me in the carriage was one well-dressed chap who started questioning me on what I did, what I didn't do and I told him that I had left the RAF, was a photographer and was starting to look for work but had not had a lot of success.

Asked me had I tried the ICI, had I tried this. I'd tried everything as far as I know. And he said, 'Well, have you tried Head Wrightson's?' I said, 'I don't know what they do, never heard of them,' more or less. He said, 'Well, I'll tell you how you get to them and if I was you I would go and try.' So I did and I got a job.

Who did you talk to, who did you meet at Head Wrightson's?

At Head Wrightson's, on the first instance, a chap called Archie Muir, who was the Chief Metallurgist, and we talked for a number of times about what I thought I could do for them and what he thought I should be able to do for them. At that point he said, 'Well, I will let you know to fill in a form applying for a job as a photographer in the Research and Development.'

And that was in what year?

Nineteen-fifty-eight. A new venture, and it was the mixture of doing the work for Research and Development with a fairly firm instruction to expand it to within Head Wrightson itself. *(Alan Simpson)*

I had five job offers. One from Head Wrightson's, one from Whessoe's, one from the Council, one from the Water Board and I can't remember what the other one was.

I chose Head Wrightson's because of the choice of apprenticeships, where you could become an electrician, a boilermaker, a pattern-maker even or a mechanical fitter, which is what I chose to do. I just applied to as many companies in the area that I thought I would like to work for. I was successful in getting five offers. But I chose Head's because of what I thought would be the quality of the apprenticeship. *(John Richmond)*

I had apprenticeship opportunities with three well known local companies and chose Head Wrightson for various reasons of which one was the fact that I was born and raised in Thornaby and only about ten minutes walk from Teesdale Works. Not to mention I had managed to sleep in on the day I was due to attend a final early morning interview at a famous chemical company locally. *(Bob Wright)*

Choosing Head Wrightson: family influence

I always looked up to my brother, my eldest brother, and I just wanted to do what he was doing. I had no other option really, I had no other interest. If I got in the Bridge Yard I'd be with him all the time you see. He put my name forward to the Apprentice School. Because as long as you had somebody working there you had a better chance. Rather than say an outsider. He put a good word in for me and that's how I got in the Apprentice School. I had to be interviewed. I had to do an exam. I finished second, so that was okay. I think there was about eighteen applied for it. I think there was only about three vacancies and fortunately I finished second in the interview. *(Dennis Johnson)*

I'd always been interested in engineering and at that time the job situation obviously was much better than it is now. I'd applied for apprenticeships at Whessoe, the National Coal Board, Head Wrightson's, Royal Ordnance Factory. But I'd always been interested in heavy engineering. Basically, my parents, my grandparents and my great grandparents had always been in engineering, on my father's side of the family they worked at places like Vickers Armstrong's. It was a bit of a family tradition but I was interested in it. *(Ken Peacock)*

I applied to a number of places actually. I applied at ICI and was unsuccessful. My father was working at Head Wrightson's and he was adamant that I should get an apprenticeship and he was quite pleased when I actually got into Head Wrightson's. My father worked in the Steel Foundry on the core floor. He'd been badly injured in the war and managed to get a job as a labourer in the core floor at the foundry. I think he had a strong interest in the fact I'd got an apprenticeship. He was pleased. *(Derek Proctor)*

Your father worked there, what was your father?

He was originally a steel erector and he finished up in charge of paint and despatch. Down at the bottom end of the works.

Were there any other members of your family working there?

My brother, David, worked for a time in the stores and Jack he was a fitter and turner. My grandfather worked there and my uncle worked there. *(Eddie Burridge)*

My father was a moulder at Head Wrightson's Stockton Forge. He'd worked in various foundries for Head Wrightson's but he was at the Forge at the time, and he went and spoke to the Bridge Yard manager and he said, 'I wanted you to come and see me.' He lived in St Peter's Road, Stockton and I went round and we must have got our wires mixed up. I thought he said, 'See me at the Forge, start on Monday morning' but what he had said was, 'come and see me on Monday morning at the Forge.' So I got there with my overalls on, and the foreman plater, George Smith, put me on the marking off benches. He said to me, 'I want you to come and see me?' I said, 'Oh I'm sorry I thought you said....' He said, 'Well, now you're here you might as well start.' So that's how I got started. I was really lucky really because all the apprentices had to go through the Apprentice School at that time in 1948. *(Norman Toulson)*

My father worked there. He was the Bridge Yard Manager. My grandfather worked there in the Bridge Yard. I had two uncles, one in the Drawing Office and one in the Bridge Yard. My father suggested that I should take the exam for the Drawing Office and if I pass go into the Drawing Office. I think there were forty-nine took the exam and two of us got into the Drawing Office from the exam. My father was there most of his life. My grandfather was there most of his life. My uncle was definitely there all his working life. So a big thing. *(Alan Sowerby)*

I wanted to go in The Forestry Commission but my father wouldn't let me. He said it wasn't a future for me so I finished up at Head Wrightson's. He mentioned my name to the manager of the Apprentice School and I went for an interview and he offered me a job. It was as easy as that. I spent six months in the Apprentice School going round the different departments and eventually finished up at Head Wrightson's, Stockton Forge. *(Barry Preece)*

I first heard of Head Wrightson's, because my uncles worked there in the Fifties. I went to Robert Atkinson School, left there at fifteen year old. My mam said, 'Get yourself down to Head Wrightson's and see if you can get a job,' which I did. There were about seven of us interviewed and when I came away from the interview and told my mam I thought it had gone alright. One of the questions they asked me was any of your family working here. Well, at the time, being a young lad, I didn't mention it. So my mam said, 'Get yourself back down there and tell them that your uncle Eddie works there, your uncle Bob works there and your uncle Matty.' Anyway I went back down and the manager said, 'Well, it doesn't make any difference son, you're one of the ones we picked anyway.' *(John Harding)*

I was up in the air what I wanted to do to tell you the truth, but then my family all worked at Head Wrightson's so I more or less got led there through them, to be honest. I had some idea of what it was like because my mother used to go down to see her father who worked in the Bridge Yard at the time. We used to go down but it was only looking through the doors and seeing how black it was. She used to take him sandwiches or just to take a message. All that people wanted to do was to get a trade in those days. I had an interview for a panel beater at Stockton Transport and there was another one. I had two or three different job ideas but Head's came along and I put an application form into Head's and I got offered an apprenticeship with Head Wrightson so that was it. Dad served his time there, my grandfather was there, my uncle was, and two uncles were there so that's what led me that way. *(Dennis Longstaff)*

I had no idea where I would go. The war had just started by the way. There was none of this night school or anything like that. I suppose I went into Head Wrightson's because my father worked there and my brothers. I left school in August 1939 and the war started in the September. I started at Head Wrightson's just after the war started. I was office boy in what they call the Blacksmiths' Shop at Head Wrightson's. They used to make forgings for all the motor car industries. They had about sixteen blacksmiths and they called the foreman Mr. Peck and the head man of that shop was a chap called Mr. Chilton. He was commercial manager of that department. In them days they had boards that they used to fill in with chalk with their time on. They used to put them in a rack and I used to gather them in on a morning and take them into the office. I used to give the checks out for the pay. They used to have a check in them days and each man when he went for his money had to hand that like a gold check in with his number on. *(Fred Watson)*

I had left school and taken a job as a telephonist and teleprinter operator but I always wanted to do something scientific, work in laboratories. My aunt got married and Mr. Purnell and Mr. Sturgess were at her wedding. And, 'Well, this is my niece.' 'What does your niece do?' 'Well, she's doing this but she would like to do something scientific.' 'Oh, we might be able to find her something at Head Wrightson so send her along.' That day they said, 'Tell her next week to go down to Head Wrightson to Enid Thurlwell.' So the first place they took me to was the sand testing room at the end of the core shop. In this little tiny filthy place and I said, 'No thank you, that's not a laboratory, that's not the work I want.' And they said, 'Are you interested in photography?' And I said, 'Well, I haven't done any photography but it sounds interesting.' So they took me straight over to R&D. *(Anne Simpson)*

Interview

I went down to the Education Office in Woodlands Road and they said Head Wrightson's have got a new scheme starting and they rang up and I went for an interview. I failed the interview but as I was coming out of the interview I actually walked with another lad called Ken Robinson and who should come behind us but Harry Soppet who was the Training Manager and Harry Soppet said, 'How have you done lads?' And we both said, 'No, we've both failed.' He asked us a few questions and I said I was in a running team in Middlesbrough High School, not knowing that Harry Soppet was a runner, and he said, 'Oh start on Monday you two, come and start at half past seven.' So because they hadn't got the full intake, they'd only got eighty-three I think and they wanted eighty-five, so Ken and I started. *(Jim Smiles)*

I was already working in engineering. I went straight from school. War was declared on the Sunday and I started at Fred Kidd's on a Wednesday, and it was my mother that found Head Wrightson's were advertising. They were looking for some people, apprentices fifteen and a half to sixteen they said, to be specially trained and be part of the forerunner of the Apprentice School. We were told that if it was a success they may later on have an Apprentice School and they did a few years later. Although I was only fourteen and a half and they said fifteen and a half, I applied and they had an interview on a Sunday morning at the Forge. There was a group of us all standing outside the offices and we were called in one at a time. I had an interview because I understood that the training there was better than I would have got at Fred Kidd's with it being a bigger company. So I had this little interview. The only thing I'd thought of was the question they would ask, 'Why do you want to leave there and come here?' So I had it all lined up for them

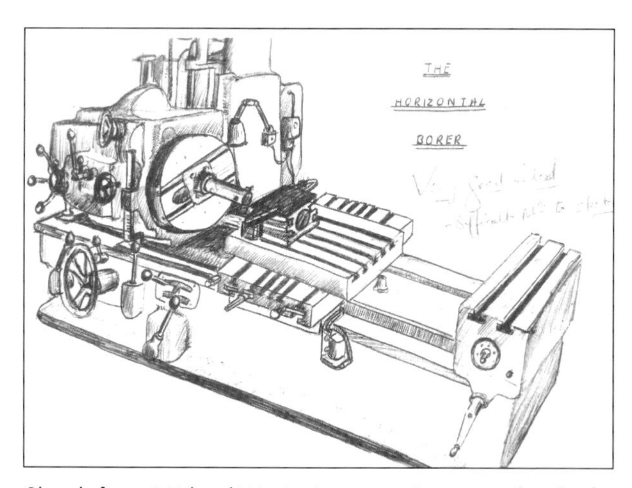

Sketch from Michael Waring's apprentice report book of a horizontal borer. Together with instructor's comments. (Courtesy of Michael Waring)

and it was obviously the right answer. I was told to wait outside and there was a group of us all milling around. Somebody came out and he had some envelopes in his hand and he shouted the names out and he gave the envelopes out. Then said to the rest, 'I'm sorry but we only have this many jobs,' and I had an envelope. *(Les Ellis)*

I'll be quite honest, it was somebody who I knew. A person I worked for just as an errand boy as a schoolboy. Up near where I live his brother was one of the managers at the Forgings Department, the Blacksmiths' Department. He just spoke to him and with him speaking for me I just had to go down and answer a few little questions to prove that I wasn't too thick and I got in the job that way. *(Derek Delahaye)*

It was a friend of mine funnily enough. His father was friendly with Frank Shepherd, and this is where the family ties come into Head Wrightson's. I didn't know Head Wrightson's existed. I hadn't a clue. I lived in Saltburn, Thornaby was a million miles away. He said, 'Why don't you get John to apply to Head Wrightson?' Now funnily enough I didn't apply, my father applied. He just wrote in and I went for an interview with Mr. Soppet, who was in charge of the Apprentice Training School. I got there and he said, 'You've come from Saltburn.' I said, 'Yes.' He said, 'Well how did you get here?' I said, 'Well my father brought me in the car,' because with him being a rep. So they brought me in the car. 'Oh well bring him up.' So I turned, I went and got my dad and anyway I said, 'This guy Soppet wants to see you.' So he came up and Soppet was on his squawk box down to Vernon in the canteen which was just below the Apprentice School, 'Could you send a pot of tea up Vernon, three cups?' And he interviewed my father rather than me. I just sat there and they did the talking. Then at the end of the interview Soppet said, 'Well I see no reason why we can't offer your son a job.' Of course, he'd asked me about my qualification, which I told him I'd got the J1 which he was rather pleased with. And my father said, 'Well you will confirm that in writing won't you?' He said, 'Oh yes,' and that was it. *(John Heath)*

I saw in the *Law Society Gazette* magazine a solicitor's job advertised for a company called Head Wrightson in Yarm. Now I hardly knew Yarm and I'd never heard of the company. So I asked around the office in Northallerton and in County Hall and I remember somebody saying to me, 'Oh yes, they're a nice, friendly, family firm, a bit backward but they'll be alright to work for.' So came up to the Friarage for the interview and fortunately was offered the job. The Friarage is at the southerly end of the High Street. It was a grand old house, very stately. It was a converted house and I was fortunate enough to have an office in the old building. It was the registered office of the company. It was the office where the senior management worked. Sir John Wrightson when I joined was the Chairman. John Eccles, who was the Managing Director and the Company Secretary, he was based there. The Finance Director was there too. The other directors were out in the various operating units which were obviously around Thornaby, Teesside and at that time Manchester with B&S Massey, which had just joined the company. I was interviewed by a chap called David Spark who was the head legal chap although I think he was called Contracts Manager. I was quite a brash young man in those days and I remember some bits of the interview that I'm not particularly

Send off for Ken Poole on his way to compete in a fabrication competition in Japan. 1970. (Wright Ahead)

proud of, but anyway it did the trick. The salary was £3,250 per annum and that was in 1973. However the real carrot was getting a car with the job. The offer letter says 'The sort of car envisaged would have a maximum list price of £1,075.' I got this dark blue Morris Marina. Down at Thornaby, of course, they had the garage that did all the petrol and chauffeuring and they used to maintain it for me. I really felt that I'd arrived. So I enjoyed that. *(Robin Millman)*

It was an exam. You had some mechanical drawings with different gears with arrows on which way they're revolving and you had to say which way it was going to move a lever or pull a weight up. Quite a few maths questions. It took place in the canteen at Head Wrightson's. The day that I went the canteen was full and I think they'd actually had two or three days where they'd had people in taking the selection test. And there must have been thousands altogether. This was in 1980. I got word that I'd passed my test and invited for an interview and that was about a month after the tests and then they just said, 'Oh we'll let you know whether you get the job or not in due course.'

Can you remember much about the interview?

Yes. They asked me a few technical questions about why I wanted to be a turner. Fortunately in the school holidays I used to go to where my stepfather worked and I used to do quite a bit of turning and milling there. I also knew a little bit about the welding side of it. But they were also asking what your hobbies were and what you'd done in your spare time, where at ICI it seemed they didn't seem to ask you anything like that; it was just all about the job. *(John Stainthorpe)*

First impressions

My first impressions of Head Wrightson's was the spirit and the camaraderie that was in there because when I started it was 1946 so you had people coming back from the war and you still had that wartime spirit within the company and it was excellent. Everybody would help everybody. It didn't matter what question you asked, they would answer it and they would show you how to do things; no problem at all. *(Jim Smiles)*

Eddie Peacock shows the finer points of moulding to two apprentices. 1971. (Wright Ahead)

The Bridge Yard was a shock. It was very noisy, dusty and dirty. We weren't actually working in there but we were taking drawings and things. Then for any alterations to drawings we had to go and pick them up, get the draughtsmen to alter it and then take them back again, and various odd jobs like that. The same with the material lists they used to have to make, they used to get them altered as well. You had to pick them up, bring them back to the office and get them altered and send them back. So you wore your feet out. We were just running backwards and forwards virtually. *(Jack Picken)*

We had a class next to the Wagon Department and the noise that come out of there was nobody's business. Frightened your pants off, you see. It was very rough and hard to live with. But you got used to it after a while. Every place had its own oddities. When you worked at Stockton Forge, the toilets were a big trough. You sat on the wood plank. The buggers used to light the paper that floated down to get you all off. Terrible. *(Thomas Wilson)*

Oh I was in awe really of the scale of things. You just felt like a dot on the landscape, huge furnaces and molten metal being poured and moulds being made and cranes and grime. The environment then was dusty and dirty but it got into my blood anyway. It certainly did get into my blood. *(Charlie Tighe)*

The big fabrication shop was a bit bewildering to a young lad. It was noisy. There seemed to be lots of men there. There were overhead cranes moving stuff about. You worked with various people as an apprentice till you got a job on your own on various types of work. It was a shock coming straight from school to go into that type of environment. *(Bill Hornby)*

To be honest I was scared stiff when I first went in. I went from school and I was only little. I remember when I first went to work in the Template Shop somebody said to me, 'I'm so and so,' he said, 'and there's your nail there.' To put my coat on. But that was how things went on. We used to have a can to take your tea. We had a fire. A coke fire. When you were only serving your time you had to keep the fire going as well and you just put your tin can round there. And I've seen people used to come and warm their egg and bacon sandwich up and things like that. All things went on like that. It was like a family affair anyway. *(Les Wilson)*

First impressions? Oh brother. I just took to it. What people don't seem to realise is if you're in school you don't start until nine o'clock, and then you go from a nine o'clock start to starting at half past seven. It's a big jump. But anyway I took to it because I knew that jobs weren't easy to get. I thought I was lucky to get the choice of two actually. But I picked Head Wrightson. *(Frank Stephenson)*

I must admit I was awfully naive when I left home. We'd had a nice sheltered life, a reasonably good life, contented, then to go into the cut and thrust of Head Wrightson's was quite a rude awakening for me. All the chaps I met were good. We had to spend time in the Forge Department, which was I would imagine something like hell, because it was noise and steam and black. All the men were black, not skin colour but that's the colour they were.

Apprentice entry exam in Teesdale Hall. 1969. (Wright Ahead)

We had all the drop forgings and the hammers and you can imagine that the ground literally shook. It was great to be in there. One of the things that I remember from those days was we were making, believe it or not this would be about 1949, 1950, we were making hip joints for people in Norway. We didn't make the machined portion of them but they were made of, I think, titanium or something like that and that was the cup and the ball. And we made them. We had the dies and we produced these things and we sent them to Norway, all those years ago. That was at one end and at the other end we had blacksmiths, as you know them, with a fire and a furnace and all that. The main man was a man called Crawford. He was a great fellow simply because after every week you got pocket money, and what you had to do to earn this pocket money was go for a barrow of coal dust. Now Trafalgar Street was notorious for being windy and to get the coal dust to go on the blacksmiths' fire, you had to go all the way round, down Nile Street and down Trafalgar Street to the Iron Foundry and fill your barrow. Shovel this barrow full of coal dust and then wheel it all the way back to the blacksmiths, and by the time you got back to the blacksmiths half the coal dust was all over you and only half in the barrow. I think you did it twice or three times a week, this barrow load carry on and you got half-a-crown pocket money. *(Bob Close)*

First weeks at work

Can you recall your first day at Head Wrightson's?

A bit nervous of course, wondering whether you were going to do the right thing and find your way round the works. It was quite interesting but nervous to find your way through the Iron Foundry, the Steel Foundries and the Bridge Yard delivering letters to who you were supposed to be delivering them to. I was always impressed. I was just amazed going through the Steel Foundry. You never knew what was going to happen next with ladles going all over the place. *(Fred Britton)*

My weeks were spent with, one day to day school, one day in the Apprentice School and three days out in the works. I started off in the foundries. In my very first week of the foundry work I went to Egglescliffe Iron Foundry and this was a culture shock at the time. Being a grammar school boy and a college boy I was fairly sheltered and the language that came out of the iron foundry was absolutely dreadful, and that was only the women. Because at that time they still employed women labourers to shovel the sand. And these women were very coarse. It was a bit of an eye-opener. My jaw dropped at listening to this absolutely appalling language coming out of them. The women just laughed about it. *(Gerald Morton)*

At this time Head Wrightson was a major employer in the area and a world-renowned manufacturer of engineering components. I had no idea at that time which particular trade I wanted to follow, but the Head Wrightson first-year induction course meant that everyone spent their first year touring around the various departments and trades. Usually two weeks in each placement. This meant that at the end of your first year you had a good idea of where you wanted to go and more importantly where you did *not* want to work. The first year was certainly an eye-opener into the world of manufacturing and engineering, but it also made you realise which jobs or trades you did not want to pursue at any cost. Certain placements soon

An apprentice being shown die-sinking methods. circa 1960s. (Company brochure)

An apprentice using a band-saw. circa 1960s. (Company brochure)

became known as 'hell holes' to be avoided if at all possible. I remember Stampings, Seaton Carew, was a strong contender amongst the lads for being the worst place to work as well as the foundries. By comparison, the Bridge Yard and the machine shops were a lot cleaner places than the foundries. They didn't have the dust and fumes that the foundries had. I suppose that the system was good in as much as you got experience or you got an insight into what each job involved within the Head Wrightson group. *(Doug Hauxwell)*

From fifteen I went down Head Wrightson's because my brother worked there. I went in the Apprentice School, which was run by Harry Soppet. Then in the Apprentice School you went round different departments for two or three weeks, like joiners, plumbers, electricians, the Bridge Yard, the Machine Shop, you spent two or three weeks just to see what it was like. At the end of your term you had to pick two choices, a first and second. Now the first choice I wanted to be a plater like my brother but unfortunately the vacancies were taken so I finished up in the Machine Shop, and that's where I started in 1949 in the Machine Shop till 1984. *(Dennis Johnson)*

I set off working as a driller's mate because I was only sixteen then and after a time I became an apprentice burner until I came out of my time in 1961/62. This was in Stockton Forge in Norton Road. I didn't go through the Apprentice School. I started in the Bridge Yard as a driller's mate but only for about six months till they found me a job as a burner. We weren't classed as a trade in the centre, only the welders and platers went to the Apprentice School but the burners didn't for some reason or other. I just started burning there, hand burning and machine burning. We did them both. *(Robert Chaney)*

I think there would be about six of us accepted onto the training scheme and we would start off the day in the Post Room. For a nine o'clock start I believe. We would be in the Post Room and the post had already arrived and the Post Room was full of little pigeon holes. So we had to take the letters out of the envelopes, which were already slit for us. We would take the letters out of the envelopes if they weren't marked 'personal' and put them into the correct little pigeon hole for the department. So sometimes they were addressed to the department and you'd put it straight in, sometimes you would read through the letter and think, 'Oh that's Invoicing or Costing,' and put them into the dockets. Then after we'd finished doing the post we were all allocated to a different department. *(Wendy Heald)*

There was a fitter and turner apprenticeship available in the Machine Shops, but the option was to go as a shop boy. A shop boy was to go

North end of Trafalgar Street, Thornaby, showing houses and the Bradford Vaults pub circa 1950s. (Remembering Thornaby Group)

up the shops for the tradesmen. I had to go and get the newspapers and get the bacon sandwiches and the fish and chips. That was for a period of about three months until the next shop boy came on the shop floor. I'd moved on to the capstan and ward lathes. Shaping machines, which again was a good insight into engineering and how to work these things and working on the ward lathes. We were doing parts for the nuclear power station, which was quite interesting, although I'd decided early on in my career I didn't want to stand at a machine all day long. *(Derek Proctor)*

There were hot-water urns strategically positioned about the place, but you took your own cup and tea in. One of the little perks that you got as an apprentice was you could become a can lad. That was one of my other little duties as well and that was a nice little earner thank you very much. I think I looked after eight cans for welders and platers. There was eight of them and you got half-a-crown a can per week. So that was giving me an extra pound a week. I remember my wages then were two pounds six and a penny. So you were almost getting fifty per cent of your wages extra, by making tea for them. They would bring their own cans in and each welder would have his own can and teabags which you looked after together with the condensed milk and you'd make the can of tea for them. *(Charlie Tighe)*

What were the first jobs that you would do?

Marking off would be the first one with template or sometimes straight from the drawings. There was a little area, where the apprentices had their benches for marking off any smaller stuff from a wooden template. I did have one spell on the rolling machine when a chap who had been on it for years and years was either sick or on holiday or something and they put me on that. I'm afraid I wasn't a very successful roller. *(Bill Hornby)*

Every morning for the first week you arrived at the Apprentice School and they went through with you how everything worked within the

Sir John Wrightson presenting Duke of Edinburgh Awards 1965. (Wright Ahead)

group. How all the various companies had their own product lines and their own management structures and that we would be visiting each one of these particular companies for maybe a month just to see how everything worked. At the time I wanted to be a draughtsman and it was accepted that I was doing an apprenticeship simply to get in one of the draughting departments. *(Colin Waugh)*

My first impression of Head Wrightson was horrible because I went into Head Wrightson's as a teenager when I left school. I was fifteen years old when I started at Head Wrightson's in the Apprentice School. The person in charge was Harry Soppet and it was all hairy-scary stuff until you got into the routine and the system. Because when you were serving your time there the first thing you did on a morning was on top of the roof doing PE. They kept you fit before they started your instructions in the Apprentice School. *(Harry Foster)*

I'd make the tea for the men and take their cans to where they were filled up, quite close to where the women had their place. So you used to get heckled off the women while you're making your tea. They frightened me really. They made you feel fear a lot. I didn't get ragged but I know someone that did. They plastered him with Swarfega. I kept well away from them. I think he had been taking his teacup or something and they grabbed him and they set their stall out to get him. Anyway I used to get two and six a week off the lads. I was making tea for about five people. I'd make about five teas and then run the messages, if they wanted fish and chips. Or if they were working over and wanted duck and peas I'd get them. There was a little back alley just out near New Street. Well, there was a fish shop there. I used to go and get the fish and chips for them or I used to go into Metcalfe's, the butchers on Mandale Road. *(John Harding)*

When you joined as an apprentice draughtsman back in forty-one. What memories can you recall of your first day?

Well, the thing I remember was wearing a brand new sports jacket, I remember that very, very clearly. It was brown, my father had kitted me out for it. I think it was nervousness. I thought as an apprentice we would be given a drawing board and getting on with it, but no, we were dogsbodies really, we were called Drawing Office orderlies. We were at everybody's beck and call, you know, 'Take these drawings to the Template Shop' or 'go and collect this or that or the other.' *(Ray Shaw)*

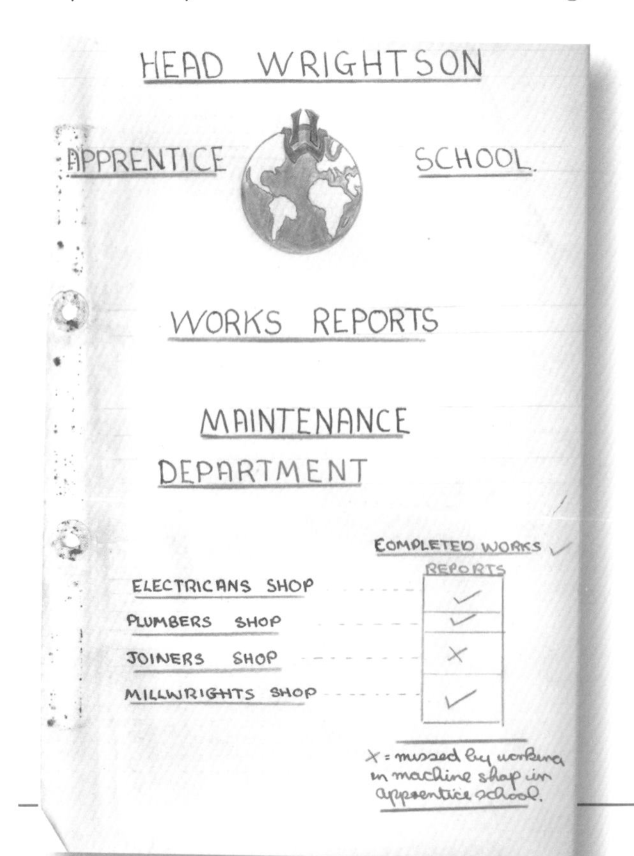

HEAD WRIGHTSON

APPRENTICE SCHOOL.

WORKS REPORTS

MAINTENANCE DEPARTMENT

	COMPLETED WORKS REPORTS
ELECTRICANS SHOP	✓
PLUMBERS SHOP	✓
JOINERS SHOP	✗
MILLWRIGHTS SHOP	✓

✗ = missed by working in machine shop in apprentice school.

Front cover of Ken Lee's apprentice report book. (Supplied by K. Lee)

Chapter 2

'It was tremendous work': jobs in Head Wrightson

The workforce at Head Wrightson had a wide range of skills and experience. Skilled craftsmen such as welders, template makers, platers, blacksmiths, fitters, turners, pattern-makers, moulders, electricians, joiners, shipwrights and burners manufactured quality engineering products. White-collar workers included draughtsmen, engineers, planners, chemists together with commercial professions such as accountancy, purchasing, legal, computing and various levels of secretarial staff.

Like other heavy industry in Teesside, the majority of workers were men but some women were employed throughout the organisation. A number of women joined during wartime in common with most other industries in the country. Whilst many women left when the war ended, there were some who continued to work on the shop floor. Women worked in many manual trades including welding, burning, drilling, core making, on capstan lathes in the Machine Shop and as storekeepers. Others were employed in more traditionally female jobs such as cooks, secretaries and clerks.

The extracts we have chosen for this chapter represent a wide selection of the jobs available in Head Wrightson. Below our contributors discuss their thoughts and feelings about these jobs and the skills they developed.

Machine burning. (Remembering Thornaby Group)

Clerical staff

I started work in the wages department in 1950 when it was situated on the upper floor of a building at the bottom of Trafalgar Street occupied by the Stockton Shipping and Salvage Company. There were 30 of us in the department including wages clerks and typists and our supervisor was a Mr. Vickers. We would go to Barclays Bank in Stockton in a taxi accompanied by Jim Rickelton, the works security officer, to collect the money for the wages and then split the coinage to allow wage packets to be made up. *(Don Raper)*

We worked the full six days a week, Monday to Friday and Saturday morning. I think we started at nine o'clock and finished at quarter past five. That's the official hours but then as an office junior you used to have to wait for mail and take it to the Post Office. You had a stamp book which you had to stamp all the letters with and account for. And of course, there were various things like parcels of drawings because we dealt a lot with South Africa. There were parcels of drawings and shipping documents. The chap who was responsible for shipping documents was notorious for doing everything at the last minute so quite often it was way past quarter past five when we finished because often we had to copy those on a fluid copier and they'd maybe want 200 copies of them. And it was a hand machine. The only thing you had in the way of a calculator was a book and it had various rates of pay on each page. At the time the men were working a forty-seven-hour week, you started off with a forty-seven-hour calculator. The men used to have time boards. It was just a wooden board which they chalked over and then they wrote on what job they'd been on, how long they'd been on a particular function of it. If they were late they had to get it signed by the foreman because they got docked pay for being late. If they were more than I think it was three minutes late they used to get quarter houred. Well, the old foremen were fairly strict. I suppose they had to be. The chalk boards were very dirty, dusty things and I used to have to enter them in wages books and job books and I suppose do the calculation of the wages. In those days the office itself was very Dickensian. We had the high desks and high stools. You sat round the office, there was the high sloping desks. Just like you often saw in things of Dickens. We used the ordinary pens with the nib. And the pen you slipped the nib in. One of the office junior's jobs each Monday was to put a clean sheet of blotting paper on the Chief Clerk's desk. Check his inkwells and things like that. *(Wilf Bradley)*

One of my jobs that I had to do was applying for the apprentices to not get called up at eighteen. Frank Shepherd put the fear of God into me because he said, 'Remember if you slip up with any of these boys and they get called up because you haven't applied for their deferment till they're twenty-one and they get killed, it's your fault.' We had a system that we pulled them out when they were getting near to eighteen. Then we applied to one of the government departments. Sent the necessary forms in so that they'd be deferred until they were twenty-one. Of course, anybody that hadn't an apprenticeship they got called up at eighteen. *(Enid Thurlwell)*

I used to go to the weighbridges every morning with some advice notes for them to go in the office to say what was going out daily. I went in there as a junior. Learnt all the goings on there. I used to go right round the works and then it was known just as Head Wrightson's, by the way. They never split it up into Head Wrightson's Teesdale and Head Wrightson's Steel Foundry and one thing and another. It was all Head Wrightson's. I used to go round the works and take every wagon number that was standing. At that time everything used to come in by rail, not road. I used to take the wagon numbers as they came in daily. I used to record them and send them round to the different departments what wagons they had standing, and I used to go round the works every morning, right round the works which was a real job. Taking wagon numbers. Were they empty, were they steel, loaded for demurrage charge? That was a

HW Middlesbrough Works Drawing Office. (HW Middlesbrough Works photo)

charge and they were only allowed twenty-four hours to off-load them, which we had a terrible demurrage charge then for the railway. When I was in the road weighbridge I used to have to make all the delivery notes out for all the drivers when they were taking things out. That was for Teesdale, not for the other companies. Everything that went out that day had to go in the office next day on what we called the yard day sheet. I used to type it out with the order numbers, everything, so all they had to do was look at it. We used to send ingot moulds out to all the steelworks. Chairs, cast-iron chairs for the railway, railway wagons, blast furnaces and all to do with blast furnaces. We sent stuff out for the nuclear power stations. *(Fred Watson)*

I settled down really in the Steel Foundry because it had a few departments. There was Sales and the Costs. I spent a lot of time in the Costs. There was about eight of us. All we were doing was putting expenditures on the little card of particular jobs. Then we had work in progress and they had to know how much was work in progress. There was actually work in progress and what they'd spent had to be noted. The patterns. And you'd know then. You used to do a balance, then they used to say, 'Oh you're a penny out,' and I really mean a penny. You had to go through all the cards again. *(Colin Fletcher)*

Computerised machine operator

I think they were the first firm in the North East to go and buy CNC machines. These are numerically controlled. The machine gets set up and then it's run by computer. What happens is that they were making, say, a piece of metal. The piece of metal was put into the machine, it had already been programmed and set up and everything like that, then you just pressed a button and the tools just automatically changed back and forward and finished. They took the component out and put another one in. I was the first one in Head Wrightson's and in the North East to work on that. One of the lads from the offices did the programming and I was taught how to operate the machine. They brought in an experienced person and they taught me how to use the machine and what I was supposed to do on the machine. Somebody did the programming and then I did the set up and the operating. *(Jack Hare)*

Draughtsman

The Drawing Office is really split into five or six divisions. You had a Colliery Division, you had a Structural Division, you had a General Engineering Division and you had a Rotary Machine Division and there was another miscellaneous one. We were in the Colliery and the Mining Division - I was anyway. The overall project ran through mainly two divisions, which was the Structural Division, who designed and detailed out the head gears and the towers for the mine. We took it from there and did all the shaft furnishings and the skips or cages and all the ancillary feeding equipment for both the surface and the underground for the mine, whatever type of mine it was. In the Coal Board they were all vertical skip or a cage and mine car circuits. In the case of metalliferous mining you had overturning skips and a different design for gold mines and copper mines and things like that.

Once you'd done the drawings what happened then?

Well, both when I was an apprentice template maker I actually followed particular jobs through the yard. I made the templates, went out and built it in the yard and followed it through to the Fitting Shop. Because a lot of our work was structural and then it entailed machine work and fitting work which was fitted onto the structures that we'd made. In the case of the Drawing Office I went as a commissioning engineer, on loan for a week and came back three months later. That was working down the mine on the surface and underground. That was my hard experience that was quite different. It was quite bloody to be honest with you at times. I remember we went down one morning at six, because we had to be at the surface to ride down with the miners, and I came out the next day at nine o'clock. Our Managing Director, John Eccles, was stood at the surface because we'd had a lot of trouble and he didn't recognise us because we were so dirty. And pretty haggard looking. But it was all very, very, very good experience. *(Barry Preece)*

I was very fortunate to be given the chance of serving my apprenticeship as a draughtsman in the Nuclear Engineering section of Head Wrightson Processes Ltd then based at the Friarage, Yarm. The Chief Draughtsman was very strict but I always found him to be fair. Every morning he would stand just outside his office, where he could look up at the clock as people arrived in the office. If you were late a few mornings in a row he would have you in the office for a little ticking off. He spent most of his day walking up and down the office making sure that no idle gossip was going on between staff members. The Nuclear Section I worked in was looked after by a big man from Newcastle, again strict but fair and determined that every drawing leaving his section would be checked thoroughly including punctuation and spelling on the notes placed on the drawing. I remember those first drawings I did would come back full of red ink marking the corrections necessary, gradually the red ink became less and less as time went on. The work involved preparing detail drawings for each type of graphite brick used in the construction of the reactor core and believe me there was a lot of them. Head's were involved in nuclear reactor design at Oldbury, Dungeness, Hinkley Point, Sizewell, Dounreay and Latina (Italy) to name just a few. I was involved in producing some of the detail drawings for the graphite core, support plates, boiler shield wall, restraint system and guide tubes on all of these sites. The design engineers and all the drawing office staff were a great bunch of people, including the lovely tea lady who would come round with her trolley and you could purchase a nice cake to go with your tea. I was extremely proud to be working at the Friarage on the above nuclear projects that seemed very cutting edge then.

Draughtsman Peter Harding at HWT Drawing Office. (Company brochure)

We had one draughtsman who was an exceptional cartoonist and every week a new cartoon would be passed round the office depicting something funny or topical that had happened that week featuring the people involved, and from memory they often featured the Chief Draughtsman. Everybody always enjoyed the cartoons and looked forward to the next one.

In 1965 the Nuclear Design Drawing Office of Head Wrightson Processes Ltd was transferred to Head Wrightson Teesdale based at Thornaby. The only advantage of the move for me was I could walk from home up to Stockton railway station, get the train to Thornaby and walk straight off the station into Head Wrightson Teesdale. I finished my apprenticeship at Thornaby and continued to work in the Nuclear Section until 1969 when the opportunity came to transfer to Head Wrightson Erection Department and become an assistant site engineer where it was felt I could use my experience to help supervise the construction of the reactor core at Hinkley Point nuclear power station in the South West. *(Ken Lee)*

There were about a 120 draughtsmen in three different offices all under Harry Welford.

There were project managers who he reported to. The project managers had quite an involvement in the projects that were going ahead that were being detailed, et cetera. You were working on producing detailed drawings, sometimes general arrangement drawings from things as diverse as the cooling tubes on incinerators to general arrangements on steelworks that were destined for India. One of my drawings I remember came back from India, it had been checked by thirty-seven people. I couldn't believe the bureaucracy of it. *(Chris Stoddart)*

So back in the Drawing Office in HWISWEL, as the acronym for Head Wrightson Iron and Steelworks Engineering Limited, we were in a

New head gear manufactured at the Stockton Forge being lifted into place at ICI Billingham. (Photograph courtesy of B. Preece)

The 61-foot-diameter dome weighing 140 tons for the Isaac Newton Telescope at Herstmonceux Observatory constructed for Sir Howard Grubb Parsons and Company Limited during assembly at Stockton Forge. (Company brochure)

drawing office which was a converted template loft for shipyard clerks. Very big, very open and very cold in the winter. There was very little heating and drawing on the old drawing boards with pencil and paper was quite arduous at that time. My earliest memories of the Drawing Office itself was being taken down three very long rooms, row after row of drawing boards and all these gentlemen many of them puffing on pipes as was the norm in those days. He took me to this gentleman in the corner, Mr. Goodwin. He was a very eccentric old gentleman, but he was the section leader and I was to work under his guidance. The first two weeks that I was on a drawing board was actually spent learning how to manipulate the drawing board for the different angles but also to practise drawing with pencils of different hardness. The second two weeks were spent learning how to write with pen and nib as they used to do in the very olden days there. All the drawing was done in pencil and the writing which had to be very upright and very neat that was done in printer's type ink, very black. Get that on your hands and it would take days to come off. So I spent about eighteen months in the Drawing Office. *(Ian Hayley)*

We had terminals which were linked up to the main one at Manchester University. You had to log in and sometimes you had to wait because the computer was busy. We had an Engineering Director called Frank Austin, he was a mathematician we got from Cambridge and he set all the programs up. We adapted to that very well, it was a big hit, it was a big help. We didn't draw on the screen, you still went back to your drawing board but we used these programs to do all the calculations which would have taken weeks. *(John Glasper)*

Electrician

I was based in the Electricians' Shop but we worked in different departments like the Bridge Yard, Machine Shop and Steel Foundry. We moved around the different departments with different instructors. Once we'd finished our apprenticeship we more or less filled in with the people who had been teaching us. We did repairing work, repairing machines, repairing overhead cranes, motors in overhead cranes and welding sets and things like that. Working on cranes meant we were working high up. There was always a way to get up. To be honest a couple of times we did walk the track. If the crane was broken down halfway along sometimes you just had to walk along the track to get to it. Difficult if you didn't have a head for heights. I was alright. *(Ron Baker)*

Erection engineer

I was seconded onto the Erection Department. So I left the Drawing Office at twenty-eight and I became an erection engineer. That entailed travelling round the country on different projects, anything from mining to rotary machines, to salt mines at Winsford, ICI, and the anhydrite mine at Billingham. I put a new head gear top on the top of that in a weekend. We did a very big major reconstruction of that. We did aluminium work at the Forge, we did a lot of aluminium fabrication and installed a lot of work into ICI Billingham and Wilton. Wilton was a major project of mine on construction. We erected some huge bunkers in there and used the first tower crane that was ever brought into this country, there. It was very varied. We had aluminium structures going out to lighthouses or you would be working underground so it was a very varied experience. Hard work because you were really troubleshooting with different squads of men at different sites with different engineers and you were running round them troubleshooting them all, between the works, the Drawing Office and the client. It was interesting. *(Barry Preece)*

Did they have a dedicated erection gang for going out to sites?

Yes they did. In 1964 I was offered the position of construction engineer after working on Herstmonceux, the Royal Observatory. This was a wonderful job, it was a dome which included the shutters openings and rotating equipment of some ninety-foot diameter to house the 98-inch Sir Isaac Newton Telescope. I was down there in charge of the erection of all the structures. Later I was working in Worthing on a hygiene unit, which was the forerunner of composting plants. Principally it was a large drum 12 foot in diameter by 110 foot long and it's like a digester which rotated and was aerated and the rubbish went in at one end and, after four to five days and the sufficient temperature reached, it was discharged at the other end. The compost was then transported to areas to be laid out in wind rows to sort for the final completion. The digesting and composting parts were new technology in the 60s. It was actually Head Wrightson again who liked to have their fingers in all the pies, and looking back to 1960, to get involved in composting, not just to make money but they had the outlook for something Green. There was a digester plant down at the 'wilderness' in Thornaby and this was worked on for quite a long time by the R&D boys and I was also involved with it. *(Allan Ayre)*

Estimator

When I left the foundry at Stockton I was asked to go to HW Steelcast at Billingham and work in the estimating and sub-contracting department. This job involved estimating from customers' drawings the cost of the pattern equipment to produce their castings. I then had to place orders with outside master pattern shops for them to manufacture the pattern equipment. *(Doug Hauxwell)*

I started off in the light bay. Then I got transferred to the induction, what they call the middle bay, which is where what they call the medium work was made and then I went into the heavy bay. I was there three years and Joe Bell come up to me he said, 'Frank Shepherd wants to see you.' So I went over in the offices, went up there and he said, 'I've got a vacancy for the Estimating Department.' He said, 'Just sit down and talk to me.' He asked me what I did out of school, out of work, did you fancy being on the staff? I said, 'Well, I think it's everybody's aim.' Anyway it was twenty minutes I was there. He said, 'Okay Eddie,' and he said, 'are you quite happy if I offer you the job?' I said, 'Yes, of course, I am.' He said 'Right, start Monday.' When I first went in, they explained to me what to do. You used to get the drawing and they'd say, 'Right, what we do is work out what size box does it go in and how much would

Drilling a heat-exchanger-tube sheet. (Wright Ahead)

you want if you made it.' You know, price wise. He said, 'You just put that down on the sheet and then if there was any core making on, how much core making you think there should be.' He said, 'That's all you have to do and then pass it on to the head estimator.' He used to fill everything in, if he thought your price was too high he'd come and ask 'Can you knock, I don't know, a pound off or one and six?' Or if he thought it was too low he used to have a look at it again. *(Eddie Peacock)*

I was about eighteen months in the Estimating Department. You had to estimate how long you thought it was going to be to machine a set of dies that were required for the production of the forging. We used to fill a form in and then it would come upstairs and there was a girl would have to type it in. I think it was like the white ticker tape. Then it would have to go through to Yarm to be put on the computer. Then you'd get it back the next day in the printed out format with prices on and everything like that. *(Barry Davison)*

Fitter

I was on the shapers eleven months. Then I got put on a lathe. I didn't like that at all. I said to Lennie Allen, 'I'm not keen on this you know; I really want to be a fitter.' 'Right ho,' he said, so the next thing I know he's put me with the fitters in the Fitting Shop. The first job I worked on was a rolling platform. For the Navy, for training gunners on. You know they'd put the gun on it. It was like a 'V' shape actually. A great big tower, spindles in and it had arms on and it pulled this deck backwards and forwards like that. It saved them being on a ship. *(Thomas Wilson)*

I did my last year and a bit in the Fitting Shop because that's where I decided I'd want to go because I found it the most interesting work of all the tasks. The machines I thought were a bit repetitive, whereas fitting it was a different task every day. They gave you a set of drawings and you went to the Parts Store, found yourself a bit of space in the workshop and just got on and built whatever you built. It was tremendous, tremendous type of work, I loved it. It was challenging and the skill level I think was really good. I went on to work for British Steel after that, and all the people I met that were from Head Wrightson's who'd moved to British Steel after Head Wrightson's closed, were exceptionally good craftsmen, they were the top league of people I've worked with. That isn't to say there weren't other good people but I never met anybody that I had worked with at Head's that wasn't a good craftsmen. *(John Richmond)*

The draughtsmen would do the drawing but for the work that we did we might have had a supplementary drawing. We might have the foreman make another drawing out saying, 'Look in order to do this particular part I want you to make this jig or this fixture.' A fixture's something for holding something, and so you might have a supplementary drawing. Whilst we did work on draughtsmen's drawing some of the time, a lot of the work we did was sketched on the back of a fag packet. The foreman would come along, or the Machine Shop foreman would come and say, 'What I want, in order for us to do this particular operation I want you to do this.' Or alternatively they often would draw it out on their hand or with a bit of chalk on the marking off table, 'Make them one of these so that we can do that.' So we worked from a mixture of drawings, and sometimes when he drew it out on his hand we had to say, 'Well can you leave the drawing please?' So a mixture of things. Sometimes you would look at the thing and you could see in your own mind how you needed to make a jig or a fixture in order to achieve the desired result.

So if somebody came to you and said, 'Right I want this jig,' can you talk me through how you would actually do that?

You would have to go and get some material. Either there would be material ordered in or go and find some suitable material. Let's say it was a big plate thing, they would probably get a proper order for some plate from the Bridge Yard which would have be machined all over nice and flat and its sides machined, and then we would mark it off, drill it and then we'd put it on what we call a jig boring machine. Then we'd have to bore the holes out to an exact pitch, using a Vernier gauge in order to measure the diameter of the hole and to measure the distance between the holes, take one from the other and then that would tell you the pitch of the holes. If it was right, fine, if it was wrong then you had to adjust your machine a little bit and take another cut through them all. Then there might be holes in different places, and so you used to work around that. You had to measure to thousandths of an inch, with a Vernier gauge. Then when we'd got it right and the holes were made to size hard bushes were put into the holes. The turners would make bushes, the inside diameter of the bush would equal the size of the drill that was going to be used. So you could take that plate and then put it on the actual job, drill the holes and they'd be there in the exact place. Do it again and again so it was producing multiple components to an accurate specification. Otherwise, if it was just a small jig you'd just go down the Bridge Yard and scrounge a bit of plate, whatever you could find. It was very much depending on the job. *(Albert Roxborough)*

Forging work. (Photograph by Jim Matthews)

Furnace man (Stampings)

I had a young family and I switched to the Forge because it was better wages, harder conditions, harsher conditions but you got paid more. I started off as a furnace man driver. Quickly graduated to be a stamper. We all started at the same time with the crew but you actually did the furnace part, they were on a twenty-four hour cycle then. One shift followed another except for a weekend. Monday morning someone else would come on and light up the furnace.

So the furnace man was pulling stuff out of the furnace?

He was the one who charged up and pulled out. But you were classed as a furnace man driver, could be a stamper but you worked as a crew. Everybody did everything.

What did you pull out, one every minute, one every two minutes, one every five minutes or...?

There's no two jobs the same. You might pull out one every two minutes, one every minute, or one every twenty minutes. It's hard to pin down, forging, there's no two forgings the same.

And then you'd be pulling some heavy, heavy stuff out were you?

In the past it wasn't so bad, the big jobs there weren't so many, it was mainly commercial stuff, middle of the range. It's all physical. Well, you can use a barrow. It's stood on two wheels, the foundry man takes it, pulls it round on the hammer and on the deck. The noise you hear is where I'm stamping. *(John Everett)*

Joiner

I used to do small things, files for the offices. Then as I progressed I was doing office furniture. Desks, stools. I used to go into the offices and do maintenance work in there. We used to do packing cases. The machinists used to cut all the timber, mark out what it was and we used to fix them together on the shop floor there. *(Bob Irwin)*

Machine Operator

When I went in I was on the marking off table for about six months. You get these jobs where you used to mark them off and get everything ready for the people to drill holes in and things like that. Then from the marking off table I went on a shaper. I was there about six months on the shaping machine. Then from a shaping machine you went on a lathe and I was on the lathe four years and then I did my National Service. Then when I came back I went on the big lathe again for about two years and then they asked me would I go horizontal boring. I liked centre-lathe turning but I was told if you go horizontal boring it's more money. So I went into horizontal boring when I was twenty-three and I did that till I was sixty-eight. You know I really enjoyed it. It was a good job. Well we did a lot of work for British Steel, what you call the clay guns. That involved some central-lathe turning and the horizontal boring. Now horizontal boring, it's fastened on a table and then your machine goes round it. When you're on a lathe it's different. The job goes round and your saddle moves along with a tool in it. *(Dennis Johnson)*

Head Wrightson's was a fantastic education for me because I learnt a hell of a lot. I'd learnt the initial things at Dorman's but this was a different ball game. There were a lot of good tradesmen at Head Wrightson's. It was a much bigger Machine Shop, a much bigger variation of machines with centre lathes, various makes and sizes of centre lathes, capstan lathes, turret lathes, grinders, milling machines, borers, planing machines. Wall borers. All kinds of machines, and it was a very busy place. *(Noel Thompson)*

My first big machine was an Elgamill, I think that had come from Middlesbrough. I had a spell on the milling machine. It was a proper bed mill. I'd say it would be about three metres long. Also I went on the Webster Bennett's. I had quite a spell on the Webster Bennett roundabout. Then I had a little spell actually in the Tool Room. Then I came back out onto the bigger lathes and I had a spell on the Craven. The big Craven lathe. I had quite a spell on there. Well, I had plenty of training on it first. I was on there working for a couple of weeks with somebody. *(John Stainthorpe)*

Maintenance

It was routine maintenance and then we'd write a report and then we'd give it to the boss and then he would say, 'Right, at the weekend this machine is down,' and we'd go over it and he'd put two or three of us on it and spruce it all up.

Did you ever find any big problems with the machines that could have been dangerous?

Oh yes. They would break, a gearbox would, a gear would smash inside. A shaft would snap. Oh there were various things. I mean it's endless, you know, what would happen on the machines. Then there was general wear and tear like on a car, you get on the machines. We had to put some adjustment in and adjust it. The machines were worked hard. They were going twenty-four hours, seven days a week some of them. *(Dick Robinson)*

So the maintenance of the site was done by the Teesdale Maintenance and we covered the compressed air, the steam heating, which heated some of the shops and also the offices.
Freddie Shaw used to strip the compressors down, either one a year or two a year. If you're shutting a compressor down you had to isolate everything to stop any back feed of air and because you were working on something which could have blown your head off, it was that strong, 100psi. We used to strip all the inlet and

outlet valves and they all used to be ground in the tool room and then all reassembled with new springs in.

How many compressors were there?

Three. We never ran three. We only ever needed two to supply the full factory. We had what they called the boilermen and theirs was a round-the-clock job to cover the compressors. That was to top up with oil, put them in the correct sequence, make sure they get a correct schedule. They also used to maintain the boilers. The compressors, which were Ingersoll Rand compressors, very big compressors, fed into three air receivers. The air would go through a heat exchanger to take the water out and then it was fed into air receivers. The air receivers then fed a six-inch line round the factory and drop off at various points.

That air would be used to drive what?

That air would be used to drive all the air tools, the air grinders, the chipping guns, the slagging guns, the pumps.

Do you remember belt-driven machines?

The only belt-driven machines were a couple in the Bridge Yard. The belt man was there when I started and I remember him well but I didn't have to use him a lot for belts because there weren't a lot of belts kicking around when I started. I did get some belts made from him. I presume it must have been an ongoing thing from the years prior to me starting where a lot of it was belt-driven. It was a full-time trade for the belt man. *(Derek Proctor)*

Management

On my arrival, or just about the time of my arrival there had been a change in Head Wrightson and the Wrightson brothers had ceased to be executive directors and the new regime meant that the then Secretary effectively became Administration Director/ Deputy Managing Director in some senses. But over the years, increasingly after a few years I began to take on some of the responsibilities including matters relating to the company's property, which was to become quite important in the future. So it was that in 1973 I was made Assistant Secretary. I continued to have a responsibility for contractual matters but some of the straightforward secretarial things fell to my lot and twelve months later I actually was given the title of Company Secretary. *(David Jowett)*

I was asked if I would like to go to India as General Manager of Head Wrightson India. Doreen (my wife) and I had an interview with Peter Wrightson and to cut a long story short we decided to go. The work, amongst other things, was completing the iron-making plant at Durgapur. We only did the iron making, which consisted of three blast furnaces plus ancillary plant and equipment. The Indian public sector iron & steel industry started its development in the mid Fifties. Three major steel plants were required but it was necessary that the countries supplying them needed to provide finance. After negotiations, Germany got the Roukela Plant, Russia the Bilhai Plant and Britain the Durgapur Plant. A consortium was set up in Britain to execute the complete Durgapur project, it consisted of: Head Wrightson for iron making, Wellman for steel making, Simon Carves for sinter making and Davy for the mills. *(Eric Brown)*

Marking off

A guy who had been marking off had been made up to a chargehand and moved from the marking off table into the Fitting Shop as a chargehand, so that was a lift for him. By that time I'd got the hang of reading all these drawings and I fancied having a go at the marking off. I went and did the marking off and I enjoyed it thoroughly. Good move I made. I became quite proficient at that. The idea of a marker off was you used to get big fabrications coming into the Machine Shop or castings which were all part of the machine that you were going to build. So before they went anywhere they used to come onto the marking off table and we used to put it on this big table and set it up square and then we used to put its centre line round it and some datums on it and

Marking off a Westling valve body. E. Burridge & A. Jackson. (HW Photographic Section)

then get the drawings out. Our job was to make sure there was enough metal on it to make what we wanted. So the marker's off job was to go to the highest point and put the line to make sure there's some metal there. Go to the lowest point put a line and make sure there's some metal there, and then within the bores to make sure there's enough metal in there, each end, left and right. And that basically was his job to make sure and put some centre lines on. So if once I found out that there was maybe a bit short of metal, that could be put right. At that time we could get a bit welded on here, put an extra pad on or do whatever. People used to say, 'How do you do that all day?' But every job was a challenge because you weren't doing the same lump of material each time. It was a different lump and a different set of drawings and each had its own problems. That was just one side of marking. Parts that had been machined came back to us and then we had to put them back on the table again and we had to re-mark them for drillings, where they needed to put some holes or keyways. When you worked in a shipyard it was unbelievable to see a ship being built from scratch and go down the slipway and then eventually sail away. That was job satisfaction at its utmost. I got a similar sort of job satisfaction knowing that that piece of metal came on to my bench eight months ago as a lump of metal and now it was part of a big gearbox that was going to do some fantastic things over the next twenty or thirty years. *(Stuart Thompson)*

Pattern-maker

At the end of our induction year we were asked to state our preferred trade and our second choice. I remember that my first choice was to be a fitter or turner but I was told that all the placements for these two trades were taken. They said that there was a vacancy for an apprentice pattern-maker attached to the foundry, so I accepted that. The pattern shop at Thornaby was at the bottom end of Trafalgar Street near the river which meant it was quite a hike from the bus stop on the main road. It was a two-storey building and there were

Stockton Steel Foundry Pattern Shop. (Wright Ahead)

about twenty to thirty pattern-makers and apprentices. Dave Gould was in over all charge of the shop and he was assisted by a foreman called Norman Treeby and a chargehand John Heighley. Health and safety in those days was virtually non-existent. Many machines were belt-driven and these were unguarded with extraction units non-existent. I remember one band saw that was started by pressing the starting button with one hand whilst spinning the top wheel of the machine with the other hand at the same time, so taking the load off the motor. When the saw picked up sufficient speed you then had to swing a lever across on the starter box to keep it running. This particular machine used to often need two people to work it when the drive belt became a bit slack, one man to cut and one to tighten the belt by pushing on it with a piece of wood to keep it tight whilst it was running. The start/stop button for this machine was located round the back of the machine, well away from easy access in an emergency. Not all machines were as bad as this, but many were, giving rise to the saying that 'not many pattern-makers pick their noses'. *(Doug Hauxwell)*

I was at the Forge until fifty-eight so I was out of my time at the Forge. Then, of course, when I went over to Thornaby you got more and more complicated patterns to make, bigger ones and more complicated things so your skill progressed. You could get patterns as big as this room. I mean a ladle if it was in here it would be practically the height of this room. And, oh, it was six foot square. It was tapered up and round at the top. You had to make that in wood. All you got was a piece of paper with the dimensions and you had big what we called drawing boards all around the shop at Thornaby and you had to draw your full size pattern out on that board and build it up. That was a building board to build it up on. When the pattern was finished and completed they were all painted up. There were special colours. Red was for the normal casting. Black was the print, in other words showing where there was going to be a hole in the casting. Yellow surface showed that it was going to be a machined area on the casting when it was finished. It was all painted up and of course, they were all checked. Every pattern was checked dimensionally, and this is what Norman Treeby did a lot of before they were okayed for the Foundry. *(John Heighly)*

Personnel

It was a very similar job to what I'd been doing in the coal industry, training people.

I used to run deputies' courses in the Coal Board which were very popular, training pit deputies, who were really the foremen. I ran some of the same sort of courses for Head Wrightson's foremen and it went down like a house on fire. John Wrightson said to me one day, he said, 'These courses you're running are absolutely first-class,' and I was quite surprised because I'd been doing them for the last eight years or so. They were courses in supervision and management, safety and handling people, of course, because the foremen had a lot to do with that. They were on the site in Trafalgar Street somewhere. I was in Trafalgar Street to start with and then the Personnel Management were moved out into the old flour mill adjacent to the Victoria Bridge on Bridge Road. There was a big mill on the site there.

Then we moved from there out to Yarm. It was quite interesting to me to see what was always a small family company growing into a very big international concern. And that's what they were doing of course. *(Joe Doran)*

Planning

There were about eight of us that did planning related to process planning sheets. Jig and tool. What you might call the sort of technical side of planning. Then there was another room at the back which had two guys and two girls who printed all the paperwork. Printed the process planning sheets and updated the progress records. It's only about a dozen people, that's all.

The Planning Department was slightly divided into two in that there was a Machine Shop and Fitting orientated group and there was a Fabrication orientated group.

And how did you find life in the Planning Department?

Oh that was great, I enjoyed the job. I can't really complain about it at all. *(Ken Peacock)*

So essentially what was your role as Planning Manager then?

Because we only had access to an offsite mainframe to do the number crunching we had to send it all the data based on the plan, which was based on the sequence of events and activities. It's like making a cup of tea. The first thing you do is put the kettle on. Then whilst that's happening you get the cups and the milk and then you pour the hot water in there and then you can pour the tea. Right, that's logical, everybody knows that. But when you're building something which is like half the size of a village then it's not quite so easy. You needed to have to look at the drawings and think on what the right way to build it is. What the shortest way of doing it, and to identify what is called the critical path, which was when you add that to that, to that, to that, so that eventually you come to the end date. So we were predicting the future. Always risks with that but that's what we were trying to do. *(Ted Sinnot)*

Plater

I was in the Marking Squad until I was eighteen and that's when you went out plating. I enjoyed the time. I've still got good hearing but to have a conversation with your mate when you were working with him you had to shout because there was riveters going, hammers going, banging and crashing all over. Oh it was bedlam, they wouldn't put up with it today, you'd have to have all these ear things on. We had nothing, nothing. When I first started we didn't even have steel toe caps, that came in very shortly afterwards. The company provided them and you paid out of your wages so much to get protective boots. You weren't provided with overalls, you bought your own overalls. I had bib and brace type with the pockets in because you needed rulers and things in your pockets. Most of the tools were provided by the company except for things like squares, set squares and things like that. When I was in the Template Shop I had to buy quite a few tools of my own. But the hammers and the pops and things, all those things were provided and basically you start off in the Marking Squad and you do the painting, because everything was painted over in white lead so that it was permanent and all the instructions were painted onto the beam and then off it would go. So I was in the Marking Squad until I was eighteen and then I went plating. *(John Heath)*

They had a piecework system then where you went to the foreman who gave you a drawing of the job, then you went to the rate fixer, and you asked them for a price for the job. Then if you could do the job inside the price you got the money that was left. Well, it worked out the worse plater you were the more chance you had of making money because they give you the easy jobs. There was what they called tray plates. Just a straight plate with a bump on there and a bump on there and they used to go on each other making a conveyer belt for carrying the coal out of the pits. Well, it just had a little jig. Drop the plate on, drop a bolt in that hole and that hole and that hole and put the end plate on then tack, tack. Used to get paid so much each for them. Dead easy. An idiot could have done it and they made more money than I did in a day. If the driller missed the hole by a fraction, which they do, you would have to put that right. The guillotine man

Working on a dished end in the Heavy Plate Shop at HW Teesdale. (HW Photographic Section)

missed the line, left three eighths of an inch on. You had to grind it off. There was a punch where one side come down the other side went up and the other side went down and that went up. Guillotines, punch. Bill Lakey was the man on it with two labourers and you can imagine twenty, thirty-foot angle bars running them along three inches apart. And he used to rest it on his knees and the punch would punch the hole in.

So how thick would be the metal with the punching holes?

Three-eighths was it, a quarter, three-eighths?. All shapes. Any shape you wanted. Good machine but it had to be used right you see. So one day the foreman template maker came up to me and asked why the platers usually fell down on the prices. So I explained all about these little things that happened; missed the line, missed the cut and then the plater has to put it right. Harry Thompson asked me to go through everything with him and write down everything why the platers couldn't make their jobs pay. *(Norman Toulson)*

Once you finished at the Apprentice School you were sent over to the Bridge Yard at Head Wrightson's, Thornaby. Well, basically, you were put in the Template Loft looking after templates, wooden templates. Then after that you were put in what was called the Marking Squad, marking pieces out for drilling steel, and then somebody higher up made the decision on what or which shop you were going to be put into. Just to basically serve your time.

I don't know what a plater does, tell me.

Well, basically it's a case of fabricating items out of steel. It could be structural steel, boilers, pressure vessels, giant power station stuff.

So in effect you'd be bending and shaping?

No, that was always done, done for us by the Press Shop. This was a case of theoretically really putting things together. It would vary from something that maybe weighed five pound or something like that. But eventually when I was working on the jigs for a particular power station it was four-inch-thick steel and

Heavy Plate shop at HWT showing two 50-ton cranes both of which had two hoists for light and heavy lifting. Stress-relieving furnace in the right background. (Remembering Thornaby Group)

they were over twenty feet long and there were two of them. *(Ken Davies - Plater)*

They used to give you a minimum amount of tools, just stuff that they could actually make themselves. We made a lot when we were serving our time in the Apprentice School like the plate square and pops and stuff. A pop is the marking off equipment. A pop used to be for marking holes actually for drilling. You used to mark the centre of the hole with a pop and put an indentation in the plate and then you would know where the centre of the hole was. That's how we used it. But the majority of the time we used to buy our own tapes if I recall, and a two-foot folding rule which was the plater's main tool. It was kept in your side pocket, the rule pocket in your overalls. You could always tell a plater by the two-foot folding rule he had in his pocket. But most of the time we'd mainly make our tools. We used to get a hammer, they used to supply you with a hammer but most of the stuff we needed had been made in the Apprentice School. The template makers used to make a wooden template which they'd lay on your plate or your angles, your angle steel or whatever. You'd lay it on and they'd already have the holes drilled in the template wood. All you would have to do is lay the wood on the steel and then you would have what they called a barrel pop which had a pop through, a machined thing to actually fit the size of the hole drilled in the wood. You just used to bat that and then you didn't have to measure anything. It was all made for you down at the template makers, that was their part. It made your job easier actually marking off because you didn't have to use the tape or anything. It was all down to the template maker's work. *(Dennis Longstaff)*

A Bradwell boiler, weighing 340 tons and eighty feet diameter and twenty-four feet long being launched into the River Tees. (Photograph courtesy The Northern Echo)

I wanted to be a Head Wrightson worker. I was fascinated by bridges even as a young boy and Head Wrightson's were the best bridge builders. It was as simple as that. And they had the best training school acknowledged. The other firms were trying desperately to get up to the level that Head Wrightson's trained their apprentices at.

So you went round all the different departments. I know you finished up as a plater. When did you, or who decided that you would be a plater?

I think it was a combination of my wishes and performances in the various departments. Because in the Foundry you were told to, 'Right get there, shovel that sand into the mould, make sure it's patted down,' and if it doesn't work you've got to do it again, and I'm thinking, 'this is not for me.' The same in the Machine Shop. We were taken into the toolmakers' section and all the machinists would bring their blunt tools back and the apprentices were given the job of sharpening them. So you put them in a machine and watched the grindstones until they were sharp, so you were stuck there like a lemon. It was boring. It was different being a plater. Once you got in, the noise, the camaraderie, the way people accepted you, not that they didn't do it in the other departments but I wasn't really interested. I wanted to be where the welding was going on, the plating, the construction, the building up from nothing to the finished article as it went from one end of the shop to the other. It was just what I wanted to do. I had no idea why to be honest. *(John Kirk)*

Project manager

What's a typical day in the life of a project manager?

Answering the phone an awful lot because you're getting your engineers on site ringing in. They're always wanting information. I found I used to have to go in on a Sunday to get on top of any work and to get away from the phone. The main thing is to do a job, get it done to time and cost. We had a Planning Office and we used to get together and talk and come up with dates that things had to be done by, and it used to work quite well I found. After Bradwell was finished they did other nuclear work I think. They quoted for Hartlepool but they didn't get it. The people who got it made a big mistake. I don't know how many years late it was but it was a hell of a lot. It was very late and the price they quoted was way out. We couldn't buy the steel for what they quoted. It would have been handy for Head Wrightson as it was so close and we had the know-how by then. *(Ron Hughes)*

Rate fixers

I did the rate fixing for the Fitting Shop and also the Heat Exchangers Shop. They were on piecework price. Their wage was made up of a basic wage and then the piecework price and I used to work out the value of a job. We always used to have a discussion. They always wanted more than I'd worked it out to. But we always finished up with a joint agreement. I worked on quite a few different projects. The main one I worked on was the Hinkley and Hunterston nuclear power stations. All the guide tubes and the core components, things like that. And I did jig and tool design for the manufacture of the guide tube. I'm pretty good with remembering numbers there was, four reactors, two at Hinkley, two at Hunterston, and there were 308 fuel-guide tubes, 90 control-rod tubes, seven flux scanning and six flux measuring. All stainless steel, all assembled in clean conditions. I did all the planning for that. Yes, all the progress reporting and everything. We made quite a bit of money on that. *(Jim Heward)*

Research and development

I went as a graduate in 1966, I was twenty-three. I had a degree in Physics, which was relevant because I was joining the Physics Department in R&D.

And how big was the R&D Department at that time?

I recall it was 107 people. There were workshops and laboratories under the main HWISWEL offices. If you recall there was the iron and steelworks offices at one side – the new bit – and they continued above. The Research and Development laboratories and workshops where they would make various samples for metal testing or whatever. Then opposite in the sort of quadrangle there were R&D offices. Then further over, outside the R&D offices at the back there were all the erection fittings that they used to take to site to erect whatever it was - blast furnace, sinter machines.

Did R&D encompass the metal testing, for the Steel Foundry, the analysis?

Yes, there was Maurice Hipkins who was I believe Chief Metallurgist. There were some laboratories there which used to do chemical and mechanical analyses of various materials. R&D was really there to serve the needs of any of the companies around. Mostly what I did was in relation to work for HWISWEL, or PEL as it eventually became. But there were people doing work for the steel foundries. I'm not sure what sort of work it was, but mine was essentially to do with pelletising machines, sinter machines and the mechanics of the materials used and research into blast furnaces and measurement of various variables on site. Things like moisture content in the sinter feed because that was critical to how effective the process was. So we'd often go out onto the site and to sinter machines up at Ravenscraig for instance, sometimes to sites at Redcar to take measurements of whatever. *(Barrie Hope)*

I had my own little research projects. I was doing work on corrosion of aluminium storage containers in cooling ponds where they store all the spent fuel rods. I was doing a project to determine which was the best coating to prevent corrosion of these things. It was a bit Heath-Robinson but we had a series of ceramic sinks that had an alkaline liquid in them. They were

HW stand at mining sales exhibition at Hong Kong.

kept at a constant temperature by immersion heaters. I checked and adjusted the pH value every day, dried them off, weighed them and put them back in situ. It was a long-term project since weight losses even after a year or so, were tiny. Alongside there were loads of projects. Project 'X,' I always remember, was a classic one which was welding of dissimilar metals. A lot of it to do with the nuclear industry and we were making the Bradwell boilers at the time. *(Colin Waugh)*

Sales

I joined the Teesdale Sales force. So you had a different background to learn, it was a heavier business, much bigger. But I was pretty lucky because I took over a job we'd developed at the Forge as a sales contact with Tioxide International, BTP as it was then, and we'd got in on a revolutionary process that they were just starting up, some vessels they wanted. They started at about nine-foot diameter and eventually finished up at about thirty odd feet diameter by the time we got to Teesdale. I took that job as a sales guy to Teesdale, so I had to keep that under my wing if you like. It turned into one of our best profitable jobs at Teesdale. It became a huge job for us. It had a lot of spin-offs as well. But at Teesdale on sales for Head Wrightson you identified a project, and having identified a project you looked at it to see what is in it for us. You identified that ICI were building a new terephthalic acid plant and what was there for us, or was there anything e.g. rotary machines? But that could be worldwide because it would be the mining side as well. It could be a new copper plant, it could be a new aluminium plant or anything really. You chased after all major projects. *(Barry Preece)*

From about 1959, 1960 perhaps until 1973 I was in the Sales Department. It involved a lot of travelling. Initially we were doing a lot of business with British Steel in South Wales so I went back to my roots, home from home. I also went to Poland because they wanted tinplate. It is a constant source of wonder that so many of these companies or countries wanted to expand to a point that now our own tinplate industry has virtually disappeared. I went to Germany and Romania but it was later that I got involved in major contracts. Basically, we would get an enquiry and from that point we'd start all the necessary introductions, the paperwork to begin with. We'd start to prepare and submit an offer. Very often it was a question of going out and discussing what they really wanted, and then you would come back and again go through the whole process of putting in a bid. *(David Auld)*

Secretary

I started at Head Wrightsons as a commercial trainee even though the course had already begun and they had their quota of six already. I think it was a question of dad pushing a few buttons and I got in. The trainees had to attend evening classes three times a week and during the day were sent to various offices to learn about the firm. We were based in the Post Room and our supervisor was also the firm's receptionist. She kept a strict but motherly eye on us. She gave us talks about the firm, told us what to do, how to do it, how to conduct ourselves, how to behave towards others and sometimes what, or what not to wear. Our office was just inside the main door of the main offices in Trafalgar Street. The first thing I had to do every morning on my way to work was to collect the newspapers from Thornaby railway station then distribute them throughout the offices. Then we handled the incoming mail. We sorted it into pigeon holes and then delivered it to the various offices. That helped us to learn where the offices were and who worked there. We worked in the Post Room for about an hour in the morning and again in the late afternoon to sort and stamp the outgoing mail but for most of the time each day we were sent out to work in a different department. Maybe a few weeks in one and a few weeks in another to learn what work was done, to see how we liked it and to see, well frankly, how much they liked us. We spent time in Personnel, Accounts, the Print Room, Communications room and others. I ended up doing a longer stint in the Purchasing Department and that's where I became a permanent member of the typing pool. The pool was part of a very large office which contained the Purchasing and Estimating Departments. There were two smaller offices for the heads of each department. I think I was in the typing pool a total of about three years.

Office girls at lunch time. L-R Norma (unknown), Frances McDermont, Dorothy Wrigglesworth, Wendy Heald, née Hudson. (Photograph courtesy Wendy Heald)

The lady who was in charge retired after I'd been there about two years and they put me in charge of it although I was quite young. At the end of each day we had to count the carbon copies of letters, enquiries, and orders and record the number of items we had typed. Then I got promotion to be private secretary to Les Reid, the Technical Manager and I worked for him until I left in 1964 because I was pregnant. I had married in 1962. *(Margaret Hope)*

They decided that they would have a Sales Office. I'm afraid I can't remember my bosses name, and he was a very nice man but he came from the Manchester area, He was based over there but he would come over every so often. But he had salesmen in different parts of the country, in different Head Wrightson's offices working for him. There was somebody in London and they all had Dictaphones with tape cassettes, which were really odd tape cassettes because they weren't cassettes, they were sheets of plastic waxed paper with a white cardboard strip across the top so they could put them in an envelope and post these. They posted them

Stepney Bridge prior to launch. (HW Photographic Section)

to me with their reports and I would thread this piece of cardboard into my receiver. It looked like waxed paper. It was shiny and I would thread them into my machine, put my headphones on and type up their reports and then send them back out to wherever. *(Wendy Heald)*

I just stayed in the Chairman's General Office and started to do little bits and pieces, helping out in various places, although Richard Miles was the Chairman, Sir John was the Deputy or Vice Chairman and Peter Wrightson, Mr. Peter, was the next one down the line. If their secretaries were off they'd send for me, would I go and do it. Well, one day Sir John's secretary was ill, she had what they had at the time, Asian flu. His PA came in and said, 'Would you like to come and work for Sir John?' I said, 'Yes,' picked up my book and I went. I thought he was joking but he wasn't you see. So I just went and sat down, did a bit of shorthand and that was it. But although we were trained to do shorthand and typing, the bosses were never trained to dictate. So it was difficult knowing the phraseology, the way they would put things.

Would you say they were quite scary people too...?

Well, they were human, and that's how I looked on people. They're human. I could go to the farm, I could go back home. And I loved the farm, and so I was lucky in that respect that I could go to work, relax, didn't put two fingers up at them but I was more relaxed knowing that I wasn't relying on them for a job.

It must have been quite a contrast working in a busy office after you'd been on a farm?

Oh yes, the animals had a lot more respect. *(Margaret Partridge)*

Shipwright

I worked all over. Outside doing dock gates. For no extra money just the job price. I went down there one day and I saw four weathers in one go. First it was snowing, then it was windy, then it was raining, it was a bloody horrible job. They launched the dock gates out of the yard and on the river bend.

But who did the propping them up and that? Who put the timbers in?

Shipwrights. There were shipwrights there. There was a shipwright squad. Because the

Walter Farquarson marking off a heat-exchanger-tube sheet. (Company brochure)

shipwrights used to buff the gates. See, they did the woodwork to get the gates shut, didn't they? And the shipwrights did all the shaping of the wood. *(Thomas Wilson)*

So tell me what did the shipwrights do?

The dock gates were made where the slipway went under them. So the extension to the slipway went up to the dock gates and then you put all the blocks in to support the gate when it was lowered onto the slipway. The dock gate itself was hinged on one side and on the opposite side was a timber where it closed. Now a dock gate would be maybe thirty-foot long or more. So these timbers were square at first or oblong. They were bolted to a plate top and bottom and then at either end they would use a metal template. Now this template was probably metal and it was worked from a centre point at either end and then there was slits in the template so that it give you a depth to work from. But in these slits there was a piano wire and in fact it went from one end to the other so that every three feet along you made a band. And to do this band you measured off your piano wire. You made a hole into the greenheart wood. When you got to the depth you put a red dot and you worked your way round and every three foot you went down the length of the dock gate. Now when that was finished with the bands you worked between each band cutting

Fifty-ton crane hook in the heavy plate shop at HW Teesdale. (Wright Ahead)

the greenheart back. Greenheart is a wood that's well preserved. It's an oil-based wood that you can use under water. It's a very hard wood. *(Bob Irwin)*

Slinger

They asked me if I fancied a job slinging, but we didn't call it slinging we used to call ourselves lifting engineers. So I said, 'Yes,' and I found out about slinging, the different ways to lift jobs in the Heavy Plate Shop. It's not an easy job slinging, you've got to be careful what you're doing with that, you know. *(Ken Davies - Slinger)*

Solicitor

I specialized in a lot of stuff relating to contracts. Obviously, if people were negotiating contracts we either gave them advice on how to do it, or participated. Technology licences stuff, that sort of thing. Technology licences, mundane sort of stuff like claims, industrial injuries, and I remember some very sad accidents, people being killed at Head Wrightson's Stampings at Hartlepool. Three people being asphyxiated at Mortlake Brewery working on a project. It was really in the days somewhat before health and safety hit the world. But there was still responsibility for one's workers. The Factory Inspector in those days used to get involved so there was stuff like that. But I think I was a corporate man really. I've never been in private practice and still never been in the idea of family law and divorces, and conveyancing never really appealed to me. So I enjoyed the work. It was very good. *(Robin Millman)*

Template Shop laying out floor. (Remembering Thornaby Group)

Template maker

A template maker in the Bridge Yard was tied to the Bridge Yard. It consisted of a large shop with a raised table roughly sixty feet by about thirty feet where you worked round this table. A series of journeymen worked round the table with their apprentices and you laid out and made templates from the drawings sent down by the Drawing Office. It was quite a skilled job and it was well paid. It was the highest paid job in the Bridge Yard at that time with the bonus system and one thing and another. It was an interesting job because you got the opportunity to actually read the drawings that were sent down and make the different templates for different parts of the project, whatever it was. I was quite happy as a template maker, I enjoyed it, but I could see that if I didn't move out of the Template Loft I'd be a template maker all my life, and even then I suppose I was a bit ambitious and the next step was the Drawing Office. So I applied to go in the Drawing Office. It was a bit difficult because one or two of the apprentices had gone into the Drawing Office out of the Template Loft, my predecessors if you like, older guys than me, and one of them in particular hadn't liked it and come back down and that had left a rather sour taste with the old Chief Draughtsman there. So he was a bit jaundiced about taking me. Anyway he did and I stayed in the Drawing Office in the Colliery Section. The Template Loft was the better paid because you got a bonus in the Template Loft. And that was one of the problems I had when I transferred to the Drawing Office. I was starting to make what I thought was reasonable money, which would probably be about seven pounds a week, six or seven pounds a week and I lost the bonuses in the Template Loft. I went onto a junior draughtsman's rate which was less than I had been getting. It was a sacrifice you had to make if you made the move. *(Barry Preece)*

Tracers

Tracing engineering drawings in the Drawing Office. We produced them for the draughtsmen. The draughtsman drew the drawing and we copied it onto linen. We had to copy every line and every word. We used Indian ink and pens with various nibs for the printing. The ink went inside the pen and you screwed the nibs on. For the tracing the pens were more like tweezers really with a screw. They weren't, as you would say, nibs for printing but for the tracing, they were more like tweezers really with a screw where the ink went in. We also used a T-square, set square, lining pens and a compass.

Were there many tracers?

Seven when I started. Seven tracers and four typists. We were in one room. Not the main Drawing Office, not to start with. You went through the Drawing Office, up the stairs and there was a department there of draughtsmen

Alf Barron operating the heavy planer in the Machine Shop at HWT. (Wright Ahead)

called Wagons. We were the tracers and the typists on the left. The Wagon Department just specialised in wagons. They were really good fun. They used to play tricks on us. Always ready for a laugh them lads. Yes. Not too serious like in the big Drawing Office because we were up there on our own. They made funny remarks when we met on the stairs. We always went out to Christmas lunch with them, to the Black Bull at Yarm. There would be about twelve or so of us, just the girls and the Wagon Department. *(Irene Henderson)*

Turner

I classed myself as a good turner. They had some very good tradesmen, very capable, very hard working. But the big money was being earned by the people on the lathes. The people on the boring machines and the planing millers and all these things were doing much bigger work so one piece of material could be on their machine for up to a week. When I first went to Head Wrightson's I was on a small centre lathe, and anybody who knows anything about lathes will know that a lathe is basically made up of a headstock and a bed and along the bed moves the saddle. The saddle has a couple of auxiliary slides, a cross slide and a compound slide, and on top of the compound slide you have a tool post and in the tool post you fit a cutting tool. And a full name for a lathe is a centre lathe so everything operates round the centre line of the machine. But you could cut things off centre, getting a bit more complicated now. Once I'd moved on to a bigger machine it had a longer bed so therefore the work was bigger. I eventually ended up on a machine which had a twelve-foot bed. But they had, they had lathes in Head Wrightson's which had twenty-foot beds. The makes of machines in Head's were Swifts, Craven's, Dean Smith and Grace, Colchester's. But I was asked to move and go on the biggest lathe in the workshop. This was after I'd been there two and a half years. So I knew the system well, I knew the jobs well, I knew the staff, the back up staff, the progress people, what we called chasers who would chase all the

HWT Light Machine Shop. (Photograph courtesy of Alan Simpson)

jobs up. I mean if the Fitting Shop are fitting something together they want to know that the part they've got is finished. And a lot of jobs in the Machine Shop would come through as a raw material and by the time it was finished it would probably have been through about four or five different machines. If it was a shaft it would have had to have been turned, rough turned, heat treated, that means hardened or tempered. Then you would have to re-machine it again, put a thread on, make sure, and then it would go to a grinder, a cylindrical grinder where it would grind certain diameters for bearings. It would have to go on a milling machine for keyways or holes to be drilled in. There were a lot of jobs like that. So those jobs had to be chased around the workshop, they had to be moved from one from one operation to another. *(Noel Thompson)*

Welders

The Class One Shop was all work that needed certification and approval for the welds and usually had Lloyds' inspection, as that type of work was generally work for the petrochemical company on heat exchangers and pressure vessels and in later years the nuclear work went through there. There was a group of welders called 'The Magnificent Seven', and it almost seemed to be a dead-man's-shoes job to get into there. But there was some damned good welders amongst them, good conscientious guys and a few of them certainly passed on their skills and their experiences to the apprentices that were about at the time. I felt as though I'd found my niche really. It was an area that I enjoyed. I was involved in the technical development of welding so it was less and less of the craft aspects of welding and more the theory of welding. Again R&D, something you realised in later years was also a training ground for not only the future managers within Head Wrightson's but certainly for lots of the local industries on Teesside as Head Wrightson's employees moved to other companies. I was very much involved in the development work. Head Wrightson's R&D was the troubleshooting centre for all of the other Head Wrightson's divisions for welding so it exposed me to visits over to Head

Welder at work at HW Teesdale. (Photograph courtesy of Chris Birks)

Wrightson's Machine Shop and Stockton works, the foundries to offer advice and guidance on welding. There was a shop-floor welding engineer in the Bridge Yard in Teesdale, but he was the day-to-day troubleshooter, so all of the specifications came from me and from the mid Sixties onwards there was more and more emphasis on the technical control of welding and the writing of welding specifications. A written specification as opposed to a verbal instruction was becoming more and more of a requirement. And all of that was controlled from R&D. So as well as being involved in the technical development of trying out new welding processes, new welding materials, looking after the physical testing of those test welds, you were also receiving the drawings to write the weld specifications for the other divisions. Plus, if there was a shop-floor failure, a defect, a crack or whatever and it was of a technological nature, you were invited over to come and assist and resolve the problem as a troubleshooter. So it was again excellent grounding. You develop some new technology, you develop some new strategy, and bear in mind it was still fairly heavily unionised, so if you had external people coming in introducing new methods and ideas there could be a resistance to it. But in some ways I was seen as one of their own. I was accepted. So what you did and what you suggested in your approach, people were encouraging you and probably more enthusiastic to embrace the ideas than they might have been. I was the first one that they'd groomed as a shop-floor welder to become a welding engineer. *(Charlie Tighe)*

Horizontal cold rolling at HWT. (Wright Ahead)

Chapter 3

'Our bread-and-butter': Head Wrightson's products

When Head Wrightson began it was a small iron foundry on the banks of the river Tees. It continued to develop until it closed completely in 1984. The portfolio of products manufactured by the company expanded and they sold to an increased range of customers. An official guide to industry of Stockton-on-Tees Borough summarised the situation in the 1970s by claiming 'the diversity of products ranges from designing and building large plant for iron and steel, colliery and mining, dock and harbour, nuclear power and process industries to steel stockholding and the supply of steel and iron castings, drop forgings and stampings. Their customers range from car manufacturers to coal preparation engineers; from copper miners to nylon producers; from astronomers to municipal authorities.'

In the nineteenth and early twentieth century, the company was well known for building bridges, viaducts and piers. It also focused on developing mining equipment and iron-making plant. As new technologies developed, Head Wrightson took the opportunity to open new markets. Nuclear engineering became a key diversification for the company and by the 1970s they had manufactured products for five British nuclear power stations; Bradwell, Dungeness, Oldbury, Hinkley Point and Hunterston. The supply of iron and steel plant to UK, European and Commonwealth markets was a significant activity after 1945. Sintering plants were also designed and built and by the mid 1970s Head Wrightson was the only UK company doing this for ferrous and non-ferrous applications. Economic historian Geoffrey North claimed Head Wrightson's expertise and their willingness to exploit new markets in this period helped maintain them as leaders in the local heavy engineering sector.

In the following extracts our contributors explain in more detail how they designed and manufactured some of these products.

Acid cleaning support plates in the clean conditions area prior to sealing in polythene.
(Remembering Thornaby Group)

Sinter plants

In iron making when the feed for a blast furnace is being prepared, large-lump ore is crushed. This produces an amount of fine ore too small for going into the furnace. So as not to waste it, the fines are made into sinter. The fines are mixed with coke and sometimes limestone and passed under an ignition hood where it is fused together (sintered). The sinter then forms part of the blast-furnace feed.

About how big were the sinter-plant machines, what sort of length?

They were quite large buildings because the sinter plant building had to include raw-material bunkers, mixing drums, screening etc. The machines would be between 30 and 40m long. *(Eric Brown)*

A handfull of sinter. (Wright Ahead)

My first move from the office was to Scunthorpe where Head Wrightson were building a sinter plant as part of Appleby Frodingham's steel plant extensions. These were major extensions and involved a number of contractors. The name of the plant expansion was SERAPHIM, which was made up from the names of the main contractors. I think they were as follows:-

SE South Extension
R Ross
A Ashmores, Blast Furnace and Iron Making
P Press, Civil Engineers
H Head Wrightson
I Idris Miles Kemp, Chief Engineer of
M Appleby Frodingham's.
(Initial of first names).

My job on the site was to record any changes made and to amend 'as designed' drawings to 'as built' drawings. On return to the Thornaby Office I was put in charge of preparing drawings, obtaining quotations and ordering material for sinter-plant projects at Hartlepool Works and Cargo Fleet Works of the South Durham Iron & Steel Co. This may sound like Project Engineering but in those days all in the Drawing Office were designated draughtsmen. *(Eric Brown)*

My very first project was design and building of a sinter plant which provides some of the materials that go into the blast furnace and that was at Skinningrove Steelworks, just local here. As a matter of fact I went right through my life when I actually left Head Wrightson to be joined by the company that took us over, which was Davy and that sinter plant was being disassembled at the very same time. *(Max Clark)*

A lot of sinter machines were made, which is a process of mixing the coal or coke dust and fine iron ore together to feed it into the blast furnace. Head Wrightson's were specialists in doing sinter machines. Basically, it was a large steel frame, probably 30 - 50 yards long with a continuous circle of pallet frames going around carrying the sinter from the feed chutes to discharge into the furnace. Where the pallet frames carrying the sinter came along the top and to the discharge end, it didn't go round on a circle, but on a bit of an arc which helped to discharge the sinter. *(Albert Roxborough)*

Equipment for steel industry

Initially we were doing a lot of business with British Steel in South Wales so I went back to my roots, home from home. This was, of course, when we produced tinplate and galvanised strip. These were the customers we were mainly supplying in the very early days. In the immediate period of first couple of decades after the war there was a huge demand for tinplate for cans and various other things and, of course, it got gradually greater because you can still see the number of tins in the supermarkets. Also in the canning industry, the soft drinks and beer, and things developed to a point where the original tin cans were made from tinplate which was of a fairly thick gauge. It then was deemed necessary to try and make it of a slightly stronger steel but thinner but it would still have the tin coating on. And again, our machinery, our equipment was providing that sort of product. Also there's always been a huge demand for roofing sheets, any sort of metalwork requires to be protected against corrosion for a fairly long period and galvanising does that, it's very effective. *(David Auld)*

Molten metal being poured into an HW ladle car. (HW Photographic Section)

We were making a hopper. That's the bit that goes at the top of the blast furnace that distributes the material as it goes in. *(Bob Close)*

Occasionally we had to go into the Foundry because they made slag ladles for the iron and steel industry. You had to go in the Foundry and set the pattern up because there were a lot of loose pieces on it. You had to fit them on. You went with a pattern-maker. You held the pieces while he put them all into place. Then, of course, when they made the mould around it you had to go in it, this was more or less the apprentice's job. You had to go in, go down in the mould and take all the screws out. To loosen the pieces so you could pull the pattern out. And of course, if you left the piece on, it destroyed the mould so you have to get every screw out. You were in and out the Foundry on little jobs like that. *(John Heighly)*

In the early days when I first started there they were doing a lot of stuff for the Consett Ironworks like Caldo converters and stuff like that. At the Forge they did the big aluminium smelting tanks for the Invergordon Aluminium Smelter Works. Scale cars for the steel industry. I remember doing the Redcar blast furnaces and the Llanwern blast furnaces. They were the twenty-metre-diameter hearths and they trial erected the hearth sections in the Heavy Plate Shop. *(Ken Peacock)*

We were building scale cars and transfer cars for the steelworks. We often did bells and hoppers out of manganese steels, and clay guns for plugging the holes on blast furnaces when they've been tapped. Everything we did was basically around steel plant. *(Billy Sharp)*

When I was serving my apprenticeship I worked on the scale cars and transfer cars, which were for steel plant. Scale cars that had hoppers in. The scale cars and transfer cars were to weigh the ore to go into the furnace. The scale car weighed it and it was on a high rail and it went along and deposited the ore out of the hoppers into the transfer car. It would maybe fill that, do two or three runs till the transfer car, which had a big hopper, was filled up and that

A selection of slag ladle cars in various stages of construction. (Turner's)

then went and was fed into the blast furnace. *(Jim Heward)*

Equipment for mining

In the first instance we used to do a lot of mining equipment, especially in County Durham where the coal was at a premium at that particular time. We used to make all the head gear and the cages that went into the head gear for the miners to go up and down. Also the cages where the coal was taken up and down, and on one occasion we built a brand-new mine at Dawdon Colliery and we all went out there to fit the equipment. That's the mining-shaft head gear and equipment altogether and so we were out of the Forge and it was the first time I'd worked away and that was one of the first jobs that we did.

The head gear would be the gear that takes the big wheels?

That's correct, yes twenty-foot diameter, I would say. The first time I got on top there I don't know whether my underpants were brown before or after I went on up but on the first occasion that I ever climbed up I would have to admit I was pretty scared. There was one little squad, and they made what's called humble hooks, which were attached to the outside of the cages that went up and down the mine shaft and if anything had happened they just slotted in a position, held it tightly. It was an absolute safety device.

About how many humble hooks would you be making then?

I would guess at least ten a week. It was quite a production line. They would go to all the coal mines in England, and to the gold mines as well in South Africa.

Was there any other work done for export.?

Yes there was. We used to make machinery purely for South Africa and at the time when we were making it, it was like washing products. When they got the gold out of the mines the water used to come down and they could see where the gold was. We couldn't

Completed twelve feet, six inches diameter by fifteen feet long ball mill for Rio Tinto Spain, awaiting shipment from Stockton Forge. (HW Photographic Section)

understand why we had to put all these great thick rails on top and then sheeting on top of that and then locks and keys on top of that. Then it dawned on us what it was, because they were frightened to death that people who were working there could get their hands in at the gold that was coming through. That was one of the criteria, that absolutely nobody could get a hand in. Everything had to be locked and it had to be really enforced so nobody could get at it. So I remember things like that vividly. *(Trevor Briggs)*

At the beginning of the war when I first started, Stockton Forge concentrated a lot on the mining industry, particularly in this area, coal. But for overseas and the metals: mining of gold, copper, tin, zinc, you name it, we were doing process plants for the mining industry. The first site visits I ever had were to collieries in Durham, in the County of Durham. For example things like the head frame. I remember Boldon Colliery, it was starting to corrode and we were asked to go and do a survey, replace all the members supporting this tower, this head frame. I remember going there with one of the cricketers that we had, Harry Thompson, he was from the Template Shop. I was only maybe seventeen or eighteen and he was about ten years older than me and he virtually took over when we got measuring up. They were swab angles, if you know what a swab angle is, where the angle had been opened up or closed, see? And when you've got this big building with all these swab angles, how the hell were we going to make it to fit? Harry was a template maker by trade and he kept me right. He was brilliant. So that was in the colliery. I learnt a lot about the geography of Durham because at the Drawing Office we used to have to go to site visits to measure up and things of that sort. *(Ray Shaw)*

We were working principally with the colliery people because a lot of the work was for the

Forty-eight inch classifier for English China Clay built by Stockton Forge. (Wright Ahead)

Coal Board and for the mining industry abroad so names like Roan Antelope and the Ashanti gold fields and Brodsworth Colliery and things like this were the names that we lived with. That was really our bread-and-butter, the colliery side. It was the mining side, when I say colliery it was mining in general. *(Barry Preece)*

Skip winding was one of the specialities of Head Wrightson's. These were big wheels at the surface and they would rotate skips containing the coal, once the skip was filled at the bottom of the shaft this was then wound up.

Was this continuous?

Yes, to get them to the top of the shaft it required a large head gear. Now Head Wrightson's were the world leaders in building head frames, pit-head frames and head gear. There were big tubs at the bottom in special shapes as these tubs would carry up to 20 tons. Skip winding the coal was a very quick procedure. *(Allan Ayre)*

Head gear manufactured and erected by Stockton Forge for Hem Heath Colliery in the West Midlands. (Photograph supplied by Barry Preece)

The major products that we made were tunnel segments, and castings for the steel industry to form the billets for the rolling mills, and the ingot mould themselves where you pour the steel into, and the base plates for them, and some of the heavy stuff like that. That's where the bulk of the work came from. But the bulk of the work was tunnel segments, which we worked on for Sao Paolo and New York. Most of the work was for London Underground and then there was Washington underground and we did the lining for Boulby Mine, which is quite unique for its depth is 4,000 feet below ground and the lining is very accurately machined to resist enormous water pressures. *(John Fuller)*

Equipment for the nuclear industry

They built the boilers and then Head Wrightson's actually put them in at the bottom of another shop and they had bolts all the way round these massive boilers. We're talking maybe thirty-foot diameter. They lagged these boilers and they what they called annealed them. They heated the metal up to a certain

Lowering the last segment of the boiler shield wall at Hinkley Point. (Photograph supplied by Ken Lee)

temperature so that once it was cooled down again it would never expand. They did that in the shop and we were the ones who went in and put all the bolts on and did that. Then when they'd finished they took them out onto the riverside and they launched them in the river and they went by tug down to Dungeness. We went down there, put big winches on the beach, we put cables on each end and we rolled them up the beach like that. A massive great big crane with two legs came and picked them up and took them over to where they were going in. They were the reactors and they lifted them by one end like that and dropped them down into the thing. I went down to Bankside power station in London because we built the boilers for them. But later they'd had a few year's service, they didn't know whether the boilers were overheating so we had to go up this gantry, where the reactors were, and we had things we used to put wood down and measure the boiler whether it had expanded or not. *(Rodney Crosbie)*

I started in Head Wrightson Erection Dept in 1969 and worked in the office for a few weeks before going down to the Hinkley Point nuclear power station site. I remember one of the senior engineers saying to me, 'Here is where we find out how accurate your drawings are.' Thankfully we did not find any mistakes and my drawing office skills came in useful

John Alderton changing a boring bar in a horizontal borer to machine support plate. (Photograph supplied by Mrs. M. Hope)

when we had to design and manufacture, on site, special lifting tools for the installation of the graphite bricks. One of my first jobs was to help supervise the building of the boiler shield wall which was built on site in a large building next to the Head Wrightson site offices, canteen, stores and workshop. The huge circular structure was in four segments and built on top of a large railway-type bogie. The bogie was positioned on a rail track which led from our building right down to where the reactor building was under construction. When the boiler shield wall was complete it was very slowly moved down to the reactor building by specially designed hydraulic rams which literally pushed this huge construction down the rail track. Quite a feat. When it arrived at the reactor building it was lifted, segment by segment and lowered onto the diagrid structure, quite a tricky operation, especially the last segment. We were all very proud of the construction, moving and positioning of this huge structure on site and we knew it was going to be photographed. So we decided a bit of publicity for Head's would be a good thing and with everybody's agreement I produced a large Head Wrightson sign and hung it on the last segment so it would be displayed on the photograph. I then went onto help supervise the installation and positioning of the support plates. This could sometimes mean working through the night. After completing the graphite core we went on to the guide tubes, then thermocouples. Something that I always remember about those Head Wrightson site days was the quality of the work produced by the fitters, welders, erectors and labourers. Many of them were Head's travelling men who went from site to site and only saw their families every month. This band of men were very dedicated and true craftsmen. I remember them together with the foreman and senior engineers with the greatest esteem and will always be grateful for the support that they gave to a young fairly green site engineer who was very new to the day-to-day problems encountered on a very large high-profile construction site. *(Ken Lee)*

We had to dry some calcium oxide pellets for the filling in the steel tubes that went into the boiler-shield-wall segments for the Hinkley and Hunterston nuclear power stations. This was done by filling stainless-steel baskets with the pellets which were then put into pressure vessels and dried using superheated steam. However, after taking the baskets out of the vessels to unload the pellets, the nuts on the retaining rods of the baskets were seizing on and were proving most difficult to remove. The chemistry department of R&D were asked if there was a nuclear-compatible lubricant that could be used to prevent the nuts from seizing. They came back with a complex sounding formula, which when translated into plain language, was simply milk of magnesia. Boots must of thought that Head Wrightson's had got an epidemic of indigestion with the large amount of milk of magnesia they were buying every week. *(Jim Heward)*

I started in Forty-four but some of us were made redundant in the mid Fifties. I was married at that time and it could have been hard but we got jobs straight away again. Kenny Howe and I were told that there were jobs at Metro-Vickers and we went there for a while. We were building locos for South Africa then they closed down. As it happened Head Wrightson's were building nuclear power stations and they wanted people so I got a job back again with Head Wrightson's but travelling the country.

We worked down in Essex, down Folkestone and Bristol on three different power stations. That took about six or seven years. When we were away we stayed in what they called camps, like dormitories. Like an Army camp if you like. We did get home at weekends however. We were paid a bit more for being away and we got our board. *(Ron Baker)*

HW did a lot of work for the nuclear power industry indeed were one of the pioneers at nuclear power engineering, both boilers and largely the furnace top where all the rods are lowered to generate the heat. The furnace top comprised a mass of different sized plates put together with masses of holes in for different things. The Tool Room made a lot of jigs and gauges for those operations. All the products had to be finished off in clean conditions. They had to be cleaned down and all wrapped up and sealed in clean conditions. A lot of the welding had to be done for the nuclear industry in clean conditions. That meant it wasn't open to the general atmosphere of the shop. The men had to wear white overalls, overshoes, hats and gloves in order to ensure that you weren't contaminating the weld parts. So a lot of things were done under clean conditions. *(Albert Roxborough)*

Head Wrightson were part of the Nuclear Power Group, TNPG, which I think was Babcock's, Wimpey, a consortium and they were building Magnox reactors of which Oldbury was one. So I spent six months on the River Severn building putting all the fuel cans inside. It was fascinating. That was another experience of engineering. All the big huge turbines and all the charging machines for loading all the radioactive fuel into the core. Because the graphite core was all being loaded with these Magnox cans, so somebody devised an appropriate winch that you could actually load them all down, put another one in and when they got to the bottom you jiggled something and the rope came off and they were all just sat in this core of graphite. So it was very good. And the cider was good down there as well. *(Michael Waring)*

Fettling a casting at Thornaby circa 1930s. (Photograph supplied by Remembering Thornaby Group)

There isn't anything safer than a nuclear power plant because it was so clean and so meticulous. See, the equipment that was going out that we were making, it was sealed in plastic bags. Everything was washed and cleaned several times before it went in the plastic bag. The bag was sealed and we had clean areas. That's how we were. *(Bob Close)*

Castings

They had three what are called induction furnaces. I think the most they did out of them was a ton and a half, and they just put the metal in them. It was just electricity through the coils, through the wall of the furnace. It was a big electrode, something about ten inches in diameter. There were three of those on each furnace. They would come down and strike an arc to heat the metal.

So how long did these electrodes last?

Oh, they used to last quite a while. I would say maybe a month, maybe even longer than that.

What sort of capacity were the electric-arc furnaces?

The electric-arc furnaces used to do ten tons and another one did fifteen tons and there was one in what they called the heavy bay, I think that did ten tons as well. When they had to cast the big wheels it used to take all the furnaces to fully cast maybe twenty-five, twenty-eight tons. So they had to have all three furnaces going together so that they could cast that job. *(Eddie Peacock)*

Finishing a casting at Stockton Steel Foundry. (Wright Ahead)

We had one big valve customer and that was Crane Valves of America, and they gave us masses of valve orders. But again, you're getting to forty-two, forty-eight inch valves, which are the big jobs. You'd get one, two, three, four maybe. You know down to the sort of two-inch valves, you'd probably have a thousand. But the problem with that was you get a thousand in low-carbon steel, a thousand in forty-five carbon steel. You get a thousand in eighteen-eight steel and you get a thousand in eighteen-ten-two steel. So you were making the same casting over a vast range of steels. *(Colin Waugh)*

The Steel Foundry was very big. It had three bays. It had what you call the Small Foundry, the mechanical side, Machine Moulding Foundry and the Big Shop which, as you can imagine, had different ranges of castings. The Big Shop did the huge castings. The Machine Moulding did the mass production jobs. And the Small Foundry, the apprentice moulders,

R. Nichol checking a casting. (Photograph courtesy of R. Nichol)

did the small work. So there was three different sections in there.

And the Big Foundry, for the big sections you'd have pits would you?

Oh yes, there were pits for them in the floor. Some of the castings they made were twenty-ton castings. We used to make gear wheels for David Brown and people like that. And you wouldn't get it in this room, the diameter of it or the circumference of it. You're talking about a ten-foot radius. Quite big. *(John Heighly)*

How big were the castings that you were making?

Just the little small ones in the small boxes. A box is about two-foot square and every day it was all laid on, you know what I mean?

And how many moulds were you making in a day?

Eventually, once you got used to making them, we used to do about six a day. We saw them being cast. The furnace was at yon end and they used to come down with the ladle and just cast them and we used to knock them all out later on.

How long before you knocked them out?

If they cast them on a morning you used to have them on the afternoon because they were only small castings. They used to cool down pretty quickly. If they were great big castings you would leave them in for days. *(Michael Nichol)*

A selection of Stampings products.
(Photograph courtesy of Caparo Forgings)

When I was at school, they used to take the kids out to various places, we went to Head Wrightson's and we went into the Pattern Shop and that's what stuck in my mind. 'Oh I like the smell of the wood,' and everything and I thought, 'oh I want to be a pattern-maker.' But it was a dying trade because fabrications were coming along and they were doing away with castings. They're still doing them now, castings, but only for specialised things. *(Dick Robinson)*

What's usually the time between casting and knocking the casting out?

Well, it depends. On big castings you might have to leave them three or four days. That's mainly because they'd still be red hot and you could bend them by moving them. Also, if you expose them to the air the cooling is affected. So you can get castings to twist. But in general we could knock an eighteen-inch moulding box out after an hour. Those castings weren't that big and virtually froze immediately the steel poured in the mould. *(Colin Waugh)*

Forgings

Most things that were made in the Forge were sold as they came out of the Forge. In other words they were what we would call 'black' as forged. They were inspected, just labelled up and sold. We used to back in with a flat-back lorry and load it with pallets straight from the hammer. You'd see them going down Brenda Road still glowing from the Forge! That's obviously a slight exaggeration.

But it's a very good picture.

But it was just sold on to a company called Moss. We made zillions of stuff for Moss Gear.

What would that be automobile or…?

It was probably trucks and buses at this time. I don't recall in the early days that we did much in cars, we still don't really. It was mostly

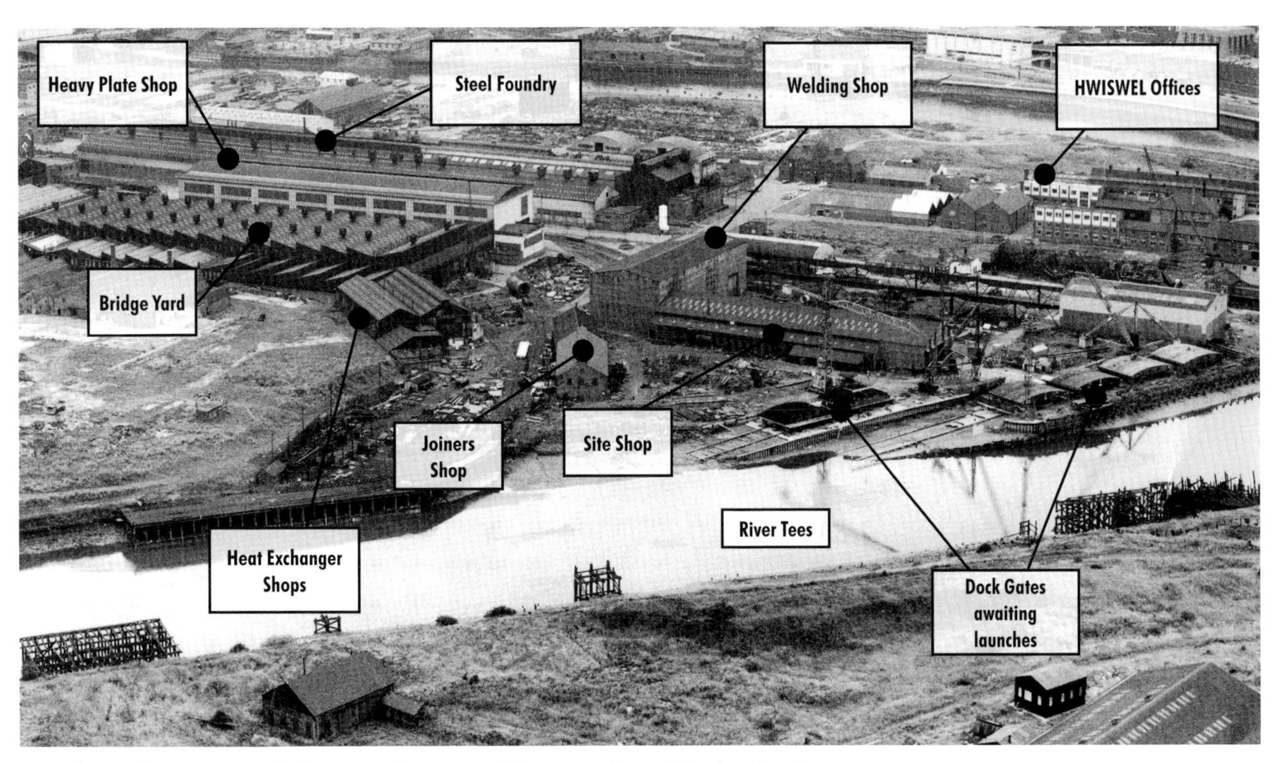

Head Wrightson's North showing slipways. (Courtesy Teesside Archives)

Heat exchanger being built in the Heavy Plate Shop at HWT. (HW Photographic Section)

trucks and buses was our sort of area. It was a bit chunkier and a bit heavier and it wasn't thousands and thousands off. There was an exception in one of the areas but most of the things at the time were small runs: two or three hundred, four or five hundred, that sort of number. *(Jim Matthews)*

I would say that nine out of ten parts on the JCB earth-moving equipment were made at Stampings. They went then to either Peterlee or to Newcastle. *(Trevor Briggs)*

Dock gates

So these dock gates, most of them were built on an old shipyard slipway?

That's right. They're all built on slipways, and launched like a ship. The tug came and towed them to wherever by sea. Sometimes some went to Scotland and they towed them there.

When they launched them was there any ceremony?

No. Only when the big one was launched and a few people got bloody wet when it hit the water because it was a big one. Actually it was registered as a ship because it was big enough. What they used to do when they went to Ireland, I understand they flooded the gate to put it in position. They flooded it so that when it stood up it, it was in place. *(Thomas Wilson)*

Big events were when they used to launch the dock gates off the slipway into the River Tees. And then after that, when they were doing all the big boilers for the power stations down at Dungeness and they used to seal them off and float them down the river. They always used to have a ceremony. Everybody used to go and watch the dock gates being launched because they'd all built them. Obviously, you have to wait for the tides coming in and then they would knock them off and slip them down the slipway. One of our MPs, who was called Mr. Jeremy Bray, wanted to shut Newport Bridge from lifting. What Mr. Jeremy Bray didn't realise was that when we were doing dock work or boilers, we couldn't float them down because the boilers had to go underneath the bridge so they had to lift the bridge. Otherwise they would have taken the bridge with them. So it was always kept open. *(Jim Smiles)*

I went back into the yard as a foreman plater, so that meant I was in charge of a section that dealt with dock gates and one in particular a flap gate, the dock gates opened vertically. The flap gate goes backwards and forwards. The ships go over the top of the gate into the dock and the gate comes up and then they pump the water out and do all the repairs. This was for the port of Tema in Ghana. Sections were built in the shop, brought down to site, the end next to the river, and I and my squad put all the bits and pieces together and they got welded. This is where the different steels came in because port of Tema, Africa, hot sunshine, the steel up and down, in and out of the water meant that it had to be special steel which meant that special welding procedures had to be adopted. I think that was my main job, making sure that they'd done all the levelling before we started work. Made sure that the pieces before they were welded were in the right spot and then get the gas heaters on, get the steel up to the right temperature. Welders came on, sweating cobs, and made sure that the welding was done, kept at the same temperature and then cooled down again. *(John Kirk)*

The river bed had not been dredged deep enough and the gate only went in about three quarters of its length and stuck there on the slipway with the front end dug into the river bed. Another one, at which some of the local dignitaries had been invited to watch the gate being launched, created quite a large tidal wave as it went into the river and the guests had to run for their lives or they would have got soaked. *(Jim Heward)*

Heat exchangers

We used to make a lot of heat exchangers for the chemical industry and every Friday we used to ship about thirty to Holland. Each one it had to be labelled. I can tell you the name of the boat, MV Venenberg. And those vessels, I had to see them painted, red lead or red oxide. I had to detail the men off to paint them. They went on railway wagons. They had five bolsters on. They used to be all different sizes. We had to enter all the incoming traffic and outgoing traffic in the books. We had an outgoing book and an incoming book, and they went down to the office every day so they could check them, because they could check them with their invoices. If there were any wagons short in weight I had to report them. Put them to one side and report them. *(Fred Watson)*

We also did lots and lots of heat exchangers. A heat exchanger is essentially a vessel, and there were various diameters, with a mass of pipes fitted through it. They would put steam through the pipes and then the gap between the rest of the tubes would be filled with another liquid which would get heated. The company did a lot of heat exchangers for ICI and various oil refineries. That was big business. They made heat exchangers from quite small ones to some massive ones, diameters to ten feet with big huge tubes in them. They were very similar to a steam boiler but much more sophisticated. Because of the pressures of the steam used and the various liquids that were going through, a very high-class of welding was necessary. The Tool Room made weld prep gauges to prepare the area of the tube plate where the tube end was welded to the tube sheet to a particular profile for welding to a high standard. *(Albert Roxborough)*

The Bradwell heat exchangers, which were for Bradwell power station, they took them down by sea and then into the Blackwater Estuary. But before that they'd built rails on the bed of the river with concrete and stuff and built some rails and they planted two bogies on those rails. They brought the vessel in from the sea into the Blackwater Estuary and stationed them over these two bogies when the tide was high. Then as the tide went down the vessel went down with it and settled on the bogies and then Sunter came along with his big Rolls-Royce engines and pulled them out. That was the Bradwell one. *(Maynard Wilson)*

Bridges

I only went on site once and that was up to Scotland, to the Forth Bridge. I went up to see them put the last piece in on the Forth Bridge.

Shop assembly of aluminium bridge at Stockton Forge 1953. (HW Company brochure)

I just went up in the work's van and was there and back in a day. I had to take a day's holiday to go and see it because I was interested in it. It's a thing not many people can say they saw, the last piece put on the Forth Bridge. *(Norman Metcalfe)*

Any bridges that moved we worked on. Swing bridges, bascule bridges like the Tower Bridge at London. That's a bascule-type bridge. We worked on bridges that moved, did the machinery for that sort of thing, worked on drawings and design for that. Static bridges were designed by the Structural Department. So one department designed and detailed static bridges but if they were moving bridges for harbours, for docks, they came to our department.
We built a slipway machinery for Suva, capital of Fiji. *(Jack Picken)*

I was fascinated by bridges even as a young boy and Head Wrightson's were the best bridge builders. It was as simple as that. We'd built a railway bridge upside down in the Bridge Yard which was the usual way to build a bridge unless it went straight out on site. But this was machined joints so that they all had to be put together. It was ridiculous to build it up on its legs because then it meant you were working twenty foot up in the air so it was done upside down with the legs up over. Everything was checked, British Rail inspectors came in and measured everything so that they knew that the bridge would fit to the concrete foundations. *(John Kirk)*

We also built the first aluminium-alloy bascule bridge in the world for Hendon Dock in Sunderland, in 1947. The only difference was that we built ours with steel rivets, we had to protect the aluminium by putting a certain type of oxide paint around and in the rivet hole. A firm in Canada were building one and they used aluminium rivets but we hadn't got down to that at that stage, but ours was

Sections for a motorway bridge being fabricated in the Heavy Plate Shop at HWT. (Wright Ahead)

opened first and as far as I know it's still there. *(Maynard Wilson)*

They did one or two bridges, aluminium bridges, one at Sunderland, one at Hull. I think the Anglesey bridge from the mainland to Anglesey was a Head Wrightson's footbridge. *(Alan Sowerby)*

The bridges that HW built were either road bridges or rail bridges, especially in London. The Barnes railway bridge, the one quite close to Fulham. Bits of London Bridge. *(Simon Wrightson)*

Transporting products

They were made in Head Wrightson's from ordinary plates. The finished job was passed on to me to get ready for delivery. I used to get instructions from the Drawing Office on what they called delivery sheets and they used to say, 'paint with one quart of red lead' or whatever they wanted. They used to order the paint in for those jobs. I used to order a lot of paint in

View down the sections for a motorway bridge being fabricated in the Heavy Plate Shop at HWT. (Wright Ahead)

for different jobs. When we were packing for shipping in cases we had to line the cases out and put other stuff in that stops them from going rusty. Every week I used to have to send a demurrage sheet in what's been off-loaded. I could work out then how much demurrage money we owed. The railway company put a charge on the wagons. When they came in the works, the next day was free, you were supposed to empty them and the next day you were supposed to send them out empty. Then they were clear. But if you kept wagons in days on end you were paying for them. That's how the railway made their money you see. *(Fred Watson)*

We once constructed a vessel for ICI which was made of a special stainless steel called Ducol WD40 and which had created many problems with the specialist welding that was needed for the material. However, it was finally completed and tested. The management were aware that the pressure testing could be dangerous so it was done on a Saturday when there were no men working in the shops. It was loaded onto a low-loader and dispatched to ICI at Billingham. Bill Porter, who was one of the planning engineers and had been involved with the contract and lived in Billingham, was horrified, when he was on his way home on the day that this vessel was on its way, to see that it had rolled off the low-loader on the roundabout at the bottom of Billingham Bank. Luckily there was not much damage caused to the vessel and it was repaired on site without much problem. *(Jim Heward)*

Absorption column for ICI's nitric acid plant at Billingham manoeuvring between St. Mary's church and the Turks Head pub in Stockton on its five hour journey to Billingham. It was 221 feet long, 17 feet 4 inches diameter, weighing 285 tons and was the longest load ever moved on a British public highway. Sunday 25th March 1984. (HW Photographic Section)

They used to get big transport vehicles in to move things. ALE I think was one company, Abnormal Lifting Engineering. I think they used to do a lot of the transportation when they used to take it out of Head Wrightson's yard. I remember them doing a long, big stack like a big chimney. I think that was going down to ICI. I remember they had a hell of a job getting it up Trafalgar Street and up over the Thornaby Bridge. There was a hairpin bend at the Victoria Bridge end and it was always a problem for Head's with all the stuff trying to get in and out, to be honest with you. The road was closed off and it took forever to try and get it round this bend, to get this long vessel out of Head's. *(Dennis Longstaff)*

The main restriction on the fabrication at Head Wrightson came about from the Highways Authority. The maximum load taken on the road was fourteen-foot diameter. Now a lot of our equipment, such as twelve-foot-diameter dryers had tyres on them increasing their diameter, and they were about a hundred-and-twenty-foot long. They had sections which were ninety to a hundred-foot long which used to be transported from the Forge. *(Allan Ayre)*

45.9m long drying column for BP Chemicals ethanol plant at Grangemouth crossing the Newport Bridge circa 1980. (HW Photographic Section)

Chapter 4

'Engineers to the World': Organisation of Head Wrightson

As would be expected of such a large company, there were several organisational changes throughout its life. The first Head Wrightson products were manufactured in Teesdale Ironworks but by the end of the nineteenth century the company had taken over the Egglescliffe Iron Foundry and Stockton Forge Works. A steel foundry in Stockton was acquired in 1927 followed by another foundry in Billingham. The Drop Stampings Forge, established at Thornaby in 1939, transferred to Seaton Carew over a two year period (1949-51). Head Wrightson Processes Limited was started in 1941 as a division and subsequently became a subsidiary company in 1946. This was followed in 1946 by the formation of the Head Wrightson Machine Company. After the war all of these different departments were turned into divisions and later subsidiary companies.

By the 1970s after several reorganisations and rationalisations, the group was divided into the following divisions. Contracting Division consisted of Head Wrightson Process Engineering Ltd who designed and contracted for the iron and steel, coal, oil and petrochemical industries. They also designed and contracted for incineration and effluent treatment plants. Head Wrightson Machine Company was also part of this division and they made equipment for manufacturing steel and non-ferrous tubes and for working, processing and coating steel and non-ferrous sheet, strip and plate. Manufacturing Division consisted of Head Wrightson Teesdale which designed and manufactured iron and steelworks equipment, nuclear power plant, colliery and mining plant, oil and petrochemical equipment and dock and harbour equipment. This division also contained B & S Massey and other subsidiary companies which were purchased by Head Wrightson in 1972. The Foundry and Forging Division comprised of Head Wrightson (Steelcast) Ltd which made carbon, manganese and alloy-steel castings, Head Wrightson (Ironcast) Ltd making cast-iron tunnel segments, Head Wrightson Stampings manufacturing forgings in steel and alloys and finally Stockton Precision Forge. The other divisions were Stockholding, Overseas, and Associated Companies all of which were based largely outside of Teesside. Research and Development Department was also made a separate division of the company in 1960.

We have interviewed employees from all of the sites based on Teesside and their descriptions of the core work of the organisation can be found overleaf.

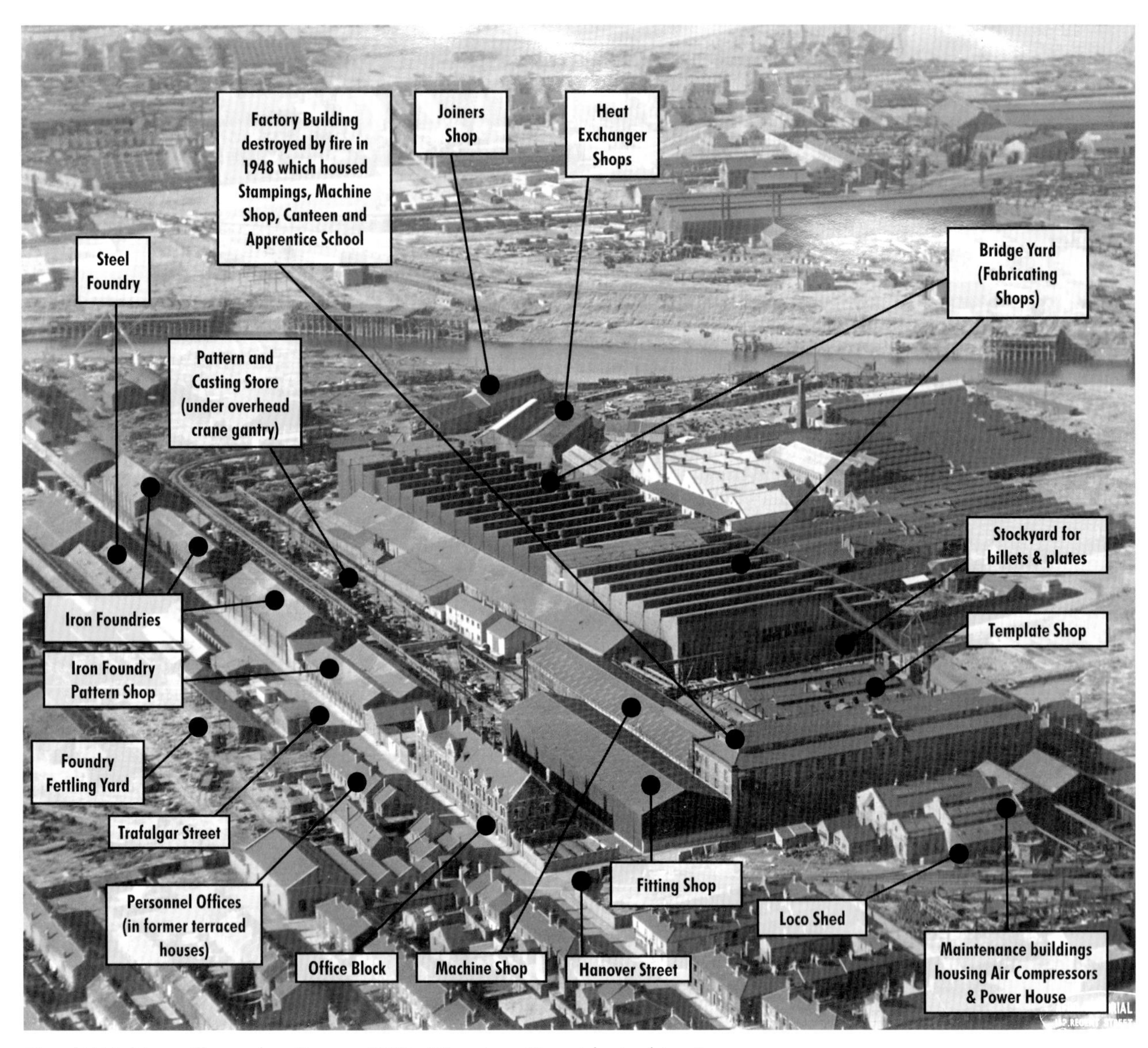

Head Wrightson Thornaby site pre-1948. (Courtesy Teesside Archives)

Teesdale Site

But, of course, in the Forge days we were much lighter in our manufacturing procedure than our big sister at Thornaby, Teesdale. They were the heavier side. We went up to about inch, inch-and-a-half plate and that was about it. Teesdale went up to four inches in cold and eight inches hot-type of stuff so they were a heavier side. *(Barry Preece)*

We built the foundations for the power stations but we didn't build them in the Heavy Plate Shop we built them in a place called the Site Shop. That was one of the memorable jobs because we did several of those year after year, and they were quite heavy things because they were filled with carbon blocks when they got them on the site. Then there were ladles and precipitators and the stainless-steel tubes for the ICI. Every job was a challenge and it was a successful challenge as well. Why on earth they had to shut that place down I'll never know. But anyway we won't go into politics. *(Harry Foster)*

Oh well, it was quite nerve-racking really because we were drilling holes in railway wagons with the windy driller. We went down the railway lines. You had to climb into them. That was an effort getting in them, and then you had to hold the handle of the windy drill while they drilled the holes for the rivets. Then you'd come out of one wagon and have to jump into the next one that was on a line, and when they were finished they were driven away. They used to have a fleet of drilling machines, in

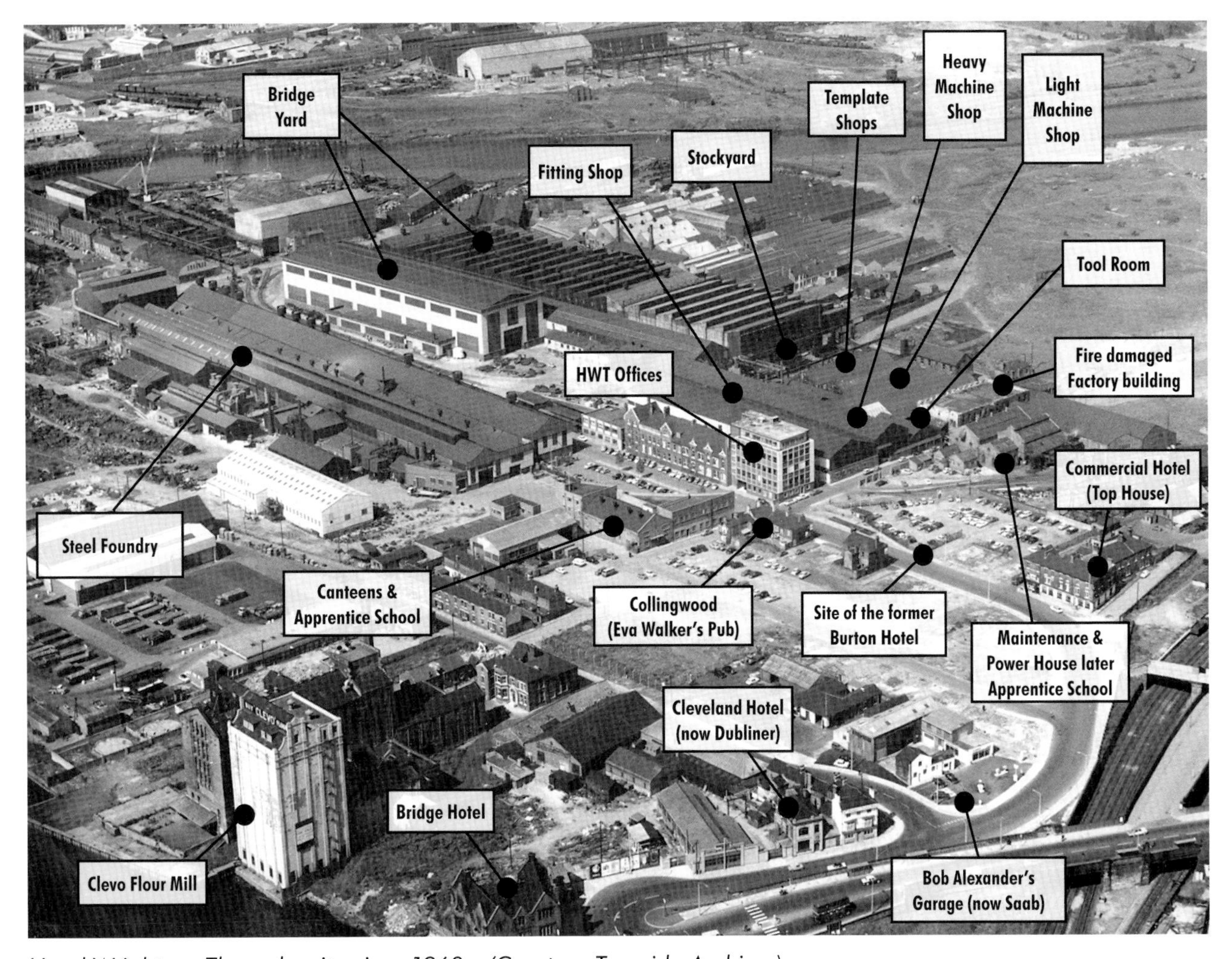

Head Wrightson Thornaby site circa 1960s. (Courtesy Teesside Archives)

the Bridge Yard where they drilled holes in plates. Then you'd have to sweep all the steel turnings that had come from the drills, sweep all them up and put them in a skip. Got very dirty but I absolutely really enjoyed working. *(Cath Harrison)*

There was some investment because when I first started in the Bridge Yard they had two planers. I think there was a thirty-foot-long and a forty-foot-long planer. And it wasn't long after I'd gone in the Bridge Yard that they got two new planers which instead of running on brass they were running on Tufnol material. They were the thing at the time. I remember doing some maintenance, we had to remove saddles and re-line the beds. The keys that actually kept the saddle straight were made out of Tufnol and you had to scrape them with scrapers. It was a very hard fibre material, very, very hard. Same principle as the normal gib keys but made out of a different material.

And they upgraded burning machines didn't they?

Well, as I said, they upgraded the two planer machines and they actually got one thirty-foot and sixty-foot long. Then they upgraded and got the first tape-controlled burning machine which is the Messer Griesheim from Germany. That was a four-headed machine which would cut through something in the region of eight-inch-thick plating. It was a terrific machine and all tape-controlled, and the actual control room was in an air-conditioned cabin. It was a super machine. But that was one of the last big purchases they made. Before the Messer Griesheim burning machine, they installed a Haeusler roll, which was a very good roll but it was actually a small rolling machine. Well they had two rollers, actually. Then there was an opportunity came up for some work on the Hong Kong Bank so they decided to purchase another roll which was one of the biggest in Europe which was a Verrina roll. I worked

General view of Bridge Yard activity. (HW Photographic Section)

with the Italians installing it. The bottom roll and top roll were about a metre diameter which were terrific rolls and they could roll up to three and four-inch-thick plates. Rolled into ten-foot diameter. They used heaters to warm the plate. It certainly assists the machine. It was set into a pit which would be in the region of fifteen, eighteen-foot deep before they put the concrete in and the foundation consisted of a metre-thick concrete. The whole machine would weigh three or four hundred tons. It was a heck of a size. It was a massive beast. I can remember they were pouring concrete for forty-eight hours. It was a heck of a blooming project.

So do you think that it was a good investment then this Verrina roller?

I think that they were a terrific investment. The problem with the Verrina rollers is once that Hong Kong Bank job dried up there was little further work. They didn't appear as though they were going out and getting work for the machine and then from that moment the machine was only working probably just the day shift. *(Derek Proctor)*

I started off doing ticket blocks, which is on the railway wagons. They used to do about fifteen a week in sets of five and it was my job to put ticket blocks on the side of the wagons. I used to be able to catch them before they got them painted so I was doing them more or less as they were on line. At the end of the Bridge Yard, near the toilets, that's where they were built and I used to have a box with nuts and bolts for fastening the blocks on. It was at the furthest end of the Bridge Yard. As they came out of the Wagon Shop at the Bridge Yard there was a continuation which was the Spray Shop and they got sprayed there and then out into the yard. If there was too many they used to take them to a place behind the Foundry. There was another Spray Shop there. So if I didn't catch them there I had to go right across to the Foundry. We were once told they made a million pounds profit and when you used to

Thornaby Pattern Shops.
(Head Wrightson Domesday Book)

go through the Bridge Yard and places like that you never saw a lot of work being done. I thought, 'Well, how can they make a million pounds?' They seemed to have mates. So if a plater was working or the mate was working the other one was standing. But I suppose they were getting on with the work because they made the profits. *(Bob Irwin)*

The Redcar blast furnace was one of the first ones I can remember them doing. It was a huge job because there was a lot of work. They had to lay it out outside the Bridge Yard. The Bridge Yard was where bridges used to be made but that was long before my time. They didn't ever do a bridge while I was there, but they did in the early Nineties, maybe to the 1930s and that's where the Bridge Yard name comes from, I believe. Then they used to have the Machine Shop which was at the other side and then the Foundry was across the road, but the Bridge Yard was where all the heavy fabrication was made up over the plates. They built the blast furnaces all in sections, in different segments they made the full circumference of it. They laid it all outside and then they'd build them and then it would all go down to Redcar. I think it went to Redcar by road. It could possibly have gone by river but I think a lot of stuff used to go by road. They used to build a lot of vessels like heat exchangers at Head Wrightson's as well, that was another job they used to do. That's where I did a lot of my work, on heat exchangers for

Thornaby stockyard: plates being moved into the Bridge Yard. (Courtesy Alan Simpson)

Matty Newton in the Class One Shop but that was all vessel work. *(Dennis Longstaff)*

I was in the Heavy Plate Shop. If you walked down Trafalgar Street what you hit first was Head Wrightson's offices. To the left of Head Wrightson's offices you had the Apprentice School building, and that was on the upper floors of what used to be Head Wrightson's dance hall and the canteen. The Heavy Plate Shop going down Trafalgar Street was on the right-hand side, and on the left-hand side you had the Foundry. And further down you had the Labs who did the testing for the Foundry, different chemical compositions for the steel. Past that it was Steve's public house, the Bradford Vaults, with a few houses at the bottom. Further down that was the Site Shop, and further down from Trafalgar Street was where they did all the carving for the dock gates. There was a big shop down there, they did all the greenheart carving for the dock gates. They did quite a few of them, years and years of dock gates, they were experts at it.

In the Large Plate Shop what was the main job in there?
Heavy industry, heavy-steel-plate industry, bridges. The plates were all bent in the rolls. It was all done in the Bridge Yard, which was a complex set up really. When we first started off as apprentices in the Bridge Yard, from the Template Shop the templates came to the young lads to mark off the beams, the joists. We used to have wooden templates, put them on the beams, pop holes in them for the drillers to drill out and then that was shipped to different parts of Head Wrightson's to be built. It was rather complex but it worked like a dream. Everything was connected. It was like making bread, you knead your dough, you roll it, you cut it. You make it, you tin it up, you put it in the oven and out comes the finished product. And basically it was the same thing. *(Harry Foster)*

I used to do torpedo cars for the steelworks and transfer cars to bring the ore from the docks to the blast furnaces. They used the slag cars to get rid of the molten slag. The torpedo car carries the hot iron when they tap the furnace and then they take it to a melting shop and they burn all the impurities out and then they start to cast ingots. The transfer cars picked the ore up off the dock and put it into storage bunkers. Then we had scale cars. We built them as well and they used to run in an alley underneath the bunkers. They had vertically operated cylinders and they used to open the bunkers up so you could get out iron ore. Dolomite and other additive sorts were all carefully weighed. Then they used to take the iron to the furnace and dump it in. The furnace had a bell at the top, a conical thing and as soon as they lifted it, the iron all rolled down and dropped in to burn. The 750 wagons were for British Rail; that was a standing order, they had to re-equip after the war. They also had some sixty-ton long ballast for laying the railway lines and we used to build those as well. Head Wrightsons didn't make wheels and axles or axle boxes, but they used to make the rest of it. Then it was all assembled in the Bridge Yard. They were pushing in one after the other, about seven a day. It was a fantastic turnover. That was just after the war. But we also specialised, as I say, in torpedo cars. The transfer cars and scale cars were self-propelled with electric motors. The torpedo cars were pulled by a locomotive. They weighed about five hundred tons so they had to have twelve axles, six axles at each end. That would give you a forty-ton axle load which is high. That transferred the molten metal from one furnace to the melting shop where it was put into a converter. *(John Glasper)*

They built the new Machine Shop onto the end of the Bridge Yard though didn't they?
That's right. I can't remember the exact date that happened but it must have been late Seventies. I can't remember exactly. It got built around about that time. But even so they never put new machines in which I thought was rather frustrating. They got an Innocenti transferred from Middlesbrough but that was a 1963 machine so were putting in old kit. We got two Sharman borers put in, which were old machines from Middlesbrough.
The Innocenti, was it a horizontal borer?
That was a ram borer. It travelled along a bed. It was a useful machine. I remember being involved in a small way ramming the beds with John Calvert with a dumpy level.
Do you think the capability of the new machines was better than the existing machines?
I would say yes because they were more modern. The Innocenti was a bigger machine. They were using it in connection to the Bridge Yard where they could do some very big vessels on the bed plate i.e. machining the ends which is what they did. But I never saw the Machine Shop fully built. There was still floor space in there which was never used. Because of circumstances it never happened. In the Machine Shop I can't recall many new machines going in although there was a multi-spindle drill installed into the Light Machine Shop. That was controlled by computer, it was the first computer machine that I can recall going into Head Wrightson's. They had a lot of teething trouble. It was

brought in to do the heat exchanger, the plates, multi drilling. *(Derek Proctor)*

We were building vessels for a methanol plant in Russia and there were several Russian engineers based at Thornaby. This was in the days of the cold war and the Russians were limited to a three-mile radius from the Teesdale site. If they were visiting any of our subcontractors in another town they had to report to the police station as they set off, then report to a police station at the other end as soon as they arrived, repeating this in reverse on their return journey. One evening Keith Hallenby, the project engineer on the contract, took the Russians out for a meal at a restaurant not realising it was outside of the three-mile radius. Next day the firm got a visit from some Special Branch officers asking for an explanation as to why the Russians had been outside the three-mile radius. It was obvious that they were keeping a close watch on them. During that period if you were making an outside call on the phone there used to be clicks and bleeps occasionally so the police were probably monitoring the phone system too. *(Jim Heward)*

The Tool Room was an enclosed section within the Machine Shop, all enclosed in with wire mesh. I think it was about thirty yards square or so, and it was where they sharpened all the drills, reamers, milling cutters and any other cutting tools. It also acted as a store. Workers would to come to the Tool Room to borrow different sized drills and reamers and cutters et cetera. It was largely two sections. There was the grinding section, which kept everything sharp, and there were the fitters who made jigs and gauges. A jig is essentially a device to assist accurate reproduction of machined components. If you wanted to drill, for instance, two holes in a plate, you would use a jig to hold the component and guide the drill so that each subsequent component would be identical and accurate. A gauge is used to help to machine or shape something to a particular curve or shape. There were also length gauges

Entrance to Head Wrightson PEL. (Head Wrightson Domesday Book)

made to two sizes, a 'no go' gauge where it would be made to, say, five inches across and the 'go' gauge made to, say, five inches plus maybes ten thou. So then you could make something that was exactly five inches within a tolerance of ten thou. So it was all accurate and precision work. I enjoyed doing that. It was basically small work and it was bench work, vice work rather than wielding big hammers. Although from time to time we did get big jobs, big layouts to do, prototypes when we'd have to work outside the Tool Room where there was more space. But largely it was precision work or prototype work or setting up big accurate layouts. In the Machine Shop if you were going to make something or drill holes or machine a component, whatever you were doing, the rate fixer would give you a price to do that job and you'd perhaps have to argue with him to get a bit better price. But then you had to do that particular operation in sufficient time so that you would earn a fair rate of pay. The machines and the fitters were on piecework, which often proved controversial because some people couldn't make their money. They couldn't do it in time and the better people probably could. But because we were on accurate work we weren't on piecework, we were on time rate. We got paid a time rate for doing what we did. What it meant is it took the pressure of rushing the work. It was more important

December 1965 R&D staff photographed at the departure of Dr. P.A. Young. He had established the department ten years earlier. (Wright Ahead)

that we got it right than got it done quickly. *(Albert Roxborough)*

HWISWEL

R&D was really there to serve the needs of any of the companies around. Mostly what I did was in relation to work for HWISWEL, or PEL as it eventually became. But there were people doing work for the Steel Foundries. I'm not sure what sort of work it was, but mine was essentially to do with pelletising machines, sinter machines and the mechanics of the materials used and research into blast furnaces and measurement of various variables on site. Things like moisture content in the sinter feed because that was critical to how effective the process was. So we'd often go out onto the site and to sinter machines up at Ravenscraig for instance, sometimes to sites at Redcar to take measurements or whatever. *(Barrie Hope)*

Head Wrightson Iron Steelworks Engineering Limited. That spelt out HWISWEL. *(sic)*
So it's just a family name we gave it. When you spoke, 'Oh he worked at HWISWEL,' we knew exactly what it meant.
So exactly where was HWISWEL based?
That was in Thornaby. That was about half a mile down the road and if you went any further back you finished up in the Tees.
So you were a mixture of different groups? Within this HWISWEL?

Craig Taylor office block used by Head Wrightson Steel Foundry as offices and Metallurgy Lab. (Remembering Thornaby Group)

This advertising campaign went out looking for people i.e. me at ICI. I saw the adverts and went for interview, so they pulled in a lot of people who had the correct skills that Head Wrightson were looking for. Then you just found that you were part of a new empire really. That was developed solely for the manufacture and design of iron and steel plant. So the thing existed, but not these new designs that Head Wrightson were au fait with building, and everybody wanted one because we had the best. *(Max Clark)*

Research and development

Most of my time in R&D I had a laboratory and in one of them in a special area we built a pilot-production-plant process for pelletising of materials for a blast furnace charge. What was called a 'balling' process. Head Wrightson Teesdale used to make these big balling machines into which you would put finely-ground iron ore, mix it with things like bentonite to hold it together, and the charge go in as powder, be mixed with moisture, come out of the other end in pellets. The moisture content would determine the strength of these because what you needed to ensure was that when they were dry they were not going to collapse. *(Barrie Hope)*

There were one or two problems on some projects where we got involved with the works people. But I think our aims were always the same. They all got resolved eventually. Where

Sir Guy at Egglescliffe 13 July 1936 on its reopening following 1930s depression. (Labour force then 60.) (Wright Ahead)

necessary if it was a problem that wanted a bit of research we used to bring R&D into it. R&D used to make models or do whatever had to be done in order to resolve the problem. That didn't happen very often, but I can remember perhaps on a couple of occasions when we used them. *(Eric Brown)*

R&D, something you realised in later years, was also a training ground for not only the future managers within Head Wrightson's but certainly for lots of the local industries on Teesside as Head Wrightson's employees moved to other companies. So it was a good training ground. I was very much involved in the development work. Head Wrightson's R&D was the troubleshooting centre for all of the other Head Wrightson's divisions for welding so it exposed me to visits over to Head Wrightson's Machine Shop and Stockton Works, the foundries to offer advice and guidance on welding. There was a shop-floor welding engineer in the Bridge Yard in Teesdale, but he was the day-to-day troubleshooter, so all of the specifications came from me and from the mid-Sixties onwards there was more and more emphasis on the technical control of welding and the writing of welding specifications. A written specification as opposed to a verbal instruction was becoming more and more of a requirement. And all of that was controlled from R&D. So as well as being involved in the technical development of trying out new welding processes, new welding materials, looking after the physical testing of those test welds, you were also receiving the drawings to write the weld specifications for the other divisions. And, plus if there was a shop-floor failure, a defect, a crack or whatever and it was of a technological nature you were invited over to come and assist and resolve the problem as a troubleshooter. So it was again excellent grounding. R&D was the showpiece for Head's and had lots of visiting dignitaries. I met Anthony Wedgwood Benn when he was Minister of Technology and he came round R&D and I was the welding engineer or trainee welding engineer in those days there. I was introduced to him and he would have been accompanied by Sir John or Mr. Peter. *(Charlie Tighe)*

I started to do ONC Mechanical Engineering at Constantine. Halfway through the system, Head Wrightson's became involved with C A Parsons and a couple of other companies on the nuclear-reactor-building programme. At that

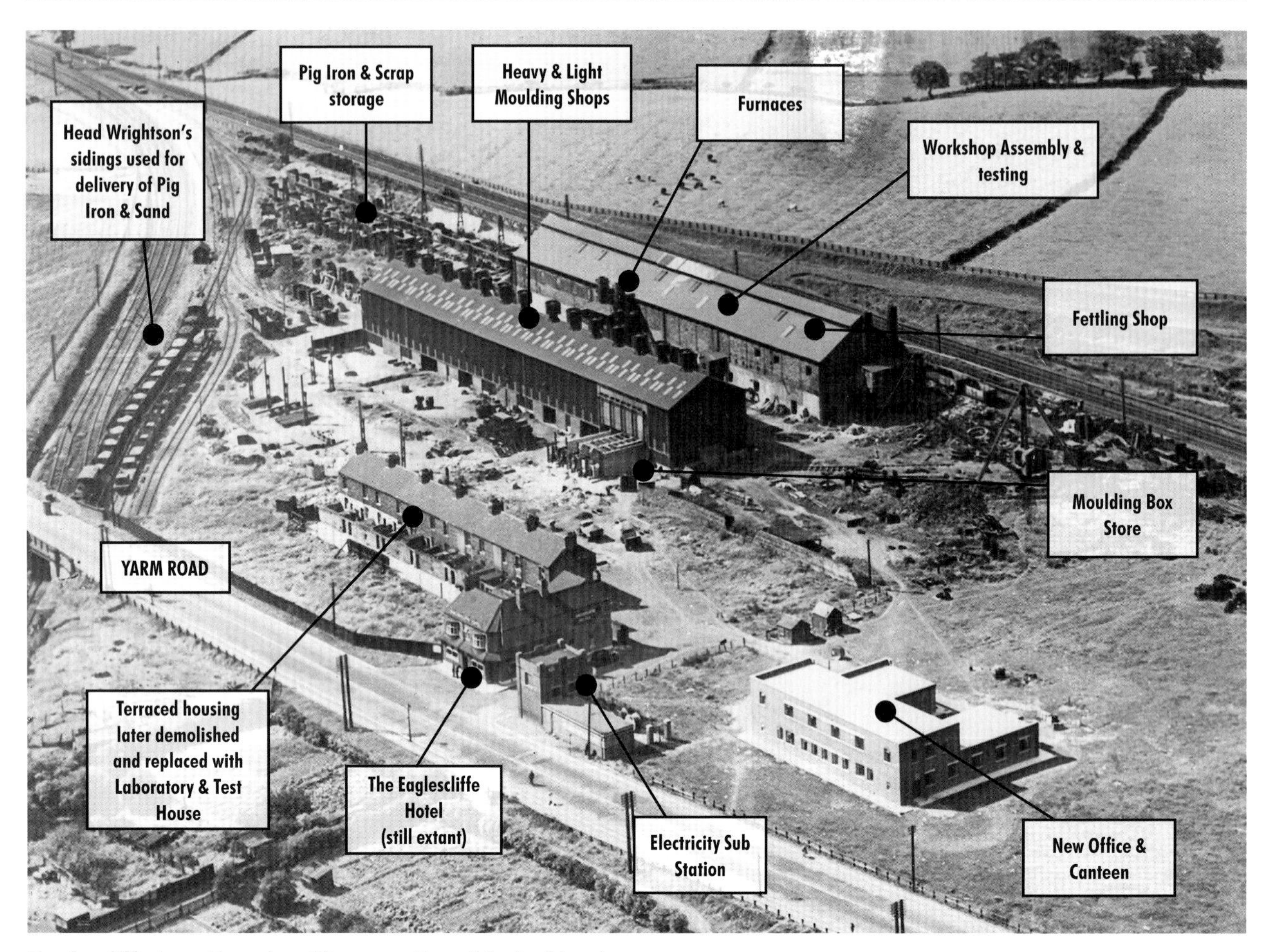

Egglescliffe Iron Foundry. (Courtesy Teesside Archives)

time the Research & Development Department was just opening up and the Metallurgy Laboratory wanted a first-year apprentice and Soppet got me in and said, 'Look, I know you want to be a draughtsman but you might be interested in this post. It could be very interesting. It's a whole new world opening up,' and it certainly was. So I arrived in the Metallurgy Department which was located in a brand-new office block, that had been specially built, and in it were some of the brightest, most flamboyant people that I ever met in my life. *(Colin Waugh)*

Foundries

So what was it like in the foundries?

Oh terrible. It was hot and mucky and dusty. And changing wire ropes on the cranes with the big cradle-ladle dryers underneath. Flames coming up, belching up. Have you seen on the television the furnace. It was similar to that, muck, dust. Oh terrible. Anyhow I muddled through. *(Dick Robinson)*

It was just loaded into a big skip by a magnet and then the crane used to go over the top of the furnace because the tops used to swing off. They used to position it over the furnace and then somebody would pull something and it just used to all drop into the furnace. They had to be re-lined every few weeks, depending how much metal had been poured into them and poured out of them.

Who would do the re-lining?

The furnace men themselves. Yes, it was all done in-house. Brick re-lined and it was like a plaster thing they put on.

So then sometimes they would have to time it so that they would get all the furnaces together for a big casting? And then they would have to check the metal, analyse it wouldn't they?

Yes, it all had to be checked and analysed and they had the labs just behind the furnaces.

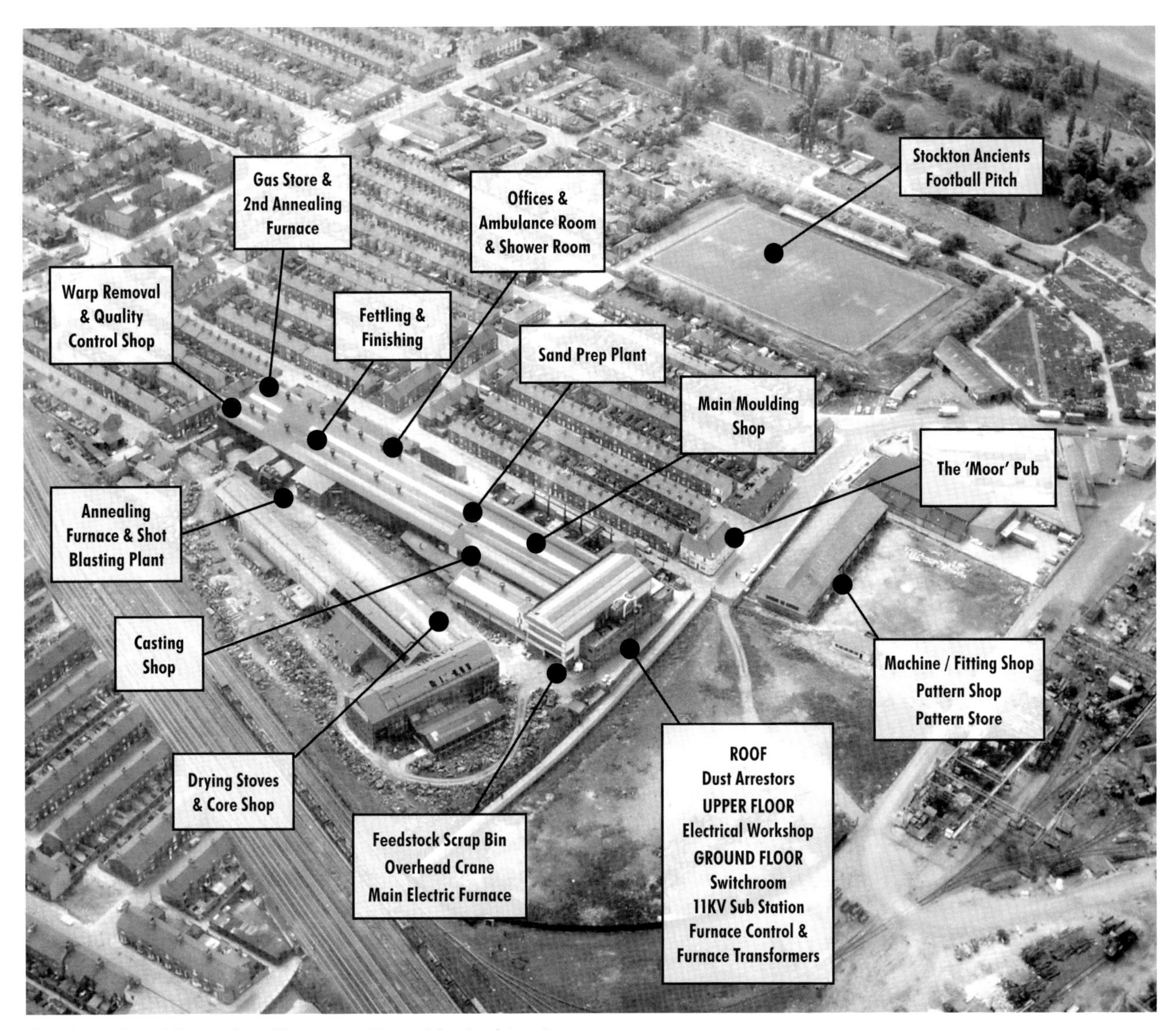

Stockton Steel Foundry. (Courtesy Teesside Archives)

There was a lab above the furnaces. And every now and again, while they were melting they would take a sample and that would be taken up into the lab and then tested to make sure everything was in that had to be in or add something that wasn't quite up to scratch. Then they did a final sample before it was tapped out to make sure it was correct for that casting.

Then how did they get the metal out of the furnace?

The furnace used to tip up at a forty-five degree angle. They used to tip it into the ladles that they were going to cast it out of. They were what they called bottom poured ladles. There was a chap had a handle and he used to pick that up and the molten steel used to come out of the bottom.

So what would the ladle carry?

I know the smallest ladle used to hold a ton or just over the ton, but they were for the induction furnaces. I think the biggest one held fifteen tons.

How did you get the slag off?

They used to skim it off in the furnaces first. Then whatever was left when they poured the metal into the mould, obviously just travelled down as they were emptying the ladle. The slag was always on the top. When it got to the end of the casting they used to tip it into what they called a bell, a big bell. Just used to tip it into that. They used to get some metal back out of it. They used to wait until it had settled off and then tip the bell up and then obviously the slag, nine times out of ten, used to break away and fall away. And then they would get the metal back out of that. *(Eddie Peacock)*

Stockton Steel Foundry Moulding Bay. (Wright Ahead)

I found the most interesting was the Foundry. I used to love to go in the Foundry because there was so much going on. You could see what they were actually doing, whereas if you went in to a Machine Shop it's just something on a machine isn't it? And the worst department I went into that I wouldn't have wanted to go in again was the Blacksmiths' Shop. They had one at Thornaby. The men were stripped to the waist with sweat towels round the neck and these big hammers coming down onto the ingots. Eventually, everything was transferred to Seaton Carew. I didn't want to go in again, I didn't like it. But I wasn't frightened to walk in the Foundry on my own. But in the Foundry the big overhead cranes carried the big ladles of molten metal. It was a risky job really. And of course, the chemists used to have to go and take a sample of the steel before they poured it. They had laboratories where they tested the sample, down what we called Richardson Duck's offices and they were also the Steel Foundry offices. *(Enid Thurlwell)*

I enjoyed both foundries really. I discovered in the early days that it was possible to weld steel, whereas you couldn't weld iron. Great pains had to be taken in preparing the moulds in the Iron Foundry to make sure there were no foreign bodies in. In the Steel Foundry this didn't matter because if a bit of muck had been left in the mould and it had left a hole, the hole was simply welded up.

Where was the Iron Foundry? Was it in the same building as the Steel Foundry?

No, no. It was on the other side of Trafalgar Street.

On the Bridge Yard side?

Exactly, yes. Ran all the way down the different shops. Ran all the way down Trafalgar Street on the right-hand side of the road. Whereas the Steel Foundry, which was a newer innovation with a new building, was on the left-hand side going down Trafalgar Street. *(Bob Waller)*

Then a lot of the London Underground, the Victoria Line. It gives you a bit of pride and I sometimes look when I'm down in London and travelling in the tube and they've got the ceiling

Thornaby Steel Foundry Induction Shop. (Wright Ahead)

off. You look up and you either see Stanton & Staveley or HW & Co stamped into the girders. *(Simon Wrightson)*

The Foundry was noisier than the Forge if you worked down where the fettlers were because the fettlers are on the chipping hammer. The moulders did the castings then they were knocked out, shot-blasted and cleaned up then it used to go up to the burners. The burners used to cut all the heads off and then they would go on the annealing plant. They would all be annealed, then they would go to the fettlers and they would cut off what they didn't want or grind them down to make into a proper casting. They just knocked the thing out to get the mould out of the sand. They were in boxes. But the massive moulds which were made at Thornaby and at Billingham, Steelcast at Billingham, they were in the ground, and they had to dig them out by the old-fashioned method and then the big cranes would pull them out of the ground. They were sixty-five ton castings, them. The fettlers got them last. They would smooth them all down, cut out all the little bits and cut off all the flashing. And then they would finish dressing off. What was moulded one week went out of the gate the next week. It was a good Foundry in the sense that there was a good turn round. *(Robert Chaney)*

The managers in the Foundry were time-served moulders, they'd come up through the shop-floor. They'd served their time so they knew what they were doing. They were men in all the departments, all the managers were shop-floor up, they knew what they were talking about. So you respected them, you respected their position.

There would be furnace men and ladle men?

Yes, there were ladle men in the Foundry. They were more or less like skilled labourers. The ladle men and furnace men, but again there were different sections.

Fettling a casting at Thornaby Steel Foundry. circa 1930s. (Remembering Thornaby Group)

Typical sample of castings at Thornaby Steel Foundry. circa 1930s. (Remembering Thornaby Group)

And then the jobs would progress through to the dressing yard?

Well, you started off with the moulder. The moulder made the mould. The furnace men, they melted the metal, the ladle men came and cast the mould. Then the casting eventually went to the knock out stage because it got covered in sand. All the sand and everything was knocked off. Then they were blasted, shot-blasted, and then they came into the Fettling Yard. To have the feeder heads and the running system and anything taken off that wasn't necessary. Then it went up to the inspection to see that there were no faults in the castings. If the surface wasn't right or there were bits and pieces on that shouldn't be on you got them taken off. Then certain ones had to go on the marking off table to be checked dimensionally and for straightness, and of course they were all governed by specifications. But there was a section that dealt with that.

And how did they get the material spec. right?

Well, that was a metallurgist's job. They sorted all the specifications out and handed them down to the Foundry. To the Metal Shop. *(John Heighly)*

We had six labourers, maybe more, in the Pattern Shop. Now they did all the sweeping up every day at four o'clock when we packed up work, or about quarter to they'd start sweeping the Shop because all the shavings and everything had to be shifted. They also were employed to find the patterns. Every week there used to be an amount of patterns go into the foundries. The orders used to come through and they used to leave all the patterns with us and paid us for looking after them. They were stored in big storerooms, on shelves and listed where you could go and put your hands on them and there was a file made out for them. There were thousands of patterns and they were all listed. They all belonged to the customer who paid for storing them and then they would send an order in and those had to be got out and then put away somewhere. They were put in about half a dozen different places or in the big field near the river. You couldn't get everything in the building so a lot were stocked outside. Some were never used for thirty years but they were still stored. You can imagine the state some were in. You had to dig them out. Most could be used but some of them were left that long that they had deteriorated and had to be renewed or titivated up. *(Ron Nichol)*

When I started off as an inspector you had to go round looking at all the castings and you would mark up where you wanted the people to trim it all off and clean it all off. Then when you were satisfied with that you had to make sure that it went from there into the machinery, and we had special machines set up just for drilling and machining segments. They were literally hand-made to do the particular job. You'd never seen that sort of machinery before. It was purely made for machining the angles on the castings. Then you had running round a rim and there was sort of a lead hammered into it and it was at both sides in case there was any water coming along or anything. So it was unusual. Then you had to set a circle up with them all. Then you get in outside inspectors to check to make sure that everything is working, it is correct, and we could machine them to that level and consistency that was required. *(Trevor Briggs)*

They said, 'Oh well, we have an opening for a foundry technologist,' which was a brand-new idea. Foundries were still using the same basic procedures they had for 4,000 years. A bit of sand and a bit of clay and you wet it and ram the mixture round the pattern and that was it. At the time they were just testing the CO_2 process which was a method of adding sodium silicate to sand and passing carbon dioxide through it to form a hardened gel, which produced far more accurate castings.

So they were injecting a gas in?

Yes. Carbon dioxide gas but at single-bar pressure, not under pressure or anything.

It would hold its shape?

Yes. After that was under way they began bringing in phenolic resin which was mixed with the sand along with phosphoric acid to harden the mix off. This was a whole new move that the foundries were making. This was mainly because the skills that were initially required, were difficult to learn quickly so these new products took all the skill out of it and improved productivity most markedly. It was far quicker to use these new sands than the old methods. Eaglescliffe Iron Foundry made just bog-standard-grade fourteen, sixteen, eighteen iron.

Yes, grey irons. To be honest it wasn't very sophisticated at all. Cupolas and sand. The Foundry churned out iron all the time. It was a much more basic job. The big orders they got were for the underground tunnels for Sao Paulo. That was a big job. It was to make the segments to make the tunnels for the trains. That was a big job. But in general they made four million, five million, six million railway chairs for British Rail and other railways around the world and they weren't too sophisticated. Literally, they had these little bumping machines that churned out millions. Every day the guy came out and knocked them out. I remember he was about six-foot-six, about the same wide. He used to turn the box over and using a pair of tongs he used to flick the red-hot castings through his legs onto a heap about twenty feet away. He had to be the toughest guy in the world to work under those conditions, though it didn't seem to do him any harm. *(Colin Waugh)*

There was a lot of messing about at the beginning because as soon as they'd finished a particular quota of tunnel segments, which was the main thing they made, they could go, and they used to be going home at half past twelve and things like that which was hopeless. The scrap rate was horrendous. When I went to Head Wrightson's the scrap rate for castings was twenty-three per cent, which is dreadful. In the gantry outside there were over 2,000 castings which were not passable as viable castings. It was a hell of a mess. We got on top of that within the first year or so. Then I introduced furan which was a resin and sand mixture instead of using wet sand. This produced very accurate castings and the scrap rate fell from twenty-three per cent to point six of one per cent in eighteen months which was, I don't think, remotely rivalled anywhere in the country. *(John Fuller)*

In addition to the Maintenance Department which included electricians, plumbers and a wire rope splicer, there was the General Office, Power House, large and small Machine Shops, Steel Foundry, Pattern Shop, Smiths' Shop, Fabrication Shop, Welding Shop which employed some very good women welders, Test House, Tool Room, garage and a canteen. There was a shipyard for the erection of landing craft but not used as a repair yard. I recollect the firm's fabrication of ladles for the Port Talbot Steelworks and they were so large that when they were transported on huge lorries up

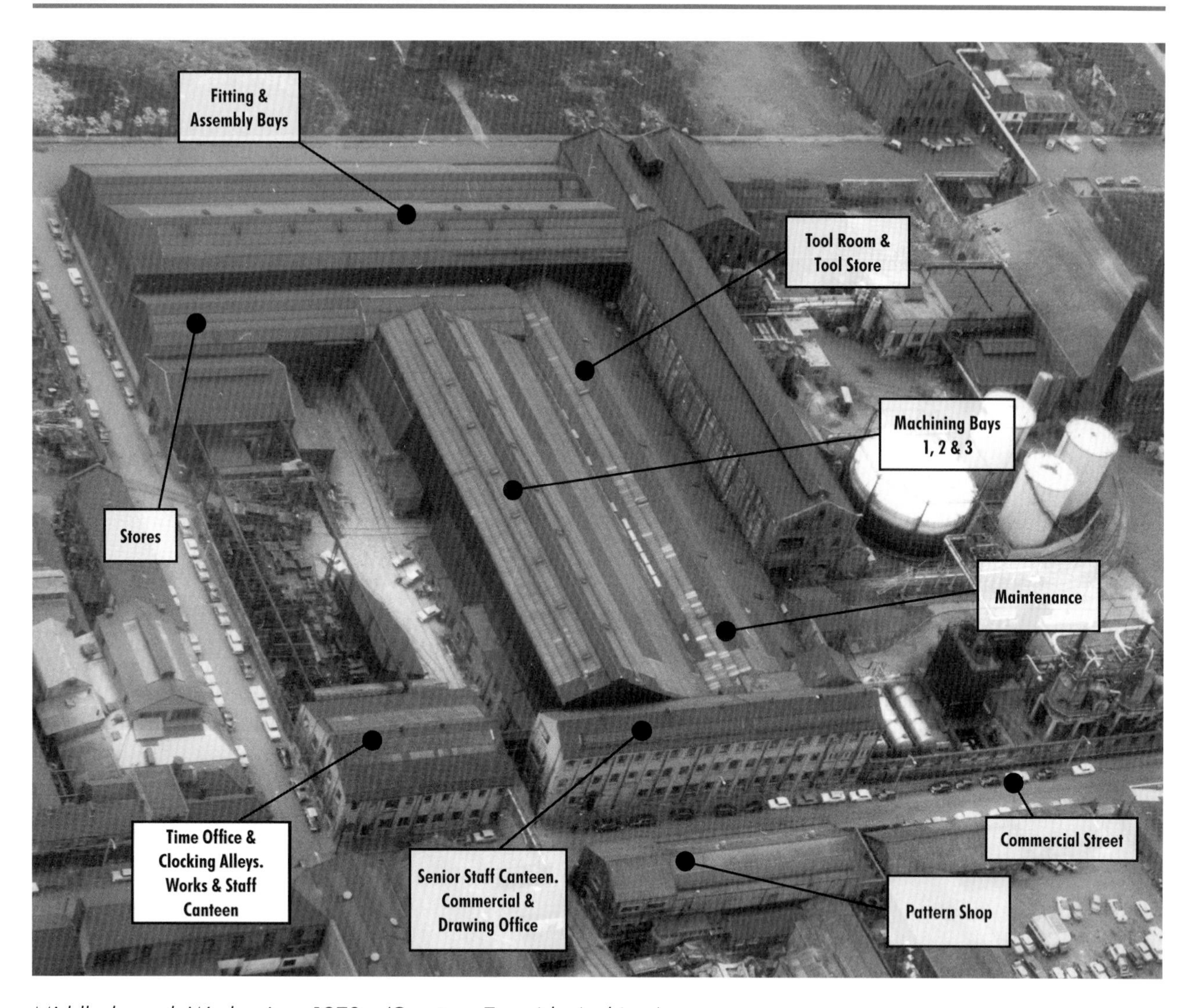

Middlesbrough Works circa 1970s. (Courtesy Teesside Archives)

Trafalgar Street they had a man on top of the ladle with a wooden pole to lift the cables which ran above the road. They also manufactured large drums for the Dover-France pipeline under the ocean. No doubt there were other large projects under construction. *(Kenneth Pelmear)*

Middlesbrough Works

The drawings were done on paper with pencil or black ink using a special pen, not the normal fountain pen or conventional pen. It was specially designed with two prongs or blades that opened up and you actually put a drop of ink in, closed them up and worked with that. The metal lower blade rested against the T-square or whatever instrument you were using. The draughtsmen all had their own pens. At that stage the equipment was relatively primitive by modern standards. Computers hadn't even been thought of. We had a basic board which would swivel and go into almost an upright position or could be laid flat. A T-square was attached either end by means of pulleys and a wire so that it would move vertically across and up and down the board. The paper we used was effectively like a greaseproof-type of paper and was transparent for printing purposes. Then of course we had a Tracing Department. If any drawings were of particular significance they needed to be traced for better life expectancy and storage. We had about nine lady tracers. The office was again fairly basic. It was on the top floor of the Machine Company. The building and the works were in Commercial Street. That was the formal address. It had originally belonged to Richardsons Westgarth who built ships' engines. It was a very old building, probably

Middlesbrough Works Bay One. (HW Company brochure)

built in the 1850s but it was quite serviceable. There was plenty of light as we had good large windows overlooking the river. From what I can remember it had a pitched wooden-timber-clad ceiling with a metal framework with horizontal cross members just holding it in position. No ceiling as such. One comical chap used to walk down the office with his beaker in hand and throw it up into the air over these cross members, hopefully catching it at the other side. This was when it was empty of course. I think there would be about fifty people working in the Drawing Office and everyone would have their own drawing board. There were also separate little offices for the Chief Engineer and Chief Draughtsman. We had the tracers in another section. We had people who issued the drawings to the works and issued parts lists because within each drawing you itemised all the component parts. This had to be transferred and typed onto other documents which went down to the works identifying all the bits and pieces. *(David Auld)*

Piecework meant that you were working against the clock. So when you got a job in the workshops you were given a time card, you were given a drawing; the materials were brought to your machine. So you got a price for the job and you had to get started. As soon as you started a job you clocked your card in a clock and when you finished the job you clocked the card again. You did know what you were going to earn, you knew what the basics were because your basic wage was made up of your basic wage plus a machine rate. Depending on what machine you were on determined what your machine rate was. The bigger the machine or the more complicated the machine the bigger the machine rate. But the more complicated it was, you were doing bigger work so you weren't necessarily doing a

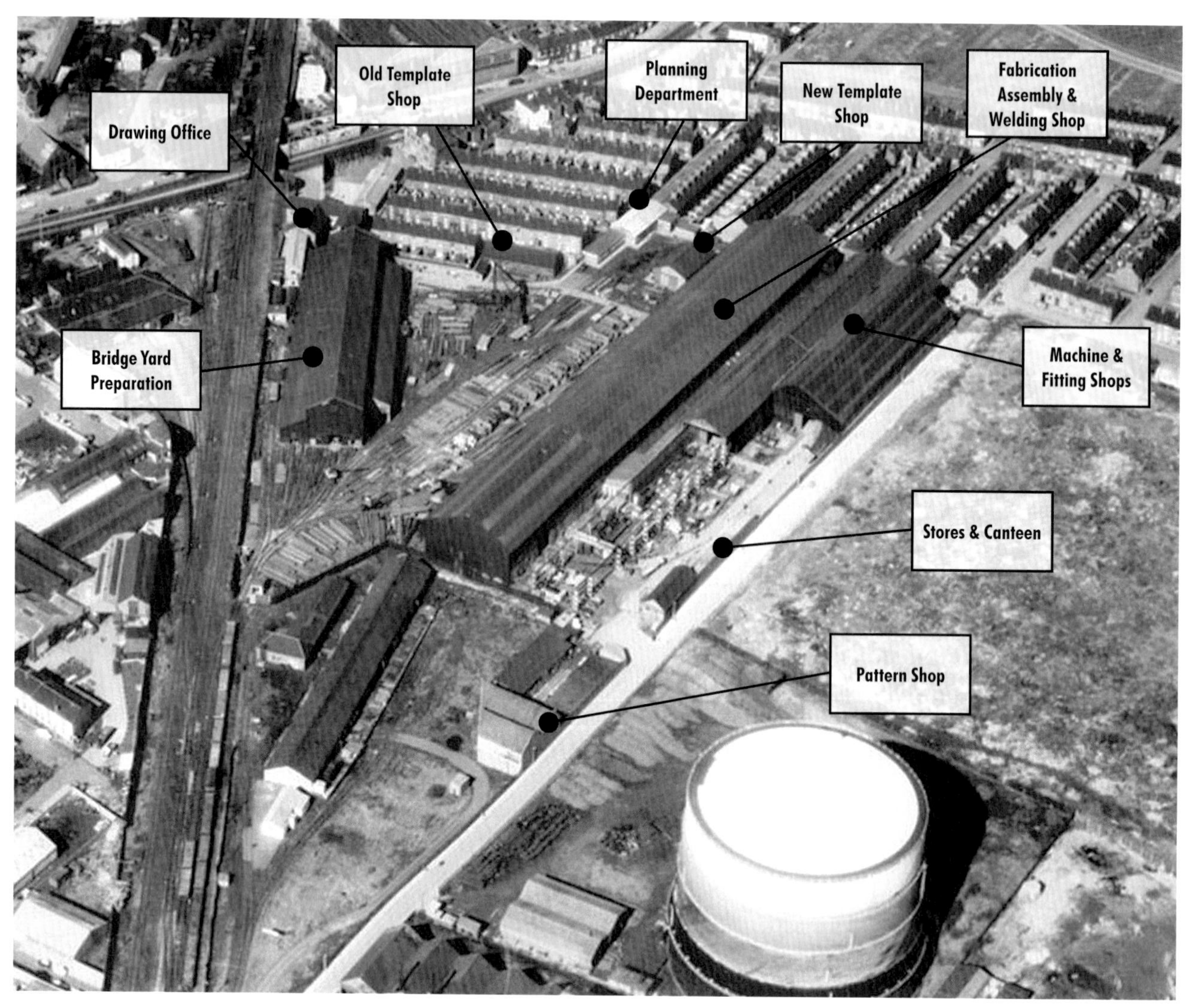

Stockton Forge circa 1960s. (Courtesy Teesside Archives)

run of say, ten, twenty, thirty, whereas on the smaller machines you would be doing a run. You could be doing literally dozens and dozens, hundreds of a component. So when you get a job like that, if you've got any kind of skill you should be making some money. Your money was worked out at time and a half or double time or treble time. For instance, if you got a job for five hours and you did it in two and a half hours that means you got double time for that two and a half hours. *(Noel Thompson)*

So I moved into what was then known as Head Wrightson's Machine Company and their premises were on Commercial Street. The first thing that put me off was the fact that it was all inside. The good side was in the winter you were warm and inside. The bad side was in the summertime it got a bit overbearing because it was a really big hangar-sized workshop with a glass roof. Although it had big doors which used to open during the summer it did get quite warm in there sometimes and it was an inside job at this. *(Stuart Thompson)*

Stockton Forge

They sent me back to the Forge for a short while and I worked with a couple of guys when we were playing about with one of the presses. They were doing a job for the MOD. I think it was these aluminium side-armour plates for the Ferret armoured car. They used to send these aluminium extrusions in from High Duty Alloys Limited. I think they actually made it and we used to press them to various radiuses and angles according to the MOD spec and then they would take them away to the firing range and fire fifty-calibre bullets at them. See what the deflection was like and then they

Stockton Forge Bridge Yard. (HW Company brochure)

would come back and say, 'Well, we need a bit more angle there and a bit more bend there.' So we made another set. So I worked on that little job for maybe only about six months and then they moved me to Thornaby into the Planning Department. *(Ken Peacock)*

The blacksmiths and anglesmiths were both in the Bridge Yard and they contributed to the noise. It was not a good experience really when looking back because a lot of people, myself included, suffer from hearing problems and I would say this was due to the noisy conditions, and ear defenders were unknown. There was no question of ear protection, it was just you, and it was one of those things you accepted. *(Allan Ayre)*

When I first started it was all belt-driven lathes. People nowadays would say, 'Crikey, what was that?' They had to have all these belts, they were all everywhere. And, of course, as electricity came in they were all individually fitted with electric motors. So I would say there was ten, maybe twenty lathes and there was the big borer and there was two roundabouts and planers. The bigger machines worked shifts.

And were the Machine and the Fitting Shop under one roof?

The Machine Shop and the Fitting Shop were under one roof. Right in the middle was the office. You went up the stairs and the people who were in charge, if they weren't wandering around, they were looking out of the window and making sure that you worked. So they had an absolute central position with windows all round. They made sure that they were watching all the time. *(Trevor Briggs)*

The main thing I remember was the colliery work. And then another job I remember was the Jodrell Bank Telescope. We did the structure for that. That was put up out in the Forge yard.

Stockton Forge Machine Shop.
(HW Company brochure)

And did you build the whole structure at the Forge? And the dish as well?

Not the dish, no. It was the structure to put everything on. But it was circular. So I don't know how it worked exactly. Everybody knew it was for Jodrell Bank. They wanted a flagpole putting on the new municipal buildings on Church Road. So they decided to do it out of fibre glass with a stainless-steel base and stainless steel for the cup that held the flag. Yes, the centre piece was fibre glass. Well, I worked on that. And every time I passed it I would see my handiwork *(Norman Toulson)*

Was it mainly the home market or did the Forge export?

Head Wrightson's were engineers to the world. Head Wrightson had the organisation for selling and marketing abroad and they used to get orders. South Africa was a prime purchasing country for manufactured equipment. In later years I worked on and installed equipment in Malaysia and Indonesia for Head Wrightson as they would manufacture, ship out and install. Their motto was 'Engineers to the World'. At King's Cross station in London you can find a cast-iron item in the shape of a big plum pudding, this was supplied by Head Wrightson's for everyone to see. 'Engineers to the World'. *(Allan Ayre)*

There was what we called section leaders in the Drawing Office. There was Structural Design Section, there was a Piping Section. There was those on the Process, mainly metalliferous mining and then there was the colliery lads, they were in various sections. The Chief Draughtsman was above the section. So that's how the Drawing Office was organised. Chief Draughtsman, and under him I think there were about five section leaders. One man in particular, Bob Howe, I was very fond of. He was a real fatherly figure, had served in the First World War and he took me under his wing for a time. He was very good. He used to say when you were doing your drawings, 'If it looks right it is right,' and I remember Bob saying that a lot of times. I say 'Bob'; he was very funny about that. A chap came up from the works with a drawing, 'Are you Bob Howe?' He says, 'I'm Mr. Howe to you.' They were very fussy about things like that in those days *(Ray Shaw)*

I stayed with Head Wrightson because the Stockton Forge was a very friendly part of the organisation. At the time there would be probably about 500 men at the Forge and you knew a large portion of them by name. Quite often with your job you would be going to the yard for various things and you got to know them. For instance when I first started each of the foremen's offices was like the General Office, very Dickensian. For instance, each office had a spittoon. They were very good at hitting that spittoon. They were very dirty, dusty places in those days - the foremen's offices. *(Wilf Bradley)*

At the Forge they did the big aluminium smelting tanks for the Invergordon Aluminium Smelter Works. Scale cars for the steel industry. I remember doing the Redcar blast furnaces and the Llanwern blast furnaces. They were the twenty-metre-diameter hearths and they trial erected the hearth sections in the Heavy Plate Shop. *(Ken Peacock)*

At the time they were modernising all the pits in England. Head Wrightson got a good bit of that work and we used to build head gears. They were erected in the Forge before they went to

where they were going. So they were a pretty big structure. Then ICI dryers which were circular. Maybe thirty-metres long, fifteen-foot diameter and they revolved round and they used to put a tyre round each end about a foot wide, six-inches-thick solid steel. They went all the way round the vessel, both ends, and it used to run on the rollers underneath. The Fitting Shop did that work. Well, we put them on initially and they machined them up perfectly round and that sort of thing. But inside the dryer were spiral plates. They were to do with churning up fertilisers and it all worked its way along and come out the other end of it.
So you had to fit all those things all the way along and you would be working inside and the pneumatic chippers would be chipping the welds away on the outside of the seam and you had to be on the inside. No wonder we're all deaf. The noise was absolutely tremendous. *(Norman Toulson)*

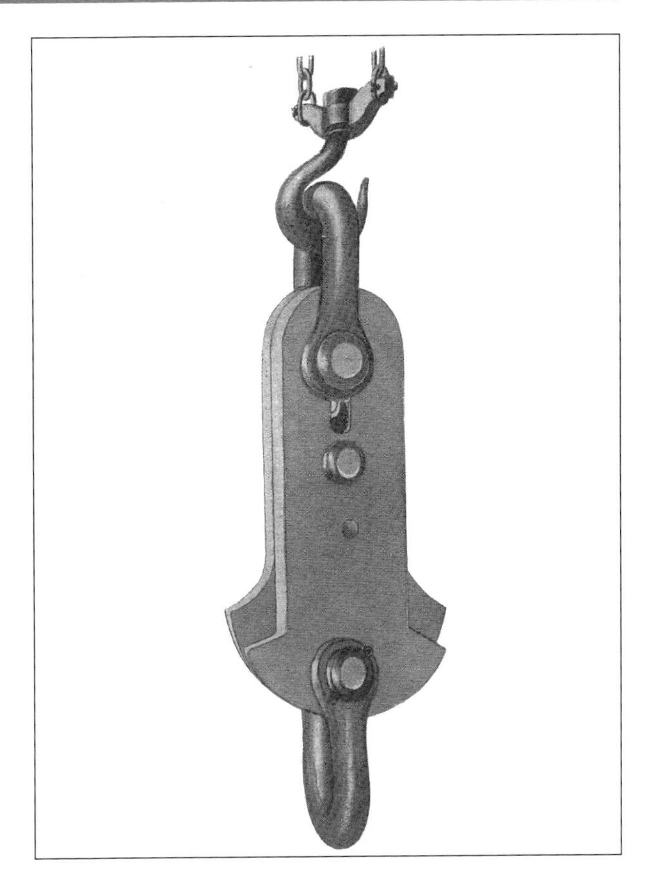

Humble safety hook manufactured at Stockton Forge for the mining industry. (HW Company brochure)

I went and worked at Head Wrightson Stockton Forge and that was a fun time. They were making a thing called an obsel plate, which was twenty-four foot of steel sheet, very thin. Two pieces, you know, as in welded together, and there were triangular sections top and bottom spot-welded down the twenty-four feet. The idea was that these were put in a big box, wires were hung down and the plates were hung down and the gas would go through and because of these triangular shapes the gases would swirl around these wires. Electrostatic potential applied between the plate and the wire, the wire attracted the dust. Every so often they were given a shake, all the dust fell down into a hopper and got used again - mainly iron-ore dust. We were making these things at the rate of something like thirty a week and the guys on the site were erecting them at the rate roughly of thirty a day so we had to start making them weeks beforehand and then store them and then ship them, which was a bit of a pain. The MD at the time said to me, 'Have a look at that, so and so knows all about it, go and have a chat with him.' 'Okay.' The net result of that was that after some chats and some talking to people on spot-welding machines and the like we devised a sketch of a potential machine. We had an idea of what we were going to do but we hadn't got all the costs. Then I went to see this MD and said, 'Well, this is an idea that we might handle this way and we could probably get to about thirty a day give or take.' 'Right,' he said, 'the Board meeting is on Friday. I need two pages from you of explanation and rough costings.' 'Oh alright.' So we went away and came back on Friday with two pages and a request for, I can't remember the exact figure, but let's say it was ten and a half thousand pounds, a lot of money in those days. But he came back on Monday and said, 'You've got it, here you are, go ahead. If you want anything drawn to create this device the Drawing Office manager will look after it.' 'Fine,' I said, 'alright.' So we then started the project of making my infernal machine. So what this did was to roughly assemble these things and we had clips to hold it altogether and then it was driven through on a continuous-belt basis. This belt came, hooked on behind it, pushed it through, a series of spot-welds, sort of eight of them, came together, 'shoosh'. Lots of sparks everywhere. Advance six inches, 'shoosh', et cetera. After twenty-four feet it came to the end, stopped. And then all the bits were added to it and it was put into some sort of pallet to go to site. The first day we were doing the trial, or the first evening, it was five o'clock. Because we didn't know anything much about spot-welding and the people who we had bought the spot-welding equipment from didn't know much about what we were doing but they wanted to make sure everything was okay. So I said to them, 'You come for five o'clock and we're going to test it on such and such a day.' Sure enough they were there. I said, 'You've got to dial all the knobs and we'll watch and listen and observe.' And of course, the plate went through, sparks everywhere and we were absolutely blinded by all these sparks and somebody came running down the Bridge Yard, 'What the f*** is going on here?' It was the Bridge Yard manager. We said, 'Well, we're doing some tests to make sure this is alright and we're just making adjustments.' And he said, 'Never mind about that, look at the bloody lights.' Oh, all the lights went out in the Bridge Yard every time the machine did a single set of welds. The electricians had connected the machine across the phases that supplied the lighting and we had a night shift working at the far end of the yard. Oh well. We have to go back to the electricians tomorrow morning! We eventually achieved more than thirty a day. The profit on the job to our company or our unit was something like seven or eight per cent, which wasn't bad I suppose. *(Ted Sinnot)*

There was Stockton Forge at Norton near to Pickerings lifts and almost opposite the former Hills wood factory and the buildings are still in use having been taken over by other people. The Forge, contrary to its name, did no forgings but tended to specialise in colliery and mining products. They made lots of things for the mining industry, both the coal mining and for the gold fields in South Africa, gold mines, diamond mines et cetera. Head gear, skip-winding plants, anything to get the men down and the stuff out. Also ball mills to grind stuff smaller and classifiers because if they're getting material out of the ground it's got to be classified or separated. So Stockton Forge made a lot of classifiers and dryers et cetera. They also made humble hooks. They specialised in humble hooks, which is a device that goes on the top of a cage so when the cage is coming up the shaft if it happened to get into what is called an over wind position, that is it overshoots its normal stopping position and is in danger of going right up the head gear to the pulley wheels, a humble hook is a device which catches and releases the cage and allows it to fall down onto a safety platform. They did a lot of them. *(Albert Roxborough)*

Stampings

Now all the laddies on the Stampings, they were all on piecework. I started off as inspector there before I went in Quality Control. You had special equipment to check the furnace, see that the furnace was the right temperature. See that the block that came out of the furnace was the right temperature to go on the hammer. While it was hot you would be able to just check a little bit but then as soon as it was cooled down you'd take a sample and then you would go through all the samples. It would say if it was sort of nine out of ten, fair enough, that would be great. Eight out of ten you would still be okay. But it was a very noisy environment but again, people really, really worked. That was one thing about Head Wrightson's, no matter where you went people really were fantastic workers. *(Trevor Briggs)*

The Stampings were horrendous, that was frightening. It was a terrifying place to work for. Once those hammers dropped there would be hot scale flying out of the sides of the machines and the noise, the forge hammer dropping was unbelievable. *(Billy Sharp)*

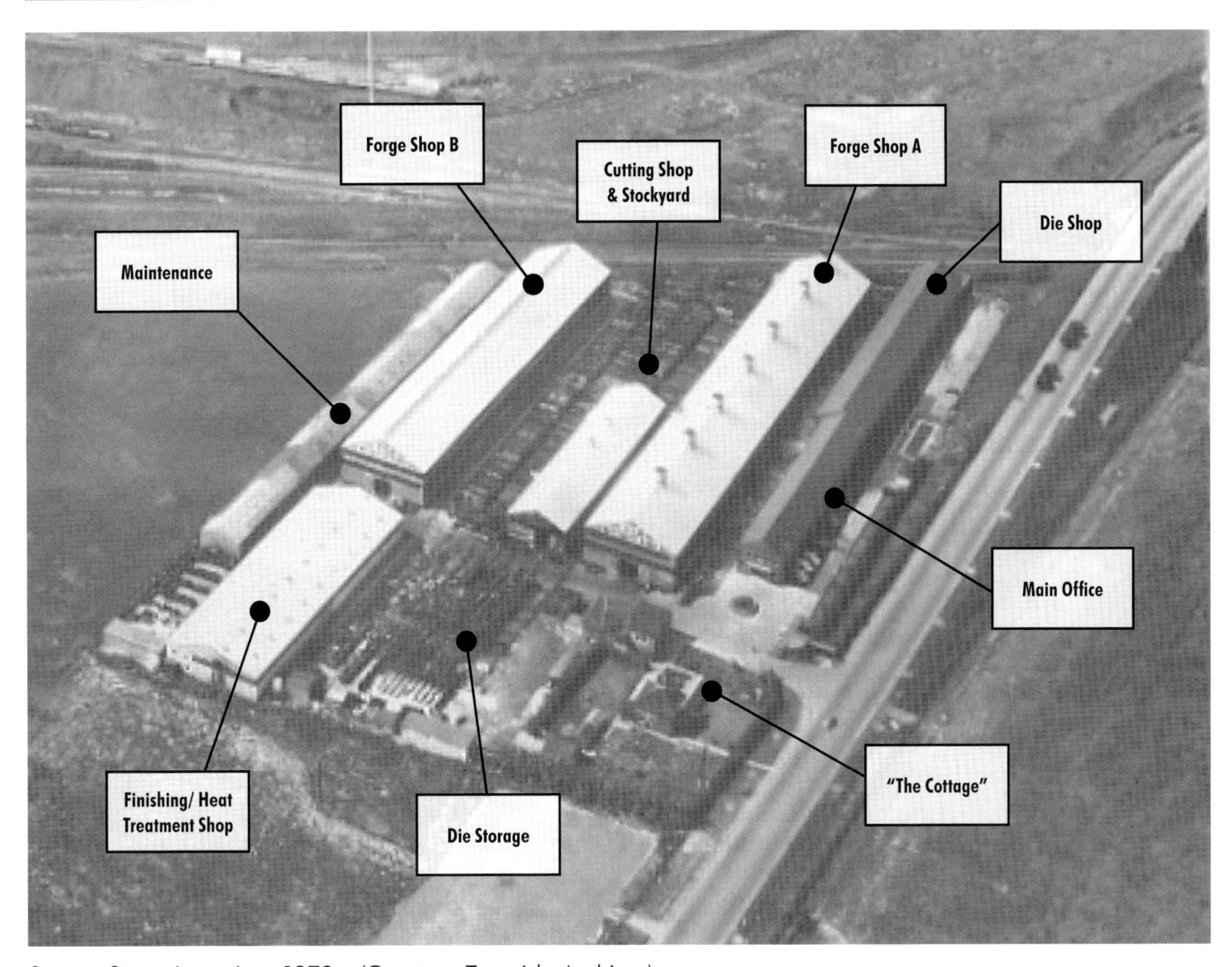

Seaton Stampings circa 1970s. (Courtesy Teesside Archives)

So you come to Stampings. What do you think of it all?

Different. It was a whole new world. You know the Forge is a strange place, I think it's a type of place that you'll either love or hate. The number of people that you find, they're either here forty years or forty minutes. And the number who've said, 'Not for me I'm out.' I found it fascinating.

Did you find it noisy and dirty, dusty and...?

Yes. But after a short period of time when the noise wasn't there you missed it. Because it's just constant and then as soon as it stops you know something's wrong. It's strange. *(Barry Davison)*

Were there many working in the Forging Department at Thornaby?

I can't give numbers but probably a couple of hundred. Because the die sinkers worked there. All the people that worked over the road from us, they had two machines that just cut up what are called the billets to the exact size for the people to use for the forgings. There was the Office Department, they had their own little Drawing Office. The Die Shop, which was milling machines and they had one or two crafty little machines for cutting dies. And the tracer traced the template and cut the die out of that template. There were quite a few people, blacksmiths, labouring people. The forging-hammers were there and it was a very noisy place. There were the drop forgings, which they called stamps. There were the power hammers and forging machines which worked on a horizontal way as opposed to the vertical.

So what's the difference between the power forge and what did you call the other one then?

There were the stamps which was basically two legs with a whopping weight in between them, that goes up and down.

And what's the power hammer then?

If you went up to Preston Park you'd see a small one in the blacksmith's shop. It's just driven by a motor which sort of compresses air. You've

HW Seaton Stampings Shop circa 1960s. (HW Company brochure)

seen the blacksmith running a big bar through it? And it's banging up and down. A work of art what they did with them. *(Derek Delahaye)*

At the Stampings they did forgings using drop-hammers and forging-hammers. A hammer comes down and makes a hot block of metal into a particular shape using a die block. A very noisy place involving a lot of heavy work. I only went to the Stampings when a trip around the various works was organised for new apprentices. I never went there for apprentice training. At that time, we didn't seem to bother with it. But they made lots of forgings for the motor industry, construction industry. They actually did some mouldings for artificial knees and hips. *(Albert Roxborough)*

The stamper places the piece into the dies and the guy's dropping the hammer on top of it. The timing of that is quite crucial. Typically, on a three-ton hammer, there would be somewhere between thirty and fifty hammer blows. The furnace man, all he's doing is loading and emptying the furnace. In those days you didn't have any temperature controls or anything like that on the furnaces. Just eyesight for the colour of the furnace. You had a control inspector measuring the temperature of the furnace now and again. I used to work in the Foundry. I thought the Foundry was scary but the noise that we got here was worse, as there were twenty-five or twenty-six hammers generally when you were working. I found the Forge scarier because you had a lot of hot metal floating around and being thrown around in the works. They would pick up a block of metal and pass it to each other. They still do it to some extent, there's very little handling equipment in there.

So what were they picking up?

Hot cut pieces from the furnace and the forgings themselves. The biggest are from the five-ton hammers and in those days was maybe about a hundred pounds. So they're pulling it out of the furnaces by hand. Most of the furnaces out there now are as they were then. They're only boxes of bricks with a burner at one end and we just push the billets through and we're dragging the forgings out when they're heated up. Depending on the unit they might put them straight into the hammer itself or they might do a little bit of manipulation beforehand like knocking them down into small units then pass them over. Then they would pass them over to the little presses which would just trim the excess off and put holes in them or whatever else you might want to do. But there was very little handling equipment and there still isn't out on the hammers. The guys prefer to handle.

I was essentially in charge of heat treatments and testing, although there wasn't much testing in those days. At the time we had a Chief Inspector but no Quality Manager as such. I was in charge of the heat-treatment furnaces but it was a very low-key business then. You weren't a quality-controlled business. That sounds terrible but you weren't a quality-controlled or quality-assured company. It was

Die sinking at Stamping. (HW Company brochure)

Bill Goring forging on a blacksmith's hammer circa 1950s. (Picture from N. Goring, his son)

a hundred per cent inspection, from memory. Everything was handled and hand counted into bins and visually inspected by a team of inspectors virtually round the clock, from memory. Everything was handballed into bins and it was all done in the Forge. We called it black because it was black, straight from the Forge.

So what were you looking for?

It's the same sort of problems now as then: bad workmanship, scrap forgings, forgings that aren't full, forgings that had been damaged in work and various things like that. Handling because everything's hot out there, so you're going to cause some handling defects if you're not careful. Things were really chucked around in those days. *(Jim Matthews)*

So I then joined my first Head Wrightson company, namely Head Wrightson Stampings, which in 1978 was losing £100,000 a month!! The company had a multitude of problems including a labour force that was grossly overpaid, by industry standards, and some dreadful decisions had been made by its former management. For example, Stampings management had predicted that their market was traditionally cyclical. Their logic was that once the current downturn levelled off then it would then enter a phase of steep growth. So oblivious to possible changes in customer component design they embarked on a stock-manufacturing programme of 'safe stock'. Unfortunately the market then double-dipped and many of the forgings produced became obsolete and nothing but scrap as designs changed. The problem was kept off site and 1,000 tons of stock, going nowhere, was left to go rusty at the Eaglescliffe Iron Foundry site. So I had a business with no order book, obsolete work-in-progress, steel stocks for more obsolete components, an overpaid labour force and too many of them. The company had also, in the interim, started up an export business which meant that it had to adapt and to become extremely competitive. In other words it had to match the highly-efficient and technically-innovative German competitors. With out-of-date equipment, over manning, and overpaid employees – it just couldn't survive doing that.

The Friarage at Yarm circa late 1960s. (Wright Ahead)

So, what was the product range then?

Originally, like most of the industry, it used the benefits of its hammer-weight-capacity range to forge higher-volume production runs, such as caterpillar track links and tractor components. However, as mechanical forging presses became larger and tool-changing technology evolved, the likes of Stampings could never match the ever increasing trend of high-speed dedicated forging lines to be found in Europe and GKN. The result was that the company was forced into the supposedly niche areas of small and medium-batch runs. Thank goodness they never tried to get involved in the automotive sector. It got involved in forgings for trucks, buses and off-highway vehicles such as tank gearboxes, excavators, graders, combined harvesters etc. It had very strong links with Caterpillar Birtley, and Volvo BM, Sweden, both of whom purchased high numbers of small quantity forgings. It also became involved in oil-related products such as valves, flanges and weldolets for people like Bonney Forge, Scotland. We did, however, still have a major issue to resolve. In crude terms the company site was like an industrial slum, with two feet of muck and dirt everywhere. You needed wellies to walk round inside and, in short, showing new or even existing customers around the site was a major embarrassment. So we set about sorting the place out. We also had to face a major sort out with the labour force, who really must have known the golden days had gone by this point in time, the bonus scheme and, of course, the staff. On a lighter note we closed the executive dining room down, we closed the senior management dining room down, and everyone moved into the remaining staff dining room. We effectively ended up with one small dining room for the staff and, of course, the works mess. *(Ian Ford)*

The Friarage

The Friarage is at the southerly end of Yarm High Street. I guess once upon a time, I don't know too much about the history, it might have been related to the friars but then it became the home, I think, of the Meynell family or something like that. It was a grand old house,

WINNING ORDER: Engineers at Head Wrightson Machine Co., celebrated clinching an export order worth £15m in June 1978. The contract for an electrolytic tinning line, which put tin on steel strip for making tin cans, was placed by a Yugoslavia state company called Zorka. The Head Wrightson winning team (L-R) is director and general manager Peter Llewellyn, Jim Scott, Alan Hurst, David Renshaw, Mrs. Jean Griffiths, sales director John Spence and Bob Olley (Image courtesy Evening Gazette Media Company (GMC) Middlesbrough)

very stately. I remember coming up and parking outside the front door and marching in. Really, it was a converted house and I was fortunate enough to have an office in the old building because they built some Portakabins and things at the back, and I couldn't really believe this gazing out of the window at the manicured lawns. It was the registered office of the company. It was the office where the senior management worked. Sir John Wrightson, when I joined, was the Chairman. John Eccles, who was the Managing Director and the Company Secretary, he was based there. The Finance Director was there too. The other directors were out in the various operating units which were obviously around Thornaby, Teesside and, at that time, Manchester with B&S Massey, which had just joined the company. *(Robin Millman)*

The Friarage is a Queen Anne house in Yarm. The offices of the Board, the Accounts Department, the Personnel Department, the Secretaries et cetera were all based there. It was only vacated some time after Head Wrightson had merged, as we said at the time, with Davy and the Yarm site was sold to Yarm Grammar School. *(David Jowett)*

International markets

Head Wrightson's overseas interests were handled via wholly-owned subsidiaries, associate companies or agents. The wholly-owned subsidiaries were H.W. South Africa, H.W. Australia and H.W. India. The associate companies were in Spain, Brazil and Venezuela. H.W. interest in other countries were handled by agents. There were also many subsidiary companies in the UK, i.e. Stockton Forge, H.W. Machine Co., H.W. Export etc. Head Wrightson Australia handled mining equipment with know-how from Stockton Forge. It also formed a base for two major

HWISWEL projects, a steel plant at Whyalla and a materials handling plant also at Whyalla. The Whyalla steel plant was quite a big and successful contract for HWISWEL, it consisted of two LD convertors together with all ancillary equipment. Unfortunately, H.W. Australia had some problems in 1974/1975 and I went from H.W. South Africa to H.W. Australia to see what could be done. Regrettably the problems were such that the H.W. parent board decided to close the company. After winding the company up, I returned to Thornaby HWISWEL. LD was a process, an oxygen steel-making process that was developed by Voest in Austria and they called it the LD process because it had been developed in two of their companies, one at Linz and one at Donawitz. *(Eric Brown)*

We did work for Cuba and Brazil. They were heat exchangers. We also did vessels for desalinisation which was like sea water to fresh water. We used to send them to water-starved countries. They used to use sea water and change it into fresh water. Some of the things they did went all over the world. *(Dennis Longstaff)*

But some of the machines that you actually built they wanted men to go with those machines to wherever they were going to put them up and it could have been abroad - Poland, Czechoslovakia, Wales - and you worked then as what we used to call 'a maker's man' and you re-assembled the machines on the site where they're going to be used. The opportunities were there but I never took the opportunities up then at that time. *(Stuart Thompson)*

We were quoting for a pelletising plant along with others, so our introduction to North Korea was to do just that. Present the case and leave maybe after six weeks there, something like that. But we had to have twin passports. You dare not show a South Korean passport in North Korea so the English Ambassador fitted us up with the necessary paperwork so that we could go in without any discouraging, disparaging material. We were treated very well. But that was one of my most horrific visits I've ever had. You were on tenterhooks the whole show. They knew exactly what we were doing. It's four hours on, four hours off, four hours on, four hours off and that's the working day. During your four hours off they knew exactly where we'd been and what we'd done. We were given carte blanche. We could go wherever we liked but they knew where we'd been and they said, 'Did you enjoy the children's park, did you enjoy the adult worshipful?' Everything was preceded by Kim Il Sung and it was something like their equivalent to God. His picture was in every room. Your bed had a picture of him on. So everything he said was game, set and match and you just had to be very, very careful. *(Max Clark)*

Tony Ogg, far left, and Max Clark, far right, HWISWEL engineers, discuss the finer points of blast-furnace engineering with Mexican colleagues. (Photograph supplied by Max Clark)

Chapter 5

'You had to appreciate how things were manufactured': training

Head Wrightson's formal apprentice scheme was established in 1945 and, according to the company, was so successful other local firms based their own apprentice training on it. The Apprentice School was established in the old four-storey factory building in Hanover Street at the southern extremity of the works. This building also housed the Stampings Division on the ground floor before its move to Seaton, the canteen and a machine shop. Following the fire in 1948 the Apprentice School was housed in an upstairs office next to the Bridge Yard prior to its move to a purpose-built school adjacent to the canteen. Here there was a foundry workshop on the ground floor, a machine shop on the first floor and a lecture room on the second floor and the flat roof was used for PT (in all weathers). Young men were not initially employed as apprentices in specific trades but were general engineering apprentices for a year. They spent one day a week in the School and spent some time in all sections of the works. Having gained some insight and experience of all the various trades, the apprentices were asked which one they would prefer to pursue. If there were places available, they were able to join the apprenticeship of their choice.

With the advent the Engineering Industries Training Board the Apprentice School expanded mid 1960s and moved into the premises vacated by the maintenance department in Hanover Street, ironically opposite to where the School started in the now demolished factory building. Here it was able to provide dedicated space for machining, fitting , electrical, foundry and fabrication skills. Classroom space was retained and expanded in the old school premises adjacent to the canteen. Apprentices now spent their first three months full time in the School which also trained apprentices from other companies.

The apprentices were expected, and other employees encouraged, to further their education in local technical colleges, studying a variety of relevant subjects and gaining appropriate qualifications. Head Wrightson also occasionally sponsored employees to study for a degree at university.

It is clear from the following extracts, that our contributors appreciated the quality of the apprenticeship scheme and the opportunity to widen their knowledge of engineering and other similar subjects.

College

I wanted to go on S1 Mechanical and the chap at the college there said, 'This is the best one for you, it is S1 Workshop.' I was on it two years. It was a three-year course and at the end of the second year he recommended that I went on to S1 Mechanical, where I wanted to be two years earlier. I told a friend of mine who was an apprentice at Teesdale and he said, 'Oh yes, they did exactly the same to me,' and he'd switched over onto a correspondence course. I did the same because at night school the second year when I was on the three shifts they'd give me homework and then I'd put it in and get some more homework but the week after I couldn't get. So I did my homework and the following week when I could get there I went and handed it in and all the instructor said was, 'Oh I've already marked that, I can't be bothered with that,' and he wouldn't look at it. So I said to myself, 'Well, if you won't look at it I'm not going to do it,' and I didn't. I don't think it pleased them because I've the certificates upstairs somewhere. At the end of that year I got First Class for Drawing and I got Distinction for Calculations and Science. I got ninety-seven per cent. Baldwin put on the thing, 'This report would have been much better had it not been for his lack of attendance and indifference to homework.' I'd just moved into the big bay on the big machines when that report was sent into Bob Snowden. He looked at it and he started to laugh and he tore it up. He said, 'That's what I think of them.' *(Les Ellis)*

I finished my HND when I was twenty-two and then I was working in the Planning Department at Thornaby. The government, which was I think a Labour government at the time, had given grants to firms to put people through higher education. They called me in one day and they said, 'We want you to go and do an MSc at Aston in Birmingham.' So when I was twenty-seven they packed me off down there for a year to do an MSc in Production Engineering. *(Ken Peacock)*

I used to go three nights a week to what was the old Stockton Secondary School in Nelson Terrace where a man called Everton Baldwin was the Principal of the School. And, as far as engineering courses were concerned, you could go as far as the Ordinary National Certificate in Mechanical Engineering, which I did, and thereafter you went on to Constantine Technical College for the Higher National Certificate. At the Higher National Certificate stage, I was released for one afternoon a week to take an endorsement certificate related to metallurgy, which was most helpful. *(Bob Waller)*

I went three nights a week to night school, right until I was twenty-one. When my father said I should go into the Drawing Office it was touch and go whether I went to college to become a physical training teacher or go in the Drawing Office to be an engineer. Anyway, my father won and I went into the Drawing Office. But then when I was twenty-one I stopped going to night school. I'd already got my Ordinary National and A1 and went to study Physical Education and I did two years taking exams for Physical Education. In 1949 I was chosen to represent Great Britain at the World Gymnastics Festival so I was a member of the team. There were seventy-two in the team, and there was the twelve of us from the North of England and I was one of them, so that made me even keener to concentrate on my Physical Education. Then I got a scholarship to a college in Denmark to study Physical Education and Engineering. That was a year's scholarship. When I came back from that I decided that engineering was the way I would go ahead and I would teach physical training part-time in the evenings, and that's what I did. *(Alan Sowerby)*

When I was doing my apprenticeship I got day-release. I went to Stockton Technical College. I got my Ordinary National Certificate before I went in the Army. I got my Higher National when I came out. All at Stockton Tech. *(Jim Heward)*

I think we went two days a week and three evenings the first year. One evening was shorthand, one was typing and one was English.

I have a feeling we did mostly shorthand and typing during the day as far as I can remember. Obviously, we worked during the day and finished at half past five. We also had to do what they called the post on the evening. We'd to go round the departments again on the evening to collect any post which had to go out. So it could be a letter which wasn't in an envelope, invoices, things like which needed to go through the franking machine for the post. One of us, we'd be taking it in turns I suppose, would take them to the Post Office. The company chauffeur would appear in a car at the front door and we would trot out through the front door, get into this chauffeur-driven car and he would drive us round the Thornaby complex to the various offices to bring their post back in to be franked again. *(Wendy Heald)*

We spent the first year in what was called the Apprentice School at Thornaby, Teesdale Ironworks. You spent one day in the offices there receiving lectures on different engineering processes and then you would spend one day a week at day-release, studying. There was the S1, S2, S3 leading up to Ordinary National and then followed on to Higher National. So I spent one day a week at Longlands College doing S2 and one evening. I had to do two evenings because some people had joined with A Levels and I had only joined with O Levels. So I would start work at half past seven in the morning and then go on to night school and probably get home about ten o'clock on the bus and then be at work for half past seven the next morning again, et cetera. I'd do that two nights a week. So there's one day in the Apprentice School, one day of day-release. I had got sufficiently high marks in my Higher National to be accepted for a Newcastle degree but when I put this to Head Wrightson's they said if I wanted to go to university then I would need to leave the company. However, if I wished to do the thick sandwich course, the Dip Tech I think it was, which was six months working for the company, six months studying, and that was a four-year course, if I would accept going on that, they would continue to employ me and they would continue to pay me my full salary. So when I was studying I would get the appropriate government grant, but when I was working I would get an elevated wage to make up what I didn't get when I was studying. That was going to be at Teesside, at Constantine College, where I'd done my Higher National so that was the option I took. *(Michael Waring)*

I was a proper plater but at the same time as I was serving my apprenticeship I went to Longlands College studying fabrication of steelwork, and S1 to S5, five years, and then the final year full Technological Certificate. That was obligatory at Head Wrightson's. If you didn't pass your exams you got a rollicking, a real rollicking, and if you were so bad they would change your status, take you off plating and make you a burner which again was one of those jobs where you burnt steel all day. It's boring. I enjoyed the school work, passed it all. First-class passes right the way through and collected prizes at the annual Head Wrightson prize-giving dos. These were basically for the apprentices but anybody that had done something wonderful for the firm would be awarded some prize or other. I have a sixty-six foot tape, in old measurements, stuck in my shed out there which was one of the prizes. It was something I couldn't afford to buy in those days. As you built up the prizes got better and better. You collected squares for marking off and helping you assemble bits and pieces. They were always tools. The final accolade was this sixty-six foot tape. Everybody used to want to borrow it because mine was one of two in the shop. We needed a long one because we built bridges, dock gates. Forth Road Bridge, we built box girders for that and they were about thirty foot sections, but they were tied together at times. I eventually went on site where we were putting the railway bridge up in Bristol. Because I graduated, I was offered the chance to go on site as a junior site engineer. It was a progression up. *(John Kirk)*

We attended engineering courses at local technical colleges with half-day-release from

Apprentice School Thornaby. Lecture room on second floor. Workshops on ground and first floor. Early morning PT on open-air flat roof. (HW Domesday Book)

HW plus two nights per week studying for Ordinary and Higher National Certificates. Training at the Forge continued in parallel with studies and at the age of 21 I started a two-year degree course at Durham University sponsored and funded by Head Wrightson. *(Bob Wright)*

Apprentice School

It wasn't an Apprentice School as such. You did go in and listen to lectures but you didn't do any training or anything of that. The main thing was you went there. Harold Soppet said, 'Right, next week you will be in so and so' or 'this department or that department.' Whether it be the Bridge Yard, whether it be the Engineering Department and from there you just went that particular week. Then you went back in the Apprentice School and then he allocated where it was the next week. I would say this went on for between three and four months. You were allocated to just jobs that they thought you could maybe do. You were allocated with a fitter or a journeyman, whatever you wish to call them. And by virtue of being there and watching other people work that was one of the most important things. Even though you thought probably at the time, 'I'll not learn anything,' by looking and watching and seeing how other people did things gradually you did. So between sort of fifteen, sixteen, seventeen you weren't doing great jobs but you were doing little jobs. Then when you were eighteen you were given more opportunities to put a lot of equipment together. *(Trevor Briggs)*

In the Apprentice School, we had a project and we made a model of the office block, the old office block, and that was cut from a big piece of wood down in the Joiners' Shop. But it was all in sections so you could take it apart and show what it was like with the different floors inside

Apprentice School trip to London 25/4/1952. The trip included a visit to the Houses of Parliament, the company's two London offices, Leonardo da Vinci Exhibition, a trip to the theatre and a tour of London markets. Included in the picture are Frank Shepherd (Personnel Manager) Harry Soppet (Training Manager) Jim Rickelton (Security Manager) Mr. J.E. Simon MP. (Wright Ahead)

the new office block. We worked on all of it. We used to go to the model shop and get brick paper. It was displayed for quite a few years, in one of the offices at Teesdale. *(Jim Heward)*

Sixty lads would be selected to be apprentices from 600 applications, after exams and interviews. You were split into houses of fifteen apprentices and then each day of the week one house would report to the School. We were Green House and we went in on a Wednesday, the technical-school lads. The secondary-school lads went Monday, Tuesday. Technical-school lads went Wednesday and the grammar-school lads went on Thursday. Then you had to write up what you'd done that week and then there would be some lessons of some description and some practical in the afternoon. So that was good. It was a day you got a later start, 8.00am, but you always started with PT on the roof. The Apprentice School was a four-storey building with an open-air flat roof and we used to be sent up there to do your PT in your shorts, bare chests. It used to be filthy, it was right next to the Steel Foundry where a lot of dust used to come flying over, and settled. If it rained, with it being an open roof and inevitably there's pools. By the time we'd thrown a few medicine balls around and had a few star jumps and rolls on the mat, well we used to be filthy. But then we had the opportunity to go and get a shower. Then you were allowed to go in the canteen, and get a breakfast, bacon butties and coffee or whatever. Then back to the Apprentice School to basically report on what you'd done that week. We had books to write up. Those books would be marked, the tutors would read them and if necessary comment on them. You had to do a day's release from work. Back to Stockton Tech, on whatever nominated day it would be for your course. Of course, you'd have a night class to do as well and when you'd finished with the Apprentice School, you still had a day-release once a week including a night class going to the Technical College. You had to get your card signed to say that you'd attended and homework was satisfactory before the foreman would sign off your time card for your day's pay. *(Albert Roxborough)*

This engine came from Horden Colliery. Somebody had tipped off Sir John or Peter Wrightson that this thing was lying in pieces in a field near this colliery. He went off and it came back on two lorries, the engine in pieces and the two coal trucks behind it. It was just dumped on the area outside the Foundry, in that area between the Foundry and the Apprentice School. Sir John decreed that the apprentices would rebuild it. Now we got the assistance of two lads who were at Constantine, they were doing a Higher National Diploma or something like that. They came along, and I don't know whether they got some old plans from somewhere of the engine but it was reassembled and any needed parts were made in the Apprentice School. It was originally made by Head and Company. It didn't have Wrightson on; it had a plate on with the words Head and Company. I think the year was 1878. It had been used to haul wagons from the colliery. So it was put back together and into working order. But they wouldn't let us fire it up, they wouldn't let us put coal in the boiler because they thought it was too thin. But after some persuasion, and it was probably absolutely crazy that we did this, we connected up a pipe from the compressed air in the Foundry. Right along this pipe and extended into the boiler, and they put compressed air in. I mean it could have blown to pieces but nevertheless we got it going, we had it running on the rails. We had test runs up and down with this great big long pipe trailing out behind it. And then after that it was put onto a stand, onto two wooden blocks. When Sir John or Peter had any of their visitors coming they always had to come and show them this engine. Anybody who was in the Apprentice School, and I was one of them, had to dash down the stairs, connect up the hose and set the engine going with the wheels spinning round. On one particular occasion he had some friends, some businessmen from South Africa. He used to come and Sir John just waved at the window. So we would go down there and we would connect the hose up and then the signal would be given and the guy would turn the air on. Now I don't know who it was but the guy who fastened the thing on hadn't got it on tight enough and the hose comes off and whips around with this compressed air and poor old Sir John's hat goes flying. I thought, 'We'll all get executed for this.' Well, his colleagues thought this a huge joke, a huge joke. But Sir John, of course, was trying to dust himself down and get his cap and shouting to turn this air off. *(Gerald Morton)*

Iconic 'Coffee Pot' steam engine built by Head Wrightson's which was returned to the company in the 1960s and refurbished by apprentices to work by compressed air. It stood at HW Thornaby works and then was displayed on the roundabout at Parliament Street, Stockton and now is on exhibition at Preston Park, Stockton-on-Tees. (Photograph by D. Proctor)

I spent the first year in the Apprentice School. I tried some foundry work, did some maintenance work, a bit of electricity work, a bit of pattern-making. A bit of fitting, a bit of turning. I enjoyed the Apprentice School, to be honest. You spent a full year. The first six months was basically classroom work. It was all lectures and a little bit of practical work. They had a small workshop in the Training School to do a little bit of practical work. The second six months you had this period where you toured round. You had a few weeks in various sections of the business and fitting and turning was the one that I chose to do. Went to Middlesbrough Works. Went to the Forge, went to the Iron Foundry, the one where they did the tunnel segments at Eaglescliffe. The Steel Foundry at Thornaby. *(Ken Peacock)*

At the time you were put into what was called the Apprentice School. You were sent to various departments at all Head Wrightson's works. Foundries, Hartlepool Stampings, Middlesbrough Machine Shop. The idea being that at the end of your time in the Apprentice School you then made a decision on what you wanted to do. They thought I would have made a first-class draughtsman. They even asked my father to come up from Billingham to see him and then they said, 'We think your son will make a first-class draughtsman, he shouldn't be a plater.' My father just said, 'What do you want to do Ken?' I said, 'I want to be a plater.' He said, 'That's it.' *(Ken Davies - Plater)*

I started at age sixteen. I started in September 1970 in the Training School, which was down by the side of the Teesdale offices. The guy in charge was a chap called Harry Soppet and I moved on from there. Did a year in the Training School and went through the various sections. Being a technical apprentice we did fabrication work, electrical work, machining work. Didn't do any foundry work but it gave us a good basic grounding for about nine months. They were in three levels. There was a craft apprenticeship for fitters and turners, machinists, fabricators, et cetera. Technical apprentices were more destined towards going into the offices at either Machine Company, Teesdale, Head Wrightson Processes, R&D. Then there were student apprentices which consisted of students who were doing degree studies. They were tied to Head Wrightson who provided them with training in between their degree courses, and there was a certain degree of loyalty to Head Wrightson once they'd completed their degree course. We were made to wear brown overalls to distinguish us from the rest of the workers. All the apprentices wore brown overalls apart from the foundry lads who wore white ones. The overalls and safety boots were provided and any gloves, barrier creams, goggles, everything. They really put safety first and were well ahead compared with a lot of other organisations at the time. We were generally in the School. But we had some contact with the works if the factory sent something to the Training School to do. There was a bit of liaison on occasions with the Bridge Yard, et cetera, but generally your work was undertaken in the Training School itself for those nine months. The last three months of your first year for the technical apprentices was spent on undertaking technical drawing instruction off a guy called Ron Miller. It was within the building where the canteen was. It was separate from the School. *(Chris Stoddart)*

I used to spend Monday in the School. You just used to do about where we'd been the week before at the time, which shop we'd been in and what type of work we'd done, who we'd helped and who we'd worked with and did we like it. What were the workmen like, the people you were with? Were they very helpful, were they not helpful?

And then did you do any practical work in the Apprentice School?

They did little bits of woodwork and then they used to show you welding, spot-welding and little bits of electrical work. *(Eddie Peacock)*

I was in the Apprentice School a year.

That would be in the very early stages of the Apprentice School?

Oh yes, Head Wrightson's was still training lads for the government and the Apprentice School was running in conjunction with it.

Where was the Apprentice School situated in those days?

When I was there it was just a conglomeration of places. The old staff canteen upstairs. Well, that was one part, and further down along the railway tracks near the Bridge Yard there was a toilet and we were upstairs in there. We used to go there for the class to learn maths and drawing and things like that. *(Thomas Wilson)*

Apprenticeship

'You should think about going into the Pattern Shop because most foundry managers

April 1980, 16-year-old Michael Gray (left) came top in the non-ferrous section of the Teesside casting competition held at Longlands College. Pictured is another Head Wrightson trainee, John Whitney, 18, who came third in the non-ferrous metal section. (Image courtesy Evening Gazette Media Company (GMC) Middlesbrough)

generally have been through the Pattern Shop. And that's the training ground and I think that's where we'd like you to go.' I said, - fifteen year old - 'I'm coming to work for money and from what I've seen the people who earn the most money are welders. I want to be a welder.' 'No, no, no, no, no, you can't do that, you can't do that, you must...,' said Harry. I said, 'I want to be a welder.' And so that's how I started. As a then sixteen year old I turned up at the Bridge Yard as an apprentice welder. Then you were sent to work with and watching welders basically. So you would be standing watching them for the day. I recall having to organise a locker which was just a bit of basic fabrication. I remember it was the days of piecework so they wanted to get everybody inducted into piecework attitude and you were given a small kind of A5-sized book. So you wrote down the different jobs you were doing, what you had been doing and what you'd been watching, the job numbers you'd been working on, a quick description of the part, and that was to get you into the habit of recording your work jobs because that eventually became your piecework book. You wrote down the various jobs that you were working on. Then after a few weeks you'd been given some practice pieces to weld on and the foreman and chargehands would make sure that you were doing bits of practising of welding, and then you were put with a plater to be a tacker for the plater. When parts are assembled together there's lots of tack-welds to done. So it was the apprentices that did the tack-welding with a plater. You started at sixteen so probably for a year, you would be tacking and then you would be given small non-critical jobs to do and they would see how you were getting on with those. Then by the time you were eighteen you should have been showing signs of having some reasonable skills and dexterity to be a welder. So they would give you

HW Apprentices who won the 1952 Inter-departmental Junior Football Competition. Jim Rickelton extreme left, Bob Summers extreme right, Harry Soppet second right, back row. (Wright Ahead)

other jobs to do and you were also given the opportunity then to have piecework and some overtime. I had limited chance for that because when I was eighteen I think others in Head Wrightson's decided I was doing reasonably well at college as an apprentice welder. Because you were doing day-release and it was one day-release and two nights per week at Stockton and Billingham Tech. I'd been doing reasonably well, I'd got an award from Sir John Wrightson for my college results at the time I recall and they said there was an opportunity to move to R&D as a trainee welding engineer which I decided to do. So I turned up in R&D and my wage dropped from about five pounds a week then as an apprentice welder to something like three pounds ten shillings as a trainee welding engineer. As I mentioned earlier, after eighteen you were given the opportunity for overtime and piecework. And clearly a lot of pals that I socialised with at the time were also apprentice welders and I was hearing stories that they were getting ten pounds a week. I'm suddenly getting three pounds ten shilling a week. So I suffered this for about a month and I went back and knocked on George Cain's door. You went in and you stood to attention, that's when you were invited in. I remember George Cain saying to me, 'Yes, what do you want?' And I said, 'I've come for my job back, Mr. Cain.' He said, 'What do you mean you've come for your job back? You're working in R&D now; you're a trainee welding engineer down there.' I said, 'I know but the lads up here now as apprentice welders they're on piecework, they're getting overtime, they're getting about ten pounds a week and I'm in R&D getting three pounds ten shillings a week and I don't think it's right.' He said, 'Get out of my office; I'll clip your ear for you. Go on get back down there from where you came, don't cross my door again.' Maynard Wilson was jumping up and down all aggressive and so that's how I became a welding engineer. There was none of this, 'Have you considered all your options son, and do you want to do this and shall we give you a bit of counselling, son?' It was a boot up the backside. *(Charlie Tighe)*

There were a fair number of apprentices. There were four groups. Red, Green, Yellow and Blue. We were told which group we were going to be in and explained what would happen to us. I was in Yellow group, which really I shouldn't have been in because they were ex-grammar school boys who were there. They were grouped supposedly on ability. Because I had this J1, I was in the Yellow group. People who were a bit further advanced than me were in the Blue group. Those who didn't have much at all were in the Green and Red, whichever way round they were that's the way it went. Three and a half days of the week you were in one of the Head Wrightson companies. You could either be in Middlesbrough Machine Company, Stockton Forge, Thornaby Teesdale, the Steel Foundry, the Iron Foundry at Eaglescliffe, Stockton Steel Foundry at Stockton. Half a day, Friday afternoon we had to go to Thornaby because we all got paid from headquarters at Thornaby so Friday afternoon was sports afternoon. The security man used to take us up to Teesdale Park, which was a massive sports complex that belonged to Head Wrightson and we'd play cricket or football or something. And on the other days you were actually in the Apprentice Training School. *(John Heath)*

When in the Apprentice School you were given the chance of being able to go to John Wrightson's estate at Neasham Hall, Hurworth, to 'beat' in one of his shoots during the game season. I was chosen and we met at the canteen in Thornaby. We were given a packed meal which contained spam and a canned drink. We were driven there in one of the people carriers. We assembled in the courtyard with all the gentry and I was given the job of helping Stephen Furness of Furness Shipping fame. We worked through the morning and then at lunch time we came upon this farm. The gentry took over the farm house with the farmer joining us sitting on bales of straw. The spam sandwiches were terrible but we could see the gentry laughing and enjoying themselves in the comfort of the farmer's sitting room. After the lunch break we set off again. There was plenty to shoot at but a lot of wasted cartridges. At the close we went back to the courtyard where everything was laid out in order. Rows of pheasants tied up in pairs, partridges, rabbits, hares and wild pigeons. We were told before we left we could be given a choice of something to take home as long as it was a rabbit. I chose a pair of pheasants and was told I could not have them. I was told that the left-over stock were going to be sold to a local butcher. *(Bob Irwin)*

I was interviewed for a job in the Drawing Office. I wanted to be a surveyor. My plan was to be a land surveyor when I was a schoolboy. They had a Civil Engineering Section there so I went and was interviewed for the Civil Engineering Section. It was only a small section, about ten or twelve, we were doing drawings for foundations for blast furnaces and sinter plants and that sort of thing. That was HWISWEL Drawing Office down at the old Pattern Shop, the old Craig Taylor's shipyard. We were upstairs. There was a great big long Drawing Office there. The Drawing Office manager was Harry Welford and we apprentices lived in fear of that fellow. Harry used to walk out of his office at eight thirty four and he used to stand at the head of the office. If you were late he had his back to you and you hadn't to say a word, it was ritual. I had to walk right the way down the first office. Then passed the Print Room where Bob Gowing worked then walk through that next section, and my desk was on the right-hand side next to it. And you knew some time during the day Harry was going to come to you and say, 'You were late this morning,' but you never knew when he was going to come. *(Gerald Morton)*

Then I started going around the various departments. This involved going to Thornaby as well. So I started off going from the Drawing Office into the Pattern Shop and spent a few months in the Pattern Shop. Then on to the Iron Foundry at Thornaby. I didn't actually do very much more than assist and watch what was being produced. You saw them making the moulds and the castings. Then you went into the actual Foundry to be with the furnace men, and they were melting the scrap and producing the molten iron. Then to the steel furnace, or the Steel Foundry, so that was another fairly long period. Then into the Laboratories, also at Thornaby, where they would take samples of the metal and analyse them and carry out all necessary tests that

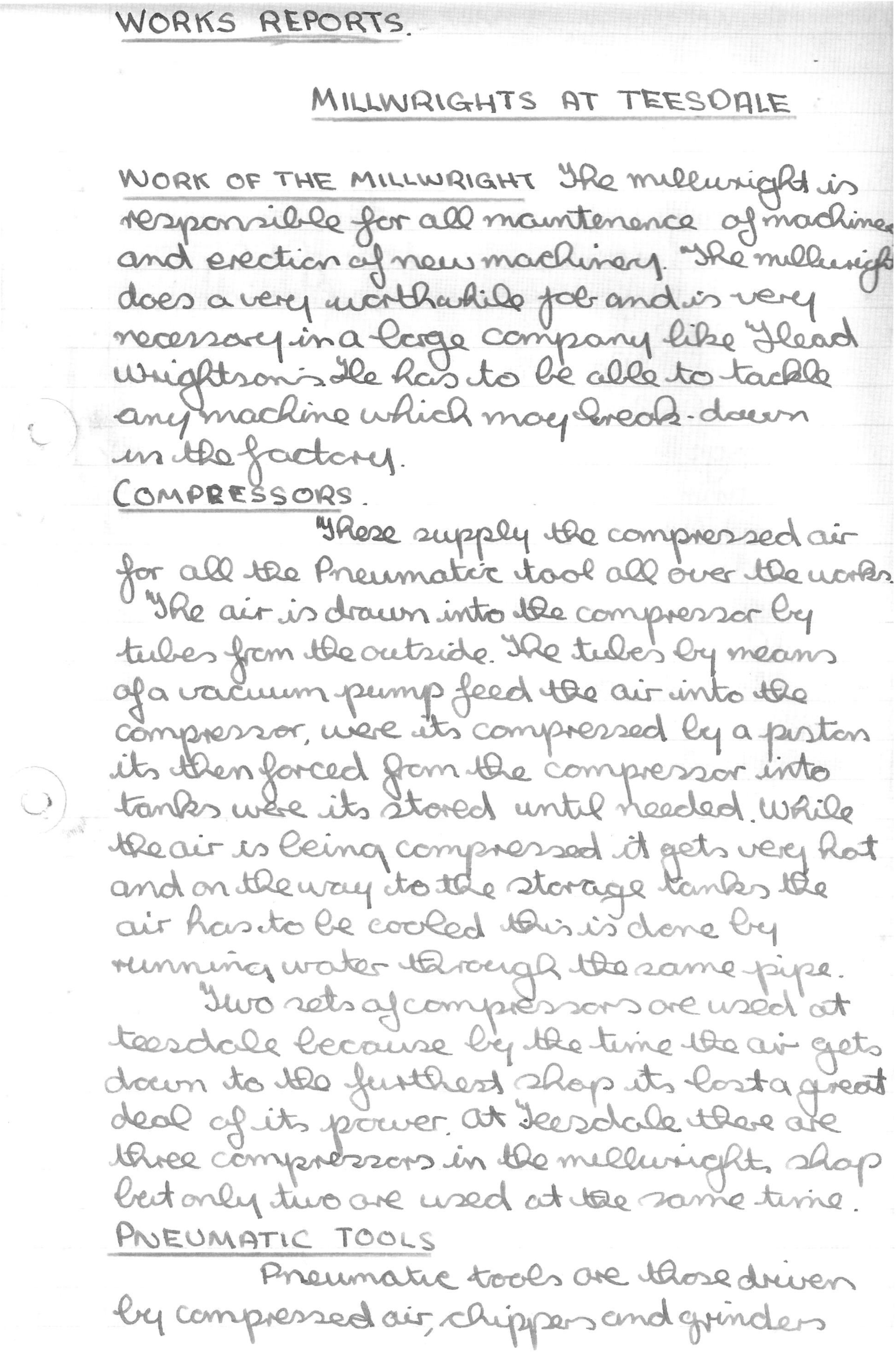

WORKS REPORTS.

MILLWRIGHTS AT TEESDALE

WORK OF THE MILLWRIGHT The millwright is responsible for all maintenence of machines and erection of new machinery. The millwright does a very worthwhile job and is very necessary in a large company like Head Wrightson's. He has to be able to tackle any machine which may break-down in the factory.

COMPRESSORS.

These supply the compressed air for all the Pneumatic tool all over the works. The air is drawn into the compressor by tubes from the outside. The tubes by means of a vacuum pump feed the air into the compressor, were its compressed by a piston its then forced from the compressor into tanks were its stored until needed. While the air is being compressed it gets very hot and on the way to the storage tanks the air has to be cooled this is done by running water through the same pipe.

Two sets of compressors are used at teesdale because by the time the air gets down to the furthest shop its lost a great deal of its power. At Teesdale there are three compressors in the millwrights shop but only two are used at the same time.

PNEUMATIC TOOLS

Pneumatic tools are those driven by compressed air, chippers and grinders

A page from Ken Lee's apprentice's works report detailing the work in the millrights.

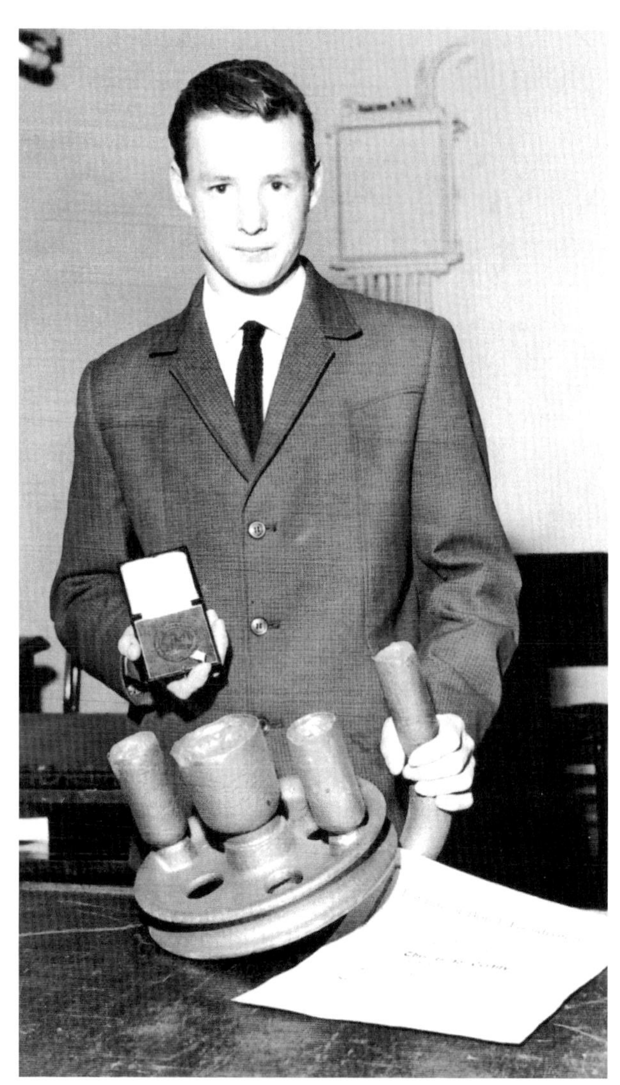

Michael Nichol, Apprentice of the Year 1967 with his winning casting. (Photograph supplied by M. Nichol)

identified whether the steel was of the correct composition. After we had spent time in the Foundry and Laboratories we returned back to the Machine Company in Middlesbrough. We went into the Machine Shop, and here you were shown how inspections were carried out, how the various machines functioned and produced the necessary components. We went into the Tool Room where they did all the necessary preparations of equipment to be used on the big machines and from there into the Assembly Shop, or the Fitting Shop as we called it. Then went back into the Drawing Office and at that stage you were just finishing off your apprenticeship and then you became a junior draughtsman. The basis of learning about the manufacturing side was very important. You had to appreciate how things were manufactured. *(David Auld)*

Your first six months at the Training School were spent in – I think there was six departments. There was Fabrication and Welding, Milling, Turning, Electrical, Fitting and Drawing Office. So you had one month in each of those sections. Then the final six months you spent in the area that was going to be your actual apprenticeship. So if you were going to be a fitter you would spend your the second six months in the Fitting Department within the School. *(Barry Davison)*

For almost the first year as an apprentice draughtsman in those days you were just running round doing errands, getting prints, taking stuff down into the works, bringing stuff back from the works and answering the telephone. I remember distinctly I'd never ever spoken on a telephone before and in 1944 not many people had telephones. It was a scary experience for me to answer the telephone. I didn't know who I was speaking to but that was part of the training, you had to answer the telephone, and the first day was doing that, answering the telephone and going down to the Print Room and getting prints and going into the works to take prints down. *(Alan Sowerby)*

I think it was different to what other people would have, because with Head Wrightson's having several foundries and workshops all over Teesside you moved around. You went to, say, Stockton Foundry for two weeks. Eaglescliffe Iron Foundry for two weeks, Middlesbrough Works for two weeks, so you got good insights into all the jobs that you could possibly go into after your year's training in the Apprentice School. After the year you did have a choice of what you wanted to do and where you wanted to go and if that was available they tried to accommodate you. *(Keith Chapman)*

Head Wrightson didn't issue indentures. A lot of companies issued indentures but Head Wrightson's didn't. In the Machine Shop Tool Room you bought cigars for all your colleagues. Largely that was about it. There was no sort of initiation ceremonies or anything. I presumably bought a box of cigars and shared

Michael Nichol, second right with some colleagues. 1967. (Photograph supplied by M. Nichol)

them all round and I think that was about it. *(Albert Roxborough)*

I was fortunate in that my father knew Mr. Lake who was the Managing Director at Head Wrightson Machine Company. Father had met Mr. Lake when travelling away on business. He'd come across him at conferences and that sort of situation. I was taken on as a third apprentice in the Drawing Office. They normally only took two in a year into the Drawing Office at Head Wrightson. During the first year the work was fairly menial, making tea and coffee for the draughtsmen and taking prints and things down to the works for the manufacture and liaising with different offices. I also did messages on somebody's borrowed bicycle to and round Middlesbrough. Some of it was quite entertaining. Perhaps I didn't really learn much that first year but I already had a pretty clear idea of what was entailed. I'd previously had an interest in railway engines and had done lots and lots of drawings and that type of thing. Consequently, there was nothing strange about the work. Also, I immediately started evening classes in technical drawing. It was required that you went through further education and obtain additional qualifications. *(David Auld)*

I started at Stockton Steel. I won the Apprentice of the Year 1967. That was for the whole area, all the foundries in the area. I got a medal with my name on it and I've got some pictures. Everybody had to make the same thing. We had to do a pulley wheel and it had three headers on it to feed the metal in and a runner at the bottom. When you poured the metal and it was full it seeped down the middle, that's why you had another head on top. As it cooled down it shrinks down the head so the head's feeding the rest of the casting. It would shrink a couple of inches in the middle and that's only on a relatively small casting, that one was a foot in diameter. *(Michael Nichol)*

You had an inspector, a checker in the shop and that was his sole job. You took your job to him and he checked it up. Everybody waited till he'd checked it and if you were wrong, then the whole shop used to start. You used to feel really humiliated. They would shout and bang hammers on the bench and shout and whistle. Then you knew you'd done it wrong and made a mistake on it somewhere. I was lucky. I think I only got whistled at two or three times. It soon made you do the job right. The men didn't make mistakes. They got to the stage where they all knew their job. The young lads it was who made mistakes. You learned when you were young. Everybody jeered you when you were young and made a mistake. *(Ron Nichol)*

I went into the Template Shop and I finished up as a template maker at the age of twenty-one. I started at fourteen and a half and I came out of my apprenticeship at twenty-one. In those days you only got full money when the Yard Manager thought you were worth it. So as a journeyman you became a full journeyman when the Yard Manager said so. Some were waiting two and three years on what they called plater's money. I went on only six months and I was sent for and I was told that, 'You can have full money from next week but if you tell anybody down there I'll stop it straightway.' That was the attitude in those days and I felt very, very guilty I can tell you. *(Maynard Wilson)*

There were about four or five different things you could do. There was lathes, there was electrical, there was welding and plating and there was foundry-type work. There were all different aspects of the job. And to be honest

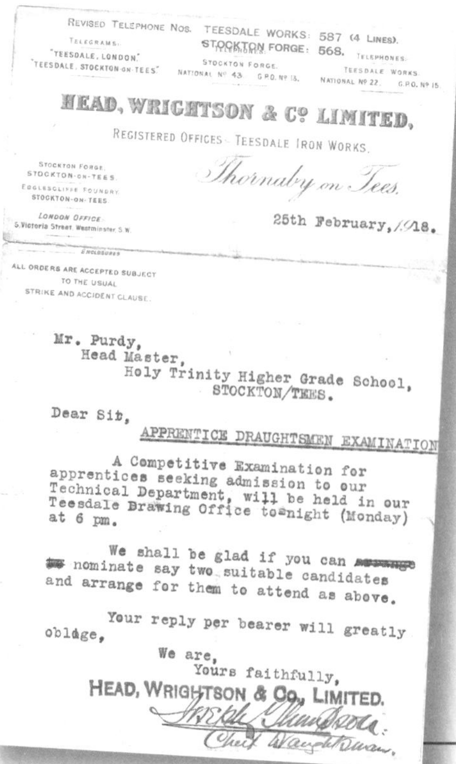

REVISED TELEPHONE NOS. TEESDALE WORKS: 587 (4 LINES). STOCKTON FORGE: 568.

TELEGRAMS: "TEESDALE, LONDON." "TEESDALE, STOCKTON-ON-TEES."

TELEPHONES: STOCKTON FORGE. NATIONAL Nº 43. G.P.O. Nº 13. TEESDALE WORKS. NATIONAL Nº 22. G.P.O. Nº 15.

HEAD, WRIGHTSON & Cº LIMITED,

REGISTERED OFFICES - TEESDALE IRON WORKS.

STOCKTON FORGE, STOCKTON-ON-TEES.
EGGLESCLIFFE FOUNDRY, STOCKTON-ON-TEES.
LONDON OFFICE 5, Victoria Street, Westminster, S.W.

Thornaby on Tees.

25th February, 1918.

ENCLOSURES

ALL ORDERS ARE ACCEPTED SUBJECT TO THE USUAL STRIKE AND ACCIDENT CLAUSE.

Mr. Purdy,
Head Master,
Holy Trinity Higher Grade School,
STOCKTON/TEES.

Dear Sir,

APPRENTICE DRAUGHTSMEN EXAMINATION

A Competitive Examination for apprentices seeking admission to our Technical Department, will be held in our Teesdale Drawing Office to-night (Monday) at 6 pm.

We shall be glad if you can nominate say two suitable candidates and arrange for them to attend as above.

Your reply per bearer will greatly oblige,

We are,
Yours faithfully,
HEAD, WRIGHTSON & Co., LIMITED.
[signature]
Chief Draughtsman.

This letter dated 1915 was found in a house clearance. (Supplied by D. Proctor)

Early morning PT for apprentices ! (Wright Ahead)

I was like any kid who left school, didn't really know what I wanted to do. I think a lot of kids today are exactly the same, they don't really know when they leave school. So you went through all the different things. Working lathes, learning mechanical, learnt electrical and at the end of the year you had to put a choice in of what you wanted to do, welder, plater, fitter, electrician, whatever. I still didn't know what to do after the end of the year and quite a few of the lads who I got friendly with put down for welders and platers so I just put down for a plater. *(Steve Featherstone)*

I said 'I'd like to be a joiner or a pattern-maker,' which was to do with wood. 'Oh,' he said, 'they're dying trades. Alright, anyhow we'll put you through the Apprentice School.' And I went through all the trades in the Apprentice School and when my time was up he said, 'Do you still want to be a joiner or a pattern-maker?' I said, 'Oh yes.' He says, 'I'm sorry but we're not taking any more pattern-makers apprentices nor joiners. Do you fancy being a plumber?' That was my second choice. I said, 'Oh plumbing,' because I'd done a plumbing course at college and he said, 'oh we're not taking any, we're not taking any plumbers.' So he said, 'Do you fancy being a millwright?' I said, 'What's one of them?' He said, 'Oh it's a maintenance fitter.' I'd done it but I didn't know they called them millwrights, I thought they were just like maintenance fitters. So that was the old name for maintenance fitting. So I said, 'Oh aye,' I fancied it. Anyhow I started my apprenticeship down at Middlesbrough Head Wrightson's. *(Dick Robinson)*

Chapter 6

'It could get dangerous': health and safety

In 1960 Sir John Wrightson used the company magazine, *Wright Ahead*, to praise volunteers who had joined the First Aid Detachment and Fire Brigade. He wrote, 'We do not always appreciate the time, skill and energy spent by a number of our colleagues who voluntarily devote themselves, without thought of reward, to our welfare and safety. I refer especially, of course, to the Welfare Committee of the Employees Council, First Aid Detachment and the Work's Fire Brigade. All their activities are carried on so unostentatiously that we are apt to forget their existence until we have a need of them... I am always impressed by the enthusiasm and aptitude displayed. This is shown in the competitive field by the First Aid and Fire Brigade successes in national competitions, which enhance the name of the company'. These volunteers were an important addition to the company's own health and safety provision. An example of this was the on-site medical facilities for minor accidents and sickness.

As in other heavy industries, the provision and use of safety equipment such as goggles, gloves and boots, was an issue of contention amongst employers and workers for many years. Often, workers were reluctant to use them as they claimed it slowed them down. But by the 1970s attitudes were changing. This new mind-set was reflected in the introduction of a new Health and Safety at Work Act in 1974. Our contributors also recognised that health and safety issues were beginning to be taken more seriously. Nevertheless, they also told tales of accidents: some minor; others unfortunately more serious; some even fatal on occasions.

The following extracts show how our contributors managed these challenging conditions.

Fire fighting the old factory building (a former jute mill) at Thornaby in 1948. (Photograph courtesy Evening Gazette Media Company (GMC) Middlesbrough)

First Aid

John had always had an interest in First Aid. He was a qualified First Aid Trainer and had nursing certificates. He ran a First Aid class in the village of Sedgefield where he lived and he was a member of St. John's Ambulance. He later changed to the Red Cross. I can't remember whether he started the courses at Head Wrightson or whether he was asked to take them over. He and his team did the training but an officer from the St. John's & Red Cross and a local doctor did the testing and gave out the certificates. Every department of Head's, every part of the works had a qualified First Aider, at least one, within the practical workshops and also in the offices. So he trained a lot of people or helped to train them. There was an Ambulance Room which was manned all the time. But the firm wanted a number of people on the shop floor who could deal with emergencies straight away even before the Ambulance Room people were called down. *(Margaret Hope)*

You used to get the odd burn and cut finger but nothing really serious that I can recall in my time. There used to be the Ambulance Room which you used to go in first, and they used to make a record of what had happened. They used to always say, 'Everything's got to be recorded.' Half the time when the lads had cut their fingers they would never go down to the Ambulance Room and they never used to bother, just suck it until it stopped bleeding, that type of attitude. *(Dennis Longstaff)*

Safety procedures

It was second nature. I mean safety is commonsense basically. For instance, when you used to sling plates we used to sling them with what they called clamps. Now if you stood underneath a plate with clamps on you were asking for trouble. If the clamp slipped that would be it, so you knew. In any event when girders were being transported by the overhead cranes you normally had a banksman underneath who would warn everybody that it was on its way. *(Jim Smiles)*

It could get dangerous. If health and safety officials had been let loose into the factories when I was a young lad they'd have shut the place down. Really they would. I've seen me scaling round a vessel clinging onto quoits, that's little angle bars welded on, just to put a chain onto a link, and that wouldn't be allowed these days. They would have used scaffolding but not in those days. There were no hard hats but you wore steel toe caps because it was beneficial to yourself to have them on. You can imagine dropping some steelwork onto your foot, which I have done because I was off work for a few weeks with a broken toe, dropping a plate onto my foot. If anything did happen to you, if you had something in your eye or if you had a cut, there was an Ambulance Room there and you were taken straight into the Ambulance Room. If it was severe, they took you straight to hospital. If you got something in your eye and you needed attention for your eye they took you to the Infirmary at Middlesbrough. So there was no waiting about. You were looked after in that respect. Actually I've got some magnets upstairs what they used to use if you got metal in your eye. It was a hazard with so much turnings and bits coming off. They were flying all over. I can remember they used to make ladles for the steel industry, molten metal. They used to pour it into ladles and all these ladles were riveted with red-hot rivets. *(Harry Foster)*

Fire Brigade

We had a fire engine. Just one you used to pull along. I was in the Fire Department. There were about eight of us and we used to practise getting the hoses out and putting the standpipe up and set the pump going and squirting water. We used to stop back an hour once a month and you used to get a little bit extra pay for doing it. *(Dick Robinson)*

His house caught on fire and all. I had to go in and try and get the kids out because we had a work's fire brigade as well. The work's fire brigade consisted of two brothers, Charlie and

Head Wrightson Auxiliary (war-time) Fire Brigade. (Wright Ahead)

David Littlewood, Alf Waton, Arthur Jackson and me. This particular day his house caught on fire. We were out there and Harry Soppet, who was the Chief Fire Officer, said to me, 'Go in there and get the kids.' Because when we came out Mrs. Walters was on the front, 'My kids, my kids are in there.' I went upstairs. I couldn't find any kids. I came out and I said to Harry, 'There's nobody in there.' She said, 'They are, they are, they're in there.' So Harry went up, came out with two kids, one under each arm. I said, 'Where the hell did you find those?' He said, 'Always remember when you go in a house and children are in, there's two places they'll always be, either under the bed or in the wardrobe.' That's where these were, in the wardrobe. We had a big works fire in 1948 when the whole of the factory burnt down and the Training School went with it. We think it was an electrical fault. But during the war, of course, there were machines and lathes and all the floors in those days were big twelve-by-twelve timbers and the timbers had soaked the oil. Well it just went like a furnace and that was in forty-eight. We had a Dennis machine and we had a little garage where it was kept and you used to turn up once or twice a month, rolling it out. Now, Harry Soppet was the Chief Officer and also the Apprentice School Manager. They actually entered the sports competition, a fire-brigade competition down in London. *(Jim Smiles)*

The electrical workshop and metallurgy lab were off a first-floor balcony. From there was a view right to the outer end of the sheds. I noticed a pall of dense black smoke rising into the roof space in the casting fettling area. On investigation, I found the smoke was coming from the semi-automatic shot-blasting plant. To protect the steel wall from the shot, thick curtains of rubber were hung and fixed as a lining. Somehow the rubber had caught fire. By that time the millwright had alerted the watchman who phoned the Fire Brigade. My duty was to isolate all electrical supplies to the plant and to adjacent areas. I managed to do that before the toxic smoke became too dense. The Brigade arrived wearing breathing sets. I had 'stood by' at a safe distance to give the leading fireman clearance to use water to extinguish the fire. It took about 30 minutes to put out the fire and cool the structure. Damage was extensive, both from the fire and water. *(John Reeve)*

Safety equipment

You had ear defenders, the safety boots, glasses. We used to get an ear test every year.
A van used to come round from the Forging Association and your ears were checked. *(Barry Davison)*

Health and safety was none existent. No safety glasses, no hearing things and it's the noisiest place you could imagine. The operators wore nothing. The blacksmiths wore a leather apron and sometimes on a stamp there was the driver and a stamper. The stamper was the guy that was in charge, set the dies up and everything. The other one just worked the stamp and pulled the hot billets out of the furnace. *(Derek Delahaye)*

I don't think it was as strict in those days as what it became later in my career, post Head Wrightson's. I don't remember wearing safety goggles at Head Wrightson's, which is probably the first thing you should be wearing when you're operating machinery. I think you only used to wear them if you were using a grinder or something where there's sparks flying everywhere. So I don't think the emphasis was great in those days. *(Keith Chapman)*

The main thing was in the Fettling Shop, you would get people with sparks in their eyes from grinding. You would get splashes. I got burnt occasionally on the eye when something would go down your safety glasses. But we wore safety glasses, we wore safety helmets, we wore metatarsal boots. We wore thick coats for insulation and we didn't do anything stupid. We wore dark glasses for looking into furnaces so it didn't affect your eyes from the arc-flashes. But it evolved rather than was just one massive idea then until the Health and Safety at Work Act came in and that said everybody had to work safely, without going into any detail. *(Colin Waugh)*

About seventy-eight I think when we had a health and safety campaign at Head Wrightson's. You all went for eye tests and you all got special goggles and glasses. They were late coming in with health and safety. I wouldn't say it was dangerous you just had to be careful. I mean they used to have women working in the Bridge Yard on the riveting section. Now when they had riveting they'd have the rivets and then they shot them to the men. But if you were walking past you had to be careful. Because now and again they just shot them like that. So you had to be careful in the Bridge Yard. Yes, seeing hot rivets flying about. *(Dennis Johnson)*

One outstanding memory in my early years at Head's was the noise when I went into the fabrication shops, with riveters and chippers hammering away on vessels, and there was no ear protection in those days, by the time you had been in the shops for an hour or two your head would be ringing for the rest of the day. *(Jim Heward)*

But you know what you're like when you're a young lad, you're grinding without goggles and it's crazy, when you think about it, going in confined spaces without masks and you did all that type of thing. I don't think they'd get away with it now. Safety is paramount now, isn't it? I did work at heights. I always remember one night I was working on this job and I was underneath and there were people working above me. I never had a hard hat on, and this piece of plate fell and I felt it. I felt the breeze of it but it went behind me but if it had hit me I'd be dead. *(Steve Featherstone)*

The union got us a change of overalls. But it did take a while to get overalls but we used to have to go to the stores and change our overalls once a week. And again, working boots. We had to buy our own at first and then eventually they got to supply us with working boots as well. They used to last until the toes were dropping out of them and they would decide to give you a new pair. That was more or less all we got. Obviously, they would supply you with gloves to protect your hands. At first there was never any stress about safety as regards eye protection and ear protection, but I suppose over my period of time at Head Wrightson things changed. When I first started they weren't very pushy but by the end they were, which was more or less the rule right through the Seventies, and then they started stressing that you had to wear ear protection and eye protection as well. But it used to be just up to your own devices whether you used them or not at first, and now it's obviously different again, you're not allowed to do anything without them now. *(Dennis Longstaff)*

They had protective gear to a certain extent. You had eye protection and if you needed gloves you could have them but most of the time then you couldn't work with gloves because you were turning the handles and things like that. Gloves were a drawback. But there were guards on the machine. You should have been behind the guard when the machine was operating, away from the danger. *(Jack Hare)*

There was everything available, but ear plugs and things like that I couldn't use. I couldn't wear the defenders because of my welding helmet, putting it up and down. So I just used cotton wool, screwed that up and put it in. But Martindale masks, they were always available. The fettlers had these proper masks with a filter on the ends that were soaked every night. They handed them into the stores and they got cleaned out and handed out the next morning with a new filter on. They could have as many filters as they wanted. But it was a pretty rough place though and it was dusty. You could see the sand and the dust in the air if you got a bit of sun coming through the doors. You could see it all, floating in the air. It was really hot with the castings, because you got the really big castings in the top shop cooling down for the fettlers to work on. They give a lot of heat off. If some had cooled they had to be preheated before the welders could work on them and you had to use oxy-propane to warm them up. We used annealing sticks to find out if they were the right temperature and they melted as soon as they got to a certain temperature. I think it was about 150 degrees Fahrenheit. And you used to touch the metal with the stick and if it melted then it was ready for welding. All the hot work in the big shop was low-hydrogen so you got money for using low-hydrogen welding rods because they used to give off terrible fumes. So you got extra money for doing that. That went on your card at the end of the day saying, I'd been working eight hours low-hydrogen work. *(John Harding)*

Accidents

We got two big brand-new machines to go in the heavy plate shop and there was a big press opposite us. Norman Pearce they called him, he worked on this, one of the biggest presses in Europe and he got his finger cut off. Put his finger on as the press come down. Just cut it off. Another time, I don't know if it was the late Sixties or early Seventies there was one chap in the Bridge Yard, they had these segments that make a circle on a wagon. They took it to the next bay and this slinger went to sling the first one off. Well, the others moved and it came like a pack of dominoes - 'boom, boom, boom'. Took his head off. Yes, because the ambulance man ran past us. But he soon came back because he'd never seen anything like that before in his life. That was a terrible accident that. I think there were less accidents then than there is now and yet there was no health and safety. I think everybody looked after themselves in them days. *(Dennis Johnson)*

There are some people from PEL who know more details than I, so this is perhaps hearsay but it was a terrible accident. The plant was to treat effluent at a plant in London and we were doing the final stages. Anyway, it appeared that somebody had to go down into a tank in the ground to do some final cleaning up and two people were going to deal with it. There were others there but two started to go down the ladder and were overcome by unseen fumes and collapsed. Somebody else went down to assist and also got overcome with fumes. It was established later that they died because of a poisonous gas. The HSE brought the case to court despite the fact that we'd done HAZOP studies. In the end his Lordship said, 'Guilty as proven, you should have thought of the unexpected.' I mean it knocks the socks off you, particularly when it shouldn't have been on the site. But his argument was, if you're doing all these studies you've got to consider the unexpected. We had to rewrite our rule books, which we did. *(Ted Sinnot)*

We worked in what they called the Aluminium Shop. It was right down near the bottom, near where the river was. It was a new plant and we started producing this molten aluminium. Anyway, everything was going fine and it's a well-known fact that water and molten aluminium do not mix. It causes a line explosion. I'd been on the job for several months and these blocks of aluminium, they used to keep them outside. Before they came into the shop where we were, they had to be completely dried, and they used to have burners there warming them up to dry them. We got set up one day and we started casting it. There was an explosion and what had happened, it hadn't been dried out this job, and I finished up in hospital for about seven weeks. I had skin grafts all over my arms and all my feet, down there. We found out after that someone hadn't done their job properly. Anyway, the legal side of it got sorted out and by the time I went back this aluminium order had finished. So they then asked me if I wanted a job in the Bridge Yard. So I said, 'Yes.' *(Ken Davies - Slinger)*

There were one or two fatalities but none that were in my vicinity at the time. There were a couple of guys I can recall were killed at the Iron Foundry at Eaglescliffe when a ladle tipped over and burned them to death. There was a guy down in the stockyard, I think he was in between a stack of plates in vertical storage that fell over and was crushed to death. I can remember that happening, but they're not things I personally saw myself and they weren't people I personally knew. *(Ken Peacock)*

I can't ever remember there being a bad accident while I was there. I know there was a couple when I'd left. One had both his legs broken when he was welding on a small dryer. The dryer was resting on a set of makeshift rollers which set off moving. The dryer came off the rollers and slipped breaking both his legs. And then another was painting inside a crushing machine when the machine was accidentally started, causing serious injury to his leg which was later amputated. *(Bill Hornby)*

It was on a night shift about two o'clock in the morning. You get to know certain noises, without the machinery working, and all of a sudden there was this strange noise. 'What's that?' It was an unusual noise anyway. I saw this chap and he was running one way and I went running another way. But what had happened, this guy had got caught up in a lathe and he was dead. It was horrible, indescribably horrible. We managed to stop the machinery. One of the foremen said, 'Oh we'll have to ring the manager.' Rang the manager. He rang the police because it was an unusual death. Unusual circumstances or something like that, classed as that. I was a senior shop steward then. I had to get involved with that case. I had to go and tell his wife. I had spoken to him that night about the fact that he wasn't wearing safety shoes and that he wasn't wearing his overalls. I remember saying to a solicitor at the time who was acting on his behalf, well for the widow's behalf, the fact that if he had have been wearing boots wouldn't have saved him from being killed. But the fact was he wasn't. The fact that he wasn't wearing overalls wouldn't have stopped him being killed but it might have prevented him being caught in the machinery. So at the end of the day that greatly affected me and, also, it dragged on for about three years before it actually came to court and then there was a settlement out of court. He was found to be a third negligent in his actions and therefore the costs were reduced by that amount. *(Stuart Thompson)*

Tommy Smith (centre) being presented by Richard Miles (Managing Director) with his award at the annual First Aid presentation ceremony in August 1957. Also seen L-R, Frank Shepherd (Personnel Manager), T. H. Robinson, Jack Bullock (partially obscured) and R. H. Danby. (Wright Ahead)

Then my final job was at Watney Mann Brewery. A water cleaning plant of some sort. We had a very bad casualty there. It was all underground, all the pipes and everything were underground. And you went down the ladder. I got a call in the office to say the site engineer had gone down and he'd been hit by gas of some sort. He'd dropped dead. He'd just dropped off the ladder. It was in seconds that he dropped. Two men from Watney Mann had gone down to try and rescue him and they'd dropped in so there were three of them dead. I had to go down overnight to sort it out, and we never did discover where it came from. We got fined. I mean it was just when health and safety had come in. We were told that they should all have had a rope round them and a man at the other end. But that's after the event. Nobody ever found out where the gas had come from. The unfortunate part of it was the site engineer, who got killed, went down to reassure the employees because the real foreman had gone on holiday. Had we'd had the proper foreman there and he'd started going down this ladder he would have known straightaway by the smell there was something wrong. *(Ron Hughes)*

I do remember a fatality early on. There was a guy working on one of the hammers. The golden rule is you switch the hammer off, ideally they're the rules. But it was still going, and it's only held up by a prop, the main weight is being held up by a prop. He did something, he kicked something, knocked it out and the thing came down on the back of his head. That's not nice. I can't remember which unit it was. It was in the early days. It must have been around the mid Seventies. *(Jim Matthews)*

There was one serious one. The time when I went back home just before Christmas to bring the family down. When we came back we found that one of the lads had got killed on one of the machines. He was working a lathe and he'd leaned over. He was wearing a woollen jumper or something and it caught on the rough part of the machine and it dragged him over the machine. Actually he ended up in bits. That happened during the Christmas and New Year period while we were in Scotland. *(Jack Hare)*

It was in the middle of a year where we were having a really good go at health and safety. It always happens when everyone's on their best behaviour. Trying to go so many days without an accident. You've seen people driving these forklift trucks? It was similar to that. He was a new driver and he hadn't been learning it very long so he was probably a bit nervous of the thing. It was a battery-operated electric thing and he was trying to reverse it. He stood on a little platform and it didn't have a steering wheel, you just have a foot throttle, and it had a lever which you either lifted up or down to move the wheels. But when you were reversing it you were moving. This was opposite to what you would normally do if you were going forwards, so I think he got mixed up and he went the wrong way and he backed it into a tailboard of a truck that he was attempting to unload, and it didn't have a barrier round. So he got a back injury and he later died as a result of that injury. It didn't kill him at that time; he died maybe three months later. *(Stuart Thompson)*

During my time in the Machine Shop I never saw any really serious accidents, and also the Bridge Yard which was a very dangerous place to work because it was noisy, you had to be very alert. I never saw any accidents although there could quite well have been because there was a lot of things, which by today's standards in the work place, the health and safety's tightened up tenfold. We used to work on the overhead cranes, as I've stated, and we had no harnesses. If a crane broke down halfway down the track I'd to walk down the track to get to the crane to fix it. You had to climb up the vertical ladder. You're talking about sixty, seventy foot. Then walk along the track, you had to hold onto the side as you go. One of the electrician's labourers was on the crane and went down to get some further tools. Then climbed up and put his foot on the track and the electrician drove the crane over his foot. Very, very lucky because his toe cap did save him but it pushed it out of the way and squashed all the cap and just bruised his toes. Very lucky, could have had his foot off. *(Derek Proctor)*

In 1952, while in the Apprentice School, I was lucky to escape injury or death while walking between the offices and the Machine Shop. The single railway line had a fairly steep incline down toward the Bridge Yard. The view down the line was restricted by a blind bend at the bottom. To get over the problem, a traffic light system was installed. The locomotive driver was required to change his end light to green. That turned the other end to red. On this day something went wrong. At Teesdale there were two locomotives. One was steam and the other was diesel. On that day the diesel was pulling a rake of trucks down the incline while the steam loco had a rake of trucks to take up the incline. I suddenly realised that the diesel train was speeding down the incline while the steam train was going up. The diesel brakes were applied but it just skidded. The driver of the steam train put the power into reverse and just avoided a collision by managing to stop and back away from the still oncoming diesel. You can imagine my state of shock following such a close encounter with near disaster. *(John Reeve)*

There was a guy died inside, varnishing a pattern. He was varnishing it with some sort of a varnish. Well, you climbed up on the outside on a ladder and then had to drop down. When it was break time they realised he wasn't there. They went looking for him and lo and behold there he was laid in the bottom of this mould. That was it, yes. He'd been using a varnish with some sort of a toxic resin. The fumes overcame him and he couldn't get out. *(Tony Lodge)*

Chapter 7

'The atmosphere was always absolutely A1': relationships in the work place

There were a number of industries on Teesside in the 19th and 20th centuries that have been described as paternalistic, ones in which the owners tried to demonstrate they were motivated by a sense of social responsibility towards their employees. They were often perceived as good companies to work for because they provided an extensive package of benefits which was designed to secure a measure of commitment and loyalty from their workers. Often such companies were family owned and this certainly was the case in Head Wrightson. Members of the Wrightson family were involved in the business for many years and followed the principles of paternalism until economic pressures meant they could no longer offer a job for life and a full range of welfare provisions. In the years following the end of the Second World War, British industry was facing a massive re-structuring programme to ensure it could remain profitable and compete with global competition. It was inevitable in these conditions that the workforce would be faced with calls to be more flexible and adaptable to market conditions.

This chapter, then, examines the impact these challenging conditions had on relationships in Head Wrightson. It involves examining attitudes to the owners and managers, trade union activity, discipline, workplace humour, and the experience of women workers.

The subsequent extracts give an interesting and unique perspective on life at Head Wrightson.

SUSAN (10) V.I.P. FOR A DAY

Thornaby launch by crane-driver's daughter

ONE of Teesside's industrial giants, Head Wrightson and Co., Ltd., of Thornaby, accorded the VIP treatment yesterday to Susan Hillman, ten-year-old daughter of a crane driver in the firm's construction department.

For 15 exciting minutes she played a key role in the launching of the eighth of 12 heat exchangers being built by Head 'Vrightson's for use in the nuclear power station taking shape at Bradwell, in Essex.

Susan was the lucky winner of a draw among the workmen to decide whose child should perform the launching ceremony, an honour accorded on previous occasions to industrial leaders and people prominent in public life.

Newspaper front page.
(Courtesy The Northern Echo)

Relationships with workmates

Everybody would help you. If you got into difficulties they wouldn't let you struggle. Nobody would see you harmed in any way at Head Wrightson's. It was a terrific family concern. When I say 'family' I mean everybody treated each other with respect and treated you as a family. If you wanted a bacon sandwich off somebody they'd break it in half and give you it, they would really. *(Harry Foster)*

I got on very well with them, very well indeed apart from one who complained that I put his work at the bottom of the pile, which I did. Everyone's went to the bottom of the pile because I worked from the top. He was a bit impatient and wanted it doing yesterday. But apart from that I got on very well with them I think. I think there was a very good working atmosphere, everyone seemed to take their work seriously but it wasn't heavy and dull. Most of the fellows were young and they were all very friendly and at times great fun. There would be laughter sometimes but at other times, when there was a rush on to finish a job, it would be deathly silent. It was a big drawing office and each draughtsman had his own drawing board and bench but the section heads had separate offices. However, the walls of each office, including mine, were only solid to waist height, the rest being glass, so everyone could see what everyone else was doing. *(Margaret Hope)*

It was a different culture to what it is now. People wanted to go to work because they enjoyed it. It was fun. Everybody got on with everybody else. There was no backbiting, there was no, 'I'm not going to train you because in five years' time you'll take my job off me.' None of that. *(Jim Smiles)*

I enjoyed the work mates and you had a good bunch of lads. That's what makes it happier when you've got a good bunch of lads you're working with. You look forward to going to work because you know you're going to work with a good bunch of lads. *(Dennis Johnson)*

Everybody was absolutely wonderful to everybody else. I've never worked anywhere else where you have people who worked there who were all sort of dedicated to one cause. They were all, I would say, dedicated to Head Wrightson's. Difficult to say that but there was no people you could say who were scroungers or who didn't do their bit or didn't work to their full capacity. The atmosphere was always absolutely A1. *(Trevor Briggs)*

Practical jokes

The initiation ceremony as a marker lad in the Bridge Yard was to catch you, take your trousers down and cover your penis with white lead, which was the marking paint. Another practical joke was because you had steel tips on your boots. When you were marking off, the welders used to come and tack your heels to the plates and walk away and shout your name and, of course, you tried to turn and you couldn't get off the plate. *(Jim Smiles)*

Played cards down in the wharf and the security guard came and I had a bloody good hand for once and we dropped everything and off like hell to get out of the way. They used to do all sorts of things. There's always ways round everything because they couldn't keep their eye on you all the time could they? *(Thomas Wilson)*

One of the favourites was for the chaps who smoked filter tipped cigarettes. They used to put ends of matches down so that when they started smoking it blew up, and things like that. When I was younger and on the shop floor I got welded to the bench, of course, because you had steel toe caps on and steel heel plates on and they used to come in and, 'ssh, ssh', with the welding and you couldn't move because you were welded to the bench, you were stuck.
I also got crucified in the Template Shop through the cuffs and the trousers. I was there for hours. *(John Heath)*

We had wooden benches with drawers with tools in. One of the tricks they used to do was knock a six inch nail through the top of the bench about four inches in front of the back of the drawer. So you would try to open your drawer and it would come so far out and then you'd think, 'Oh there's a file or something sticking up and jamming it,' and you were trying to find out what was stopping it. And in the end you'd give it a good pull and nine times out of ten you pulled the back of the drawer off. *(Jim Heward)*

There was a bit of joking. In the works you would normally have a tin mug and they occasionally ruined it by nailing it to the bench so when you went to pick it up it wouldn't move. And the other terrible thing was they would drill a small hole just below the lip and consequently the moment you started to drink it would all run down your chin. These jokes were only played occasionally and it didn't happen to everybody. *(Dennis Longstaff)*

Every morning the section leaders of each department, about five or six of them, would walk along the main passageway in through the Drawing Office to the Chief Executive's Office. They discussed what today's mail had brought in, any enquiries, any orders and discussed developments on the various jobs. So while all the section leaders were in that big office there was a little bit of mayhem, a bit of horseplay. We used to throw paper balls at each other and that sort of thing. We were upstairs and we used to kick them about. It used to get silly. Major Miles' office was below us and he sent his secretary up to say, 'Will you ask the draughtsmen to stop because they'll bring the ceiling down?' We did let our hair down a little bit, for ten minutes while they were in that meeting and then it was back to work again. *(Jack Picken)*

It was one bait time and it was when we were in the Oxyacetylene Section and we were sat round the section having our bait and I'd made a little box with a hole in it and I'd actually filled the box up with gas not realising that acetylene was a heavy gas *(sic)* and it wouldn't come out of the box. I was winding everybody up saying, 'Oh I'm going to light it,' and they all said, 'ah don't be daft,' thinking that the gas would have went out. I thought, 'If I just play around with it another minute or so all the gas will be out.' Anyway, when I eventually did light it, it went off like a firecracker, actually bounced up and hit the roof. You would have thought it was a bomb going off. I got the shock of my life. All my mates got the shock of their lives and Mr. Thew and Mr. Watson came running out full of hell, 'What the hell's going on?' And for something like that you could have very easily got the sack for it. *(John Stainthorpe)*

I can't remember what wage I got or anything else. Then I also got another job while I was in the Bridge Yard - I used to collect all the welders' books, because the welders would write all their hours down in the book, and I would collect all the books in off the welders, take them to the office and then hand them back. So I did that as well while I was at Head Wrightson's. Never got to drive a crane or anything like that. I once worked in the Tool Shop as well. They had a Tool Shop where people had to come for tools. While this Danny was off on sick they asked me to go and work in the Tool Shop that was in the Bridge Yard. It was just like a hut full of drills or whatever tools they needed and they had to sign for what they took out to make sure they brought it back. I remember somebody telling me, 'Now about ten o'clock Danny's pet rat goes along that beam.' So I put two pair of bicycle clips on the bottom of my trousers and I sat on the counter. I used to say, 'You can come in and help yourself. I'm not getting off this counter. There's a rat about.' I mean you did see like rats, you know, scurrying about at times and I'd run for a mile. *(Cath Harrison)*

Relationships with women workers

I can tell you one funny story about the girls in the London office. They came in to see me one day and said, 'We've come to see you about

Lady crane driver. (Wright Ahead)

sexual harassment,' and I thought, 'oh dear.' And they said, 'Yes, we're not getting any.' So that was the end of that meeting. *(Joe Doran)*

I went into the Light Machine Shop under Alan Hewitson. First of all I was working on a shaper at the top of the shop. Everyone started on the shaping machine and then there was no swearing there because there were three women on the capstan lathes in there, and old Ernie Orpen, their supervisor would have words with you. If Margaret, Vera or Hilda said you were swearing, you were spoken to. They were remnants from the war years and they were working on capstan and turret lathes. I was led to believe Sir John Wrightson had said he would never ever finish them because of their wartime service and they would leave of their own accord rather than be finished ever. *(Billy Sharp)*

The women had their own area in what they called the induction bay. They had their own way in and way out. The big core shop was just past what they called the Heavy Bay Foundry, they were all separate. But I think there was never any bother. *(Eddie Peacock)*

What I did find embarrassing, being perhaps fairly innocent, were lots of ladies when we went to the foundries at Thornaby, in what they called the core shop. They were making some of the smaller sand portions or moulds. These were perhaps the little bits that went on the inside of some of the bigger ones. If you were producing a big valve casting it needed to have an outer casing or an outer shell and, because it was hollow inside, had to have a core. These girls used to do that sort of work. It was quite menial work in a way but quite hard and it must have been terrible on their hands. But it was the first time I realised that women swore as badly as men and it was a real shock to the system. I must have been innocent in those days. *(Dennis Longstaff)*

In the Foundry you made moulds and the cores were the small shapes that went into a mould to make up the overall mould and the women made the cores in an area of a shop called the core floor. They were controlled by a character called Tommy La Roche, he was the only man there and you as an apprentice had to watch yourself because the idea was to get your pants down. If you didn't watch yourself they'd debag you. So it was quite a place. I managed to avoid it. I was pretty fast in those days. But I know guys that didn't. There were women in the machine shops as well at one stage but of course, through the war there were a lot of women working there, a lot of women. *(Barry Preece)*

The highlights for me? I think what it did for me as a woman. I was doing what was then considered a man's job. It was actually to do it and to do it properly and be recognised for what I was doing. It gave me sort of a platform to do what I wished to do.

A woman in a man's world - you were getting a man's wage or did you get a woman's wage?

Management and foremen training day at the Friarage circa 1970s. (Wright Ahead)

No, I got a woman's wage. There was one time when I'd been admitted to the Institute as a Licentiate. Which is the first step along professional recognition. And that alerted newspapers, quite a number of newspapers, 'We want your picture, you're a woman industrial photographer, a woman in a man's world.' Many a time I would turn up when these two young men were still training and I was the photographer and they'd come with me as an assistant. I'd walk into, say, Head Wrightson Machine Company to do something. I think Mr. Mather was the M.D. They would come down whoever was in charge of the commission and they would walk in and straight to the man. 'Right, I'm wanting this shot, this shot, this shot from this view and a close up of this, and they'd say 'no, no, I'm not the photographer she's the photographer.' You see many a time that would happen. Well, it was unusual to have a female photographer. But after a while they all got to know. They were, 'Oh sorry, sorry. Are you sure you'll be able to do it? Can you climb up there, can you do this?' Yes, it was a bit daunting sometimes if you had to walk into the Heavy Plate Shop. You'd walk down with the camera bag on and it would be wolf whistles and jeers. Well, I shouldn't be in there but you had to do your work. And eventually I think you earned their respect.

Did you have to climb?

Yes, yes. And then that was a funny old thing, wasn't it? You'd have to climb up ladders and women were not allowed to wear trousers at work. We can't have you wearing trousers at work. So Alan said, 'They have to go out, they have to climb.' Right, okay if you're going out on a job in the Bridge Yard or the Foundry you can change before you go out. Walk over to do the job, come back and then you had to change into what was office wear. *(Anne Simpson)*

My dad was really against me going but I said, 'Well, I've already said I'll start Monday.' But when I got there I was, of course, scared stiff. I had really only worked in shops and sweet factories, so to go into a big works where there was cranes, it was quite something, but I absolutely loved it at the end. It was the best job I ever had because it had such a sense of humour with all the men, although there were swear words and they turned round and saw you there and they would always apologise and say, 'Sorry Cath, we didn't know you were there.' *(Cath Harrison)*

Women are more dexterous than men to make things and pick things up, and small things particularly. So what they were doing was making the cores in sand to go in the sand box so that the casting, after they'd poured the hot metal in it and it cooled and had gone solid, they could take all this out. Then the core that's actually in the middle, the sand by that time will have totally dried and been burnt, if you like, by the hot metal and it would just pull out. So you would then have a hole in the casting the shape of this core. Now to do those again you've got a pattern box to make them and you stick carbon dioxide in it and it's delicate work. You can't have ham-fisted people or hairy erectors doing things like that, it just don't work. But again, from the language that came over the wall I think these ladies were a little on the rough side. *(Ted Sinnot)*

Relationship with managers

In them days they were pretty strict. If you wanted to go to the toilet you had to go and see the manager. He used to say, 'Alright, I'll give you five minutes.' And that was it, five minutes you were back on the job again. Because he'd come round and make sure you were there. Nothing like now. To be honest we were like school kids; put your hand up, 'Can I go, go to the toilet?' Very strict. *(Dennis Johnson)*

We used to have a nurse on the site, a lovely lady called Mrs. Whitehead. Two guys had got burnt. There'd been a bit of a little explosion and she treated them and sent them to hospital and then he found out. They were working on a very important job, these people. He went in to see her and gave her the roasting of her life for not getting his permission to send these people to the hospital. They went to the hospital and they had twenty-per-cent or twenty-degree burns or whatever so they were treated and told not to return to work for at least ten days. He put that nurse through a lot of argy-bargy she needn't have had, shouldn't have had because she was only doing her job. I went in to him and tried to get him to publicly apologise to her but he wouldn't. But in the end he did apologise to her privately but I wanted him to do it in the canteen in front of everyone but he wouldn't do it. So there was daggers drawn on that. *(Stuart Thompson)*

Well, if Mr. Hutchinson was there it was 'Mr.' Hutchinson or 'Sir'. I had no problems with referring to anybody as 'Sir' or 'Mr.'. I was taught by my parents to respect age and I always did that. Going back to Bradwell. Sir John was then Chairman and he was making a visit on behalf of the Nuclear Power Corporation, and my father and Sir John were both members of the Airborne connection. Sir John was the President, my father was the Chairman of the branch on Teesside. I remember we were in this reactor this day, everybody was being told that Sir John Wrightson was coming down and all the engineers from all these other companies, 'Oh we're going to meet Sir John.' He walked into the reactor and all these blokes were lined up going to see him and he said, 'Now then young Partridge how are you doing?' They looked at me, these engineers, he wanted to speak to me. But that was the Head Wrightson set up. If they were walking round, any of them, they would stop and talk to you, and of course, you addressed them as 'Sir' completely out of respect. *(Pat Partridge)*

There was no nastiness in the bosses, that's what I found. *(Norma Pelmear)*

Then there was the case of a little girl whose mother died. Something went wrong with the anaesthetic that she was being administered and she never recovered. The baby was born and survived. But obviously there was a case of negligence by the hospital, or there appeared to be. Anyway, the father who was actually a colleague of mine, and in fact eventually moved down to Bournemouth, was very distraught. The company Managing Director took it on himself to arrange for lawyers to be brought in to take on the case. Obviously, the company eventually recovered all the costs but they were willing to participate and go to that level of help. I would say that that was typical of Head Wrightson and the general atmosphere was always very pleasant. We socialised with the top bosses at one or two events. There were Christmas parties at their homes and that type of thing. *(David Auld)*

Discipline

The only time I've been disciplined was when I worked in the Purchasing Department where discipline was fairly tight. People worked, walked and talked quietly. That was at the very beginning, you know, first three years. I can remember this vividly because a chap called Harry Smith was waiting for a phone call. It was very urgent apparently, very important to him, and every time the phone rang he jumped. For some reason he had to leave the office and as he was going out of the door this particular phone call came through and I shouted to him across the big office. The Chief Estimator had a visitor in his office when I shouted, which gave a very bad impression. I really got hauled over the coals for that. The Chief Estimator was furious. Another thing I can remember was to do with the Chief Purchaser. He'd been invited to an event. The invitation was written in the third person and he told me to write and accept it. So I wrote a very good letter - 'Dear Mr. so and so', finishing with 'Yours sincerely'. 'That's no good,' he said and tore it up. So I thought, 'Oh I've made a mistake with spelling or something.' So I redid it, took it up to him again. 'That's no good,' tore it up. So I asked Sheila Cross, the fantastic head of the typing pool, and she explained about answering it in the third person. So when I took it back to him Mr. Walker said, 'Now you'll never forget will you that whenever you don't understand anything, don't be afraid to ask?' That lesson has stuck with me all my life really. *(Margaret Hope)*

Well, you had to behave yourselves but now and again little things happened. Like I was stood marking off at the benches one day and a few of the lads were kicking a ball about, which they shouldn't have done. It rolled over to me and I just kicked it back. I wasn't playing or anything. George Smith saw me and I got sent home. Yes, he sent me home and suspended me for two weeks. I lost two weeks' wages I think. I wasn't even playing, I told him that. *(Norman Toulson)*

Anybody went out of line and they were sent home for three days. That was normal. One thing I can remember particularly well, outside the shop where the canteen was, it was sloping down and there was a wagon there. A low-loader thing, and we'd pull it up and you'd jump on and have a ride down. So we'd ride down to the Fitting Shop and then, 'Oh let's have another go,' and somebody pushed it up again and had another ride down. Up and down. It was still within lunchtime. I know this day it came down to the shop doors and we stopped and some of us said, 'That's it, it's time to start.' So we went in, and two or three of the others said, 'Oh we're going to have another go.' I said, 'Well, you do if you like, we're going in,' and they pulled it back up and had a ride down. What they hadn't realised was as there was only a few of them there wasn't enough of them for a brake. And they went into the Fitting Shop doors and knocked them off their hinges. The foreman just came along and looked at that and looked at them and said, 'Right, out.' And they were all sent home. *(Les Ellis)*

I can never ever actually recall anybody actually getting sacked. I can remember someone being disciplined for three days suspension or something like that, and it was always something like petty theft or something like that rather than your attitude to work. They'd always find something alternative for you if you struggled to do one certain part of the job. They'd find you something which suited you and you could manage and you'd get by and that's how they used to work with that. *(Dennis Longstaff)*

It was a bit of fun seeing a person all of a sudden put in his mouth a cigarette. You weren't supposed to smoke in the Template Shop. No, because there was wood and things around. But they tried to smoke. And when the foreman came up, well they used to get the fag in their mouth. *(Les Wilson)*

I lived near Head Wrightson's and I used to have to go to the common to hang our washing out. It would be halfway through the day and I'd say to Ernie Lister, 'It's raining, I've got a line of washing out.' 'Oh go home and take them in,' he said, and I used to run home, sneak it because they used to have a watchman on the gate. So you used to have to see if he was there and sneak behind a wall and nip up and take the washing in and then go back to work again and then sneak in as you'd sneaked out. Probably, instead of going out the Bridge Yard door you'd nip through the Fitting Shop, pretending you were going to the Fitting Shop, and nip out of their door. It was good. I enjoyed working there. *(Cath Harrison)*

Strikes

About the early Seventies we wanted to have a pay rise and they wouldn't give us one. I knew the Managing Director, they called him Wood. Anyhow, he threatened, he said, 'I'll lock the gates.' We thought he wouldn't do that but he did. We were on six till two, we went to work on the morning and the gates were locked. We couldn't get in. So we had to wait until the day men came. The gates were locked and wouldn't let us in. So we were on strike for a week. Then we used to go up Head Wrightson's club and have a game of cards on a morning. Just pass the time away. It was sorted out in the end but on strike for a week. *(Dennis Johnson)*

I had to take the men out on strike actually, which was the first strike that there had been within Head Wrightson's Group at the time. It wasn't an easy thing to do. Negotiations had been going on for about six months over a wage increase. They used to start locally, me and the Works Manager, along with the foremen sometimes and then in the end you were talking to the Production Director. To cut a long story short we made a deal. Then about two weeks later, when that wage increase should have been in the pay packets it wasn't there, so I had to go and see about that. So we went out on strike on a Friday. The Manager's words, as they said it would be, 'Well, I'm not talking to no one till you come back.' So we made arrangements to go back on a Monday dinner-time but not to start work, to sit in the canteen, make ourselves available for work. That was the deal. And then negotiations were going to go on, and so in the end it got ratified again. But the worry it caused me at the time was unbelievable. They got it because it had been agreed to. But that was the first time I felt like, 'Well I don't trust you.' So that broke a trust between me and that certain gentleman. *(Stuart Thompson)*

We never came out on strike. We had one in all my time I can remember and that was a general strike. I think the upshot of the strike was where previously we'd worked on a Saturday morning, I think we worked a forty-eight-hour week and then all of a sudden we went on strike. Then Saturday mornings became overtime and I think we got a rise. But thereon after, you would normally work just a five-day week. Then if requested you would work overtime on a Saturday morning, or even on a Sunday of course. But that was, as I recall, a general strike, it wasn't aimed particularly at Head Wrightson's or anybody else. I never got in, not that I can recall anyway. *(Bob Close)*

Trade Unions

We didn't really have a large amount of grief as in many respects some aspects of the semi-skilled employees antics were a serious embarrassment to the full-time union officials. I think that because the wages were so high the Forge labour force obviously weren't prepared to take the financial pain of going on a prolonged strike. We had a few token half-day walk outs and a bit of working to rule, whatever they were, as we brought the Forge numbers down. What we endeavoured to do really wasn't so much drive the Forge people out, but it was to improve working practices, create a safer environment, pay fair wages yet still manage to achieve good manning levels with commensurate levels of productivity to enable the company to regain its competitiveness. Dealing with the skilled unions, who were incidentally the lower paid on the site, was totally different. Dialogue was always constructive and they would usually eventually accept that some change could be very beneficial. The key was always to clearly explain the plan and the intended consequences and benefits to job retention and skills enhancement. In the Tool Room, for example, where we had a very large labour force, we reduced manning by the introduction of new technology in that we invested in CNC spark erosion (EDM), wire erosion and CNC vertical boring machines. This investment also yielded significant benefits in the enhancement of skills related to die design, and the manufacture and fitting of hammer dies and press tools. And in Maintenance we ran a very tight ship. We managed the work, and we introduced planned maintenance on machines so the tradition of the night shift doing nothing, or very little of what was actually required from them, disappeared. We strived to always keep equipment in good working order and to be in control by carefully evolving and running to a very practical yet transparent plan. We knew what we had to achieve and so we kept driving and pushing the business onwards. *(Ian Ford)*

The trade union fellows on the whole are perfectly good decent fellows like anybody else. They've got their point of view and it's up to them to present it. In the 1970s it was the time of roaring inflation, if you remember. So wages were going up and up and up out of all recognition. I had a lot of meetings with the Boilermakers Society, or the Boilermakers Union. I can't remember the name of the chap at Head Wrightson who was the representative. I can visualise, I can see his face now but I can't think of his name. He had a hearing aid, but that was one of the problems we had, they were all claiming compensation for hearing. That became the fashion at that time, and quite a lot of them were successful. *(Joe Doran)*

We were in the ETU. Electrical Trades Union. You had to be in. It was a stipulation, if they brought the electrician in they had to be in the ETU. I used to go to the Salutation pub in Billingham to pay my subs and I used to go maybe once a month. *(Tony Lodge)*

You joined the union when you went there straight away because it was a union shop so you had to be in the union in any case. That's how I joined the union. The AEU.

Where did you go to join it?

The old Co-op down on the Green at Billingham. There they had a dance place upstairs and a theatre. You went along to the left and at the end there was a room. Subs were always paid every fortnight. You had to pay because you got your card marked and then when the shop steward asked you for your card and if it wasn't paid he used to say, 'Right, out.' He'd send you home. When I become a shop steward I had to do that as well - mark the cards. Checking them every quarter. But you see the only reason why I went as a shop steward is because some lads were getting mucked about by the gaffer. Because we had a system among the fitters. When you worked overtime you'd work Sunday or whatever and they weren't sharing the overtime out properly. Some weren't getting any, some were. I worked out a system for the foreman to do it. He didn't like it but it worked. *(Thomas Wilson)*

I don't recall ever having strikes at Head Wrightson. Plenty were threatened, of course, but never really came to anything. And we went through the Engineering Employers Union Procedure several times right up to the top and things were settled there.

What pressures were you under from higher management then, if any?

Well, oh nothing serious, no not real pressure. They obviously wanted the unions to be working okay.

Can you recall any personalities from the union side that you negotiated and dealt with?

Well, Jackie Hunter of course of the AEU, and then there was Arthur Johnson, Boilermakers, and there was a chap for the T&G, he was called George Doige. And then of course, there was AST, ASTMS, well ASTMS grew out of the AS, ASCW were the Association of Scientific Workers. ASTMS was part of DATA which was the old draughtsmen's union, and the ASCW combined into the ASTMS, Association of Scientific, Technical and Managerial Staff, I think they were called. They were very active. There were not a large number of them but they were very active. We had a Staff Committee, which talked about matters of mutual interest, but it wasn't supposed to negotiate but in fact we inevitably talked about things like that. One of my main responsibilities was fixing salary levels and wage levels because you've got to pay people the right wage. I did that by talking to all the other personnel people in the district and keeping an eye on the cost of living and the RPI and so on. Then I used to put my proposals to the Board, about twice a year it would be. I'm amazed that in fact the Board always accepted what I said. The only time they ever changed it was when I think I was suggesting a seven and a half pence increase, and they put it up to eight.

I always remember having the negotiation with the Construction Engineering Union and they were going to go on strike because the shop steward came in to me and said, 'It's too dangerous up there Sir.' They were working on steel bars about a hundred feet above the ground. 'They'd got this red dust everywhere, it's slippery, it's dangerous, and we can't do it. But give us another three pence an hour and we'll do it.' As I said, really good negotiation. In my day that was the time when industrial tribunals started under the Industrial Relations Act.

It became quite fashionable for people to just go to the tribunal because so many companies would just pay you a hundred quid to keep you quiet because it saved time and it saved management time. Well I think that was wrong. We'd always contest a tribunal. We did that and we won every one of them. But of course, when people know you're going to contest it they don't take frivolous cases along. It also has a very salutary effect on managers because they know if they've made a mess of things they might finish up in a tribunal, as they sometimes did. So it's good for the management as well to have these tribunals. *(Joe Doran)*

I was in the Boilermakers as an apprentice. I stuck in the Boilermakers until about 1972. The boilermakers paid their dues at a pub called the Sadlers in Thornaby next to the Five Lamps. It was upstairs and so you had to stand in a queue to pay your dues, which was nine pence a week or a fortnight. Then they said, when it was coming up to the 1970 election, 'There's nine pence and there's a three pence political levy.' I said, 'Well, what's this political levy?' I would be about twenty-three at the time. 'It's a fighting fund.' I said, 'I didn't realise we were at war.' He said, 'Well, no it's to fight. If Ted Heath gets elected it's to fight the Heath government. We're building up a fighting fund.' I said, 'Well, I'd support Ted Heath.' So I said, 'I'm not prepared to go against it financially. I want to contract out.' Well, by now there's a huge queue behind me, so they've got to hunt about in drawers looking for this form to contract out. Of course, everybody wants to get off to their pint. So talk about intimidation. Anyway, I stuck by my guns, contracted out and saved myself the three pence a fortnight political-levy fee. But I did eventually leave. I'd decided that it wasn't providing me with any benefits. A number of the things they were doing in the early Seventies I disagreed with philosophically so I think round about 1974 I'd resigned the union. Even though I was still at Head Wrightson's it didn't cause a problem, I was fairly well accepted by that time. *(Charlie Tighe)*

I thought I was in a trade union. I'd paid my subs for quite a while and then it turned out the guy who was taking the subs was on the fiddle and he'd been pocketing the money and he actually finished up in court. I found

I wasn't actually in a trade union at Thornaby. The union I thought I was in was DATA, the Draughtsmen's & Allied Technicians Union. *(Ken Peacock)*

When you were eighteen you had to join a trade union. It was compulsory then, you didn't have a choice, whereas now you don't have to be in a union. But then you had to be in a trade union, and we were all in the Boilermakers as they called them. We went to the Mandale Hotel in Thornaby on the first contribution night, then we moved on to the Queen Street School in Thornaby to pay our contributions there. We used to get holidays, tea-time breaks, longer breaks, shorter working hours, that's what the unions used to do for our money and that's what you used to pay for. They all used to represent each trade to go to the management and fight their corner if there was anybody in any bother. If you'd been disciplined they would go and back you up if you want. For want of a better word they would try and defend your corner or get you leniency off the management if you'd been a bad lad. *(Dennis Longstaff)*

We seemed to be bedevilled with redundancies right throughout my career to a greater or a lesser extent but it was starting to intensify in the late Seventies. I can't particularly put dates on it but there were redundancies. There was a distinct rundown. I was a shop steward at the time and you'd be called in and they'd say, 'Well we've got to make 'x' number of people redundant and these are the names we've picked.' You're sitting there thinking, 'Well, I hope my name's not among it,' which it wasn't. On one occasion they'd called the shop stewards in, they've told us we're making so many redundant and these are the names we're making redundant and there was some sort of dyed-in-the-wool Head Wrightson names among them. Then I thought the management had gone round and told these people. After lunch I went to one particular fellah and said, 'Oh I'm sorry, mate, but there's nowt we can do about it,' and they hadn't told him. So hard times but you've got to fight for your job while you can. But it was a losing battle, it was definitely a losing battle, they wanted you to do more multi, multi-skilling. *(Albert Roxborough)*

I was in the ETU, Electrical Trade Union and for my sins I was a shop steward. I even became President of the ETU on Teesside. I enjoyed being involved with talking to people.
All the years I was at Head Wrightson, and the position that I did hold, we never had a strike. The only time we had a situation was when the Confederation wanted everybody out in the whole of the area. But we didn't have a strike in Head Wrightson's whilst I was there. It was because the company itself would listen to what you had to say and if you asked for too much they would tell you, but at least they were prepared to talk with you. *(Pat Partridge)*

In them days we used to walk instead of talk. There was quite a few. There was nothing sustained, if you know what I mean. You might get one shift would walk out because of a problem and the next shift might not come in, and that would be it. And then again, the night shift come in and so the next shift, the following shift, the ones who'd walked out said, 'If they've gone in we might as well go in, we're not getting anywhere.' *(John Everett)*

You had to be in a union, if you weren't in a union you didn't have a job. I remember doing a rotary kiln, building it in Head Wrightson's and then we had to go to British Chrome. We went to British Chrome to commission it. I remember going onto the British Chrome site, and there was a shop steward, a big union man at British Chrome and they called him George Dick. He came up to us, he said, 'Can I see your union card because if you haven't got a union card you're off the site.' He said, 'If your union card isn't up to date with your payments you're off the site.' So the union was very, very strict, and it was strict in Head Wrightson's too, but the union looked after you, and the management was a bit wary of the union people as well. So the union had a big influence on the company and the workforce. *(Harry Foster)*

We went to a union office in Borough Court in Middlesbrough. There were shop stewards there from all over. There were full-time officials there and a couple of union solicitors there to show us all the procedure - things like this. Then we got registered officially as shop stewards in the national book of shop stewards. The course lasted about two years on and off and then in between we used to go just as sort of passengers to these industrial tribunals, to listen and learn all the procedures. Then after that I was elected as chairman of the shop stewards' committee for Head Wrightson, just for talking, a sort of spokesman for all the stewards. But of course, before this took place we, the shop stewards, we'd already had a meeting and decided what the procedure would be.

Now there were Works Councils, were you ever involved?

We were on the Works Councils, yes. Actually I think they were pretty good. We met with the management regularly every month. I felt they were definitely useful.

Can you recall any problems that you had about the Seventies?

I can only remember we had one dispute. I think and it only lasted one day. We didn't have many problems at all when it was Head Wrightson's, we seemed to get more niggly problems when it was Davy's. One thing I will say about Head Wrightson's, our local management down there, John Jeffels, people like that, we got on marvellous with them. I think all the shop stewards did. We were all on first name terms and even at meetings all the shop stewards and all the local management respected each other. But when Davy's took over we seemed to be sort of out of touch with the higher management. Davy's took over in seventy-eight and the top management structure changed but not for the better. *(Ken Davies - Slinger)*

They were all in the pattern-makers' union. The UPA. United Pattern-Makers' Association.

And where did you meet to go for you to pay your subs?

They were in the Jubilee Hall in Leeds Street, Stockton, near the station. They had their meeting up there. I never went because I wasn't particularly a union man.

Was there any reaction to your coming out of the union when you became chargehand?

Other than the union officials didn't like it, they couldn't stop me. But I said, 'Look I don't need to be in a union, if I'm off work I get paid.' They said 'We can give you this benefit and that benefit.' And I said, 'If I'm off work I get paid, I get more holiday, I don't need you, to be in the union.' Because it wasn't a closed shop. *(John Heighly)*

The T&G shop steward was invited to a meeting in Newcastle of all the top brass of the Transport and General Workers, who he didn't know, and when he was there they asked him to make a speech. He was totally unprepared so they prompted him and asked him how he got on with Head Wrightson's and how he got on with his Managing Director, which was me. When he got to that point he said, 'Oh he's a decent sort of a lousy bastard.' That was in a public meeting as well! A decent sort of a lousy bastard which apparently in union terms was quite a compliment. *(John Fuller)*

Each subsidiary company had a Works Council and the representative was usually a union official from each department. Well, really it was a workers' representative from each department not necessarily a union man, although unions were represented in their own right, but whilst it could have been any one of the employees, it was usually a shop steward. There would be a manager from each department and the Personnel Department was represented. The MD would be chairman, which was good because there was access to top management once a month. So, you couldn't fault that. They'd had these Works Councils for a long time. Then they were reviewed and

Harold Macmillan, Prime Minister and former MP for Stockton, photographed outside the canteen with members of the Works Council and directors, Sir John Wrightson and Mr. Peter Wrightson, together with Frank Shepherd, Personnel Manager, in March 1959. (Wright Ahead)

upgraded. There was also a group Works Council comprising representatives from each subsidiary company. *(Albert Roxborough)*

Special visitors

We had a visit from Harold Macmillan when he was Prime Minister and Lady Dorothy.
And, of course, they were going round the works and my boss had to get an itinerary out for the visit. They always did everything like that. So I went into his office and he said, 'Oh I've got you down on this visit.' He said, 'You're lady-in-waiting.' He said, 'Look there's only one woman on the visit, that's Lady Dorothy, and so we need a woman.' So he took the itinerary up to Sir John. Sir John looked through it, he said, 'What's this Miss Thurlwell lady-in-waiting?' He said, 'Well, Sir John, there's no woman in the party and Lady Dorothy shouldn't have to ask a man if she wants to go to the cloakroom.' 'Good thinking, Frank,' he said. *(Enid Thurlwell)*

The Prime Minister, The Right Honourable Harold Macmillan, Wednesday the fourteenth of January 1959. Now at the time Head Wrightson's had a contract with the Bradwell nuclear power station, and they were making heat exchangers of some sort or other. They were quite bulky things so rather than transport them by road they put them onto a barge and they launched the barge off the Head Wrightson's slipway which was down the bottom and past the Pattern Shop. Then they were towed down to Bradwell in Essex, and they had about eight or ten of these things I think they made. Macmillan came to launch one but he had a tour of the works first of all. But there's a funny story about that. So many boys were chosen to be a guard of honour and we got these white overalls. We had to stand at attention while Harold walked between us. Then as soon as he'd gone we'd sprint round the back of the shop to come out where he was coming out of the other end and stand guard of honour at the other end. About twelve or fourteen of us had been picked. I suppose we were called the blue-eyed boys. But there's one man in particular. He was a big lad, much bigger than the rest of us, he was a big fine lad. Harold Macmillan felt that he had to go and shake somebody's hand as he went down. So he shook Gerald's hand. We'd go out and when he came out again he'd go and shake his hand again, and he shook his hand about four or five times and nobody else's. But I'd got one in the end and I asked him for an autograph because he was talking and wandering about and I got his autograph. So that was quite a day. *(Gerald Morton)*

R&D was the showpiece for Head's and had lots of visiting dignitaries. I met Anthony Wedgwood Benn when he was Minister of Technology and he came round R&D and I was the welding engineer or trainee welding engineer in those days there. I was introduced to him, and he would have been accompanied by Sir John or Mr. Peter. *(Charlie Tighe)*

Wrightson family

There's no manufacturing industries here now. In Thornaby we had about five or six iron foundries and Head Wrightson's had Eaglescliffe Foundry, Stockton Forge, Stockton Steel, Head Wrightson Machine Company, Middlesbrough Works, Head Wrightson's Stampings at Seaton Carew. It was a good firm to work for. It was a happy atmosphere. Everybody knew everybody. I knew all the top lads and they knew me. Sir John Wrightson. And I even knew his father, Guy Wrightson.

What was he like then?

Oh if he saw a bolt he'd tell someone, 'Pick it up it's worth a penny that.' *(Fred Watson)*

One of the things Head Wrightson's were very keen on, Sir Guy in particular, was continuity. If a man worked in Head Wrightson's he loved it if his son worked in Head Wrightson's, and he liked that continuity. 'Oh I remember your grandfather.' I used to go round the works every Christmas with the Yard Manager, as he was then known, and Sir John. I used to pull people out for him to see and shake hands with and to wish them, 'A Happy Christmas'. That was done every year. Sir Guy in particular would say, 'I remember you, your grandfather worked here didn't he?' That was a highlight if he could meet people who had families who'd worked in Head Wrightson's. They believed a great deal in that because Sir Guy's attitude used to be, 'If I had a good man, that man's sons et cetera would be good as well,' and that was one of the things that he used to love to do every year. *(Maynard Wilson)*

Through Sir John Wrightson we joined the TA, and we got time off. Sir John Wrightson allowed you time off to go on the camps. I joined the TA just for extra money I think. I was in the Boys' Brigade at first and then I went into the Cadets and then the next step up was the TA so I was always into something. We got paid time off to go on a camp for two weeks. We went to Germany with the Regulars. The company was quite happy to let you have the time off for that. Sir John Wrightson was right into it. He said he didn't mind letting people off to do that. *(John Harding)*

It was very regimented then. Even some of the older clerks you called them, 'Mr.'. You didn't call them by their Christian name.

And what would you be called? Would you be called by your surname or your Christian name?

Well, often by your surname. For instance, Sir John Wrightson would often come over to the Stockton Forge and if the General Manager wasn't in his office he'd just stand in the passageway and bellow out, 'Wardell.' Oh yes, he didn't pick anybody passing by and say, 'Find Mr. Wardell for me.' He used to just stand in the passage and bellow, 'Wardell,' who was the General Manager.

If Sir John Wrightson did come in would you be expected to stand up?

We didn't stand up but we made sure we had our heads down. We also had Mr. Wilfred Wrightson, he was domiciled at the Forge. Now he was a different kettle of fish altogether. He was a quiet gentleman and very gentlemanly. *(Wilf Bradley)*

I thought Head Wrightson was a very good company to work for, very good indeed. It all

HW directors with the Mayor of Stockton, Claude Booth, outside the Thornaby canteen circa 1951. Also included are L-R second left, Mr. Peter Wrightson, Sir John Wrightson, Ald J.L.F McGann (Thornaby Council) Mr. Richard Miles. The five remaining gentlemen have not been identified. (HW Photographic Section)

stemmed from the man at the top, as it always does, so I have great admiration for Head's and Sir John Wrightson and John Eccles, and for the company. When Sir John retired I was asked to present him with a wood-turning lathe on behalf of the company. A garden party was held at the Friarage at Yarm to mark this occasion. *(Joe Doran)*

Old Sir Guy used to come round on his daily walkabout and he stood and watched me for ages. I was most embarrassed. I had little to do with him other than that personal experience. He used to do his walkabout and going down different sections. One of the things I gleaned was that he had an extremely good memory because he would challenge a foreman of the department who would show him round about a certain job, and the next time he came round he'd remembered what he asked him to do first time which hadn't been done. So he was a good strict man. Sir John was another more youthful version of Sir Guy. *(Bob Waller)*

There was a big commissionaire who was at the main entrance to the main offices. Can't remember his name now but Sir John always told him that when he was dropped off by the firm's car at the offices that the commissionaire had to make sure that nobody got in his way into the offices. One day a man called Wolfe, who was a general labourer, was sweeping the pavement and gutter outside the main entrance when Sir John arrived. He had to walk round this gent and on entering the offices he remarked to the commissionaire, 'It's your job to keep the Wolfe from the door.' *(Bob Irwin)*

We didn't have many instances where we met Sir John Wrightson but you did meet him at times such as Christmas time, he used to come round the shop floor. Sir John Wrightson and his buddies used to come round the shop floor and shake your hand and wish you, 'Merry Christmas.' But he kept his gloves on. *(Harry Foster)*

The funny thing about being at the Machine Company was that we were somewhat divorced from the rest of Head Wrightson's. It was strange, there was very little liaison. My wife and I did go to Sir John Wrightson's retirement garden party at the Friarage. I think we must have been representing the Machine Company that particular time. The retirement party was quite an occasion. It was in marquees on the lawn and there were lots of speeches. I think it was at the time that John Eccles was going to take over in one of the leading roles. I think this would be in the mid Seventies, probably about 1973, that sort of period I think. *(David Auld)*

I remember Cec Rounthwaite came to me and said, 'Sir John has to give a talk to some learned society or some industry association and wants some views on the increasing use of computers in industry. I would like you to write something for him.' So I did and he built whatever it was into his speech. He was very grateful for that. He came to see me afterwards.
He thanked me for it. I do remember he would come round at Christmas and shake the hands of those that he fed. That's when you got the real feeling of it being a family business.
It wasn't like the chief executive of a multinational business coming around, it was more personal.
I do remember going to his house at Neasham Hall, and this was when I was in R&D. We had this contract with this LKAB, a Swedish iron-ore mining company, and they were sending two of their directors over to set up the project. Sir John wasn't there but he was allowing us to use his home for entertaining these important visitors. We were in this panelled room, all nicely oak panelled, suit of armour and a huge fireplace and roaring fire, and we were plied with whatever it was you wanted, a gin and tonic, dry sherry, whatever your requirement was. And we were sitting chatting and then all of a sudden the wall opened, concealed doors, and the butler said, 'Gentlemen, dinner is served.' We all went into this alcove, which was bigger than most people's living room, and we were served food and wine and had a very pleasant evening. And to show you how things have moved on, I would have been probably in my mid twenties. That was the first time I had ever had scampi. Now you can get scampi anywhere and everywhere these days. I wasn't entirely sure what it was at the time. *(Barrie Hope)*

Anne and I went and photographed his house, which took three days. We produced a book for him. From then on I was referred to as 'Simpson'. Earlier on, I'd put some pictures into the Royal Albert Hall, that was a big exhibition for industry. We were the only one that got five accepted. The agreement was they would send these things back. I was so annoyed because they were being wrapped wrongly and they were battered a bit when they got back and I thought, 'I'm going to write to this chap,' and he was a Sir somebody. So I wrote back and said I was disgusted by the way, considering we were producing these free and everything totalled a considerable amount of money. Anyway he must have got really ratty so he wrote to Sir John. This man's complained about my attitude. Sir John was walking through one time and said, 'Ah Simpson, this guy has had a word with me and although I agree with you entirely - don't do it again.' *(Alan Simpson)*

Father was Peter, and he was the joint MD with his elder brother, Sir John, and he was very well loved. I have talked to quite a lot of people over the years and they were very, very fond of him. I think it was a very successful family business in that they chose everyone very beautifully and they were very hard working people. But, unlike some bosses, they did not run roughshod over them. It was a family business and they were very much part of that family business. They were employees but I think they were closer than that. They were very well looked after and I think that that wonderful feeling went both ways. My father and his brother appreciated the workforce and vice versa and this relationship worked beneficially.

And what were your father's particular skills?

Oh he was tremendous at selling. He used to do a lot of business abroad, and he was a great personality. He found it very easy to talk to people. Very easy to convey his enthusiasm and he was very knowledgeable. *(Simon Wrightson)*

Chapter 8

'The social side was excellent': benefits and facilities

In common with other paternalistic firms, Head Wrightson offered its employees a varied package of benefits for much of its history. A small weekly contribution funded the activities of the Works Council which organised a wide range of benefits and faculties. Medical treatment and recuperation, for example, was provided at Manor House Hospital in London or Ropner Convalescent Home at Middleton-one-Row. There was also a small hardship grant available for employees who were absent from work for a period of four weeks. The Works Council were also keen to support sporting and social facilities.

Teesdale Park included a bowling green, two football pitches, three tennis courts and a cricket pitch, pavilions and changing accommodation. Inter-departmental sporting competitions were a regular feature of life at Head Wrightson. An annual pantomime treat for all children of employees was also funded as well as day trips for pensioners. Furthermore, employees of Head Wrightson had access to a pension scheme which offered sickness benefits and death grants.

In the following oral memories our contributors share their feelings about the benefits, facilities and social life they enjoyed through their employment at Head Wrightson.

Opening of the Tennis Pavilion at Teesdale Park in 1938 by Mrs. W. Wrightson, (with bouquet) Mr. Wilfred Wrightson (brother of Sir Guy Wrightson) is to her right. The Tennis Pavilion later became the Bowling Pavilion. (Remembering Thornaby Group)

Members of the Senior Staff Guild at a garden party at Neasham Hall the home of Sir John Wrightson circa 1952. (Photograph supplied by Mrs. Hope)

Senior Staff Guild

My father, Les Bell, was the senior of the section and a member of the Senior Staff Guild. I don't really know much about the Guild. I'm not sure whether it was a management tool or simply a social body. They did organize visits to other firms and had social outings. I remember mother's delight in getting dressed up when they were invited to Sir John's garden parties.

And who would go to them?

Well, all the senior members of staff and their partners I would think. The directors, the senior heads of department and people like that. *(Margaret Hope)*

There was the Senior Staff Guild; one of the stalwarts of it was George Wilkes. I was asked to join the Senior Staff Guild. I think as you became section leader, manager or director you were entitled to be in it. I actually became President of the Senior Staff Guild for several years. We used to organise various things. One of them was a coach load of us to go up to Lumley Castle for a medieval banquet. We used to organise events in the grounds of the Friarage. There would be bowls, archery, which when you think of that in these days of risk assessments, there were these proper arrows and targets and arrows flying around. And quizzes, we used to organise them. Sometimes it would be teams from PEL and teams from R&D and we'd meet in a local pub and we'd have a primitive buzzer system. So there was all that sort of thing going on. We tried to organise treasure hunts. I think we had twelve car treasure hunts. I don't think we had what I would call a great social network at Head Wrightson's but we did have some. *(Barrie Hope)*.

Catering

One of the things that I found when I arrived at Head Wrightson was that I would lunch in the management mess. At the Friarage at the outset there were three layers of lunch. One for the staff, which wasn't particularly well used I think. They preferred to go to the pubs in Yarm. The management mess in

Opening day, 1957, of a hostel (now the Clairville Hotel, Eaglescliffe) for HW staff living away from home. Included in the photograph are Ronnie Purnell, Frank Shepherd, Bill Hutchinson, Mr. & Mrs. Miles, Bob Sturges. (Wright Ahead)

which I ate, the Deputy Chief Accountant was President of the Mess. I think that's what he was called. Finally, the directors' dining room. The directors ate in the dining room in the house. The rest of us ate at one end or the other of an outhouse as it were. We didn't have the key to the executive washroom, and I don't know whether that's just apocryphal or not but certainly it was hierarchal. On the main site in Thornaby there were in fact five levels of dining. There was the works canteen, the staff, the senior staff, the management, which was the layer that I would have been at, and the directors. In fact two things happened food wise. Because of the staff at Yarm eating in the village that facility was closed and the management mess moved into the house and was served from the same kitchen as the directors. And one thing that happened, of course, was that whereas in the management mess we got bottled beer, the directors had at Yarm an anteroom where they met before lunch and had a drink. If ever I was over in Thornaby meeting a client with someone from the subsidiary we would eat and drink with them and there would be the drinks available. *(David Jowett)*

But to be fair, at the bottom end of the shop there was always an urn with hot water in and if any of us felt that we wanted a drink we used to go down, make ourselves a pot of tea and have it. But you never stopped your job. And the only concession was if Bob Snowden came round, and especially if he had a visitor, we used to put the tea out of the way. Out of sight. But we never knocked off for a break; there was no official knocking off time. *(Les Ellis)*

You just had your lunch break and I think when I first started you used to have an hour for dinner. You didn't have any breaks morning or afternoon. We weren't supposed to and if you were caught you were in bother.

Did you manage to sneak a one then?

Oh yes, every day you did. You found some time. We had a little cage which was for keeping stuff in and us lads used to use that. I don't know what the fellows did but that's what we used to do. So we always managed to get an unofficial break. We had a gas ring they'd set up themselves. A bit of pipe with a gas ring on and it boiled water. I cannot remember whether it was in a pan or a kettle but that's what we used to do. *(Derek Delahaye)*

They were good meals. I don't suppose they were anything exceptional. But they were adequate hot meals. The canteen was well patronised, there was plenty of people got in. You had to get in there promptly. You had to make sure you got your dinner in time. *(Eddie Burridge)*

When we got into management later, we got the key to a particular toilet and that was for the management and we had our own key. It was the same for the eating arrangements. Twenty years later when I was Chief Draughtsman, as part of the management team, we used to have our own management mess, which I remember it being decorated and the manageress was a woman called Mrs. Astle. She had it all decorated in red, the management mess. I remember John Eccles coming in and saying, 'God,' he says 'it looks like a high-class brothel.' He had that changed. But that was the management mess and the standard of food there was good considering the time, the war. But when I was an apprentice we used to go in the works canteen, but we had a special table reserved purely and simply for the cleanliness. In other words, we were in office things. And the chaps in the dirty overalls would be sat at a different table but got the same food. I remember Mrs. Astle would call, 'Anybody who wants seconds?' And the apprentices were always hungry. The apprentices would dash up, and it was time and time again, jam roly-poly. *(Ray Shaw)*

We had a menu for the week, a different meal every day but there was no choice each day. Obviously, the directors had different to what the men had. For the workmen you'd plate up the meal whereas the directors, they would be served in tureens. They would have the table set with glasses of water. They could have alcohol in one part, you know, they used to be able to have a drink.

It must have been hectic though. How many men were you putting through, how many meals?

I'd say about a 150 on the men's side and maybe about 40 sometimes on the management side. It was brilliant because you built up, then it was wind down. Then once all the men were served and all the directors were out of the way we would sit and have our lunch. The men only had about forty-two minutes so it was quite hectic. They used to have dinner tickets. There was a little takeaway hut where you made sausage buns, bacon buns and egg buns and they used to come there on a morning to buy their sandwiches. So instead of coming into the canteen during the morning they used the little shop. It sold sweets and drinks and we used to take trays of sausage sandwiches down, bacon sandwiches, egg sandwiches into the actual little office and they all used to come over and buy them. They used to have their orders, say, for one shed or the other shed. Then they used to have vending machines as well. We used to go over and fill them on an afternoon, and in the offices they used to have vending machines there. I started work at eight o'clock and worked till four. It was a fairly long day but it went quickly. *(Barbara Mifrej)*

Teesdale works canteen opened on Monday 24th September 1951. (Wright Ahead)

I do remember the Thornaby Bridge Yard, which was a huge place. When it came to tea time this chap gave me a tin thingy with a cup on the top of it and inside was condensed milk, tea and sugar. He said, 'Go to the urn over there or round that column and fill it up.' I thought, 'Well if I'm going to learn anything from him, I'm going to have to do this otherwise I'll upset him.' I went round, and this urn, I kid you not, it was encrusted and it was bubbling away merrily. There was a bit of a queue and I was thinking, 'Is this water alright?' But the tea it was beautiful. *(Ted Sinnot)*

Tell me about the canteen at the Stampings in those days?
There were four of them. Four canteens we had. In the early days it was almost a nonstop canteen because they served you with breakfast in the mornings. You'd have a break from nine to nine thirty, you had your breakfast and a cup of tea. I'll work up the tree. There was the staff dining room and staff canteen, which was generally works staff. So you had the guys who would work at the Forge, you had the guys who worked in the Fitting Shop, that sort of level. Next to that where reception is now, that area was known as the junior management dining room. Who on earth were junior management? And then the table we're sat at now, which was in the conference room downstairs, was the senior management dining room, and that was silver service when I came. You had a very nice lady dressed in black and white who would serve you every day. *(Jim Matthews)*

Sports

I played football, cricket, bowls, darts and I got involved in all of them. First in the Machine Shop, played for the Machine Shop, the football team in 1968 when we won the cup. We beat Stampings 3-1 and that was a terrific game, a terrific night and in the club. I was only twenty but I had a skin full. I don't know how I got home yet. And then when I went in the Bridge Yard we formed our own team and came away from it. I played cricket for the Maintenance. I never got into the elite team in the Machine Shop because there were some good cricketers there. Canny team the Machine Shop. The club, the whole site, was just a nice size. You had the two levels and down below you had the cricket, there were tennis courts down there. Up above you had a different level; you had the two football pitches up there. I think it was a good little layout. The actual club itself which was on the top level of the entrance in that was a nice sized club, it wasn't overly big and gave a good atmosphere. *(Derek Proctor)*

The social side was excellent. Can't remember how many years I played in the football tournaments and the cricket tournaments at Teesdale Park at Thornaby. There were a couple of football pitches. There was a cricket pitch. I think there was a bowls rink and a tennis court. And the social club itself. There was a couple of times where we actually invited major customers down and had a day of playing cricket or football or whatever against the major customers we had. *(Barry Davison)*

I was in the tennis section. Mrs. Lonsdale oversaw the sports scene and each sport had a secretary. I was looking after the tennis. So I was the tennis clerk.
Did you play tennis?
Yes. Not very good. I have a handicapped left arm from birth. I had to serve the ball with my right and hit it using the same hand.
How big was the tennis section?
Oh, it was canny when it came to the end. I used to arrange the draw for the tennis tournament. We used to play with places up at Skelton. Just arrange things like that. *(Colin Fletcher)*

There were quite a lot of anglers down at Middlesbrough and I used to ring or get the Personnel Manager of Middlesbrough to ring the Personnel Manager up at Thornaby to ask Sir John Wrightson if we could go and fish on his water because he lived up at Neasham Hall. He had a stretch of river. We used to go up there. There used to be about twenty or thirty of us go and have a little competition. I used to try and organise it once a year. Then it just petered out. *(Dick Robinson)*

We had Head Wrightson's Club at Teesdale Park. They had a nice club there and we used to have inter-departmental cricket teams. Bowling. Yes, we enjoyed it. I played for Head Wrightson's football team for about fourteen years. We had a good football team.
And did the company allow you to have time off for any of that?
For the departmentals, yes. If I was on two till ten and I was playing for the Machine Shop

Head Wrightson Sports Ground Teesdale Park. (Wright Ahead)

Thornaby Foundry inter-departmental football team. (Photograph supplied by J. Harding)

they would allow me time off, or if I was playing for Head Wrightson's, they'd say, 'Right.' If I was on two till ten and I was playing football, they'd let me go at, say, six o'clock if it was a night match. I'd probably come back about nine, after the match and then work till ten. Oh yes, they were good at that. *(Dennis Johnson)*

Goodness gracious, the sports side of the company was fantastic. They ran football inter-departmentals, cricket inter-departmentals, bowls inter-departmentals, tennis tournaments, everything. They used to have somebody in the company who'd be the secretary of that particular section and they would go to the sports fund, because we all paid from our wages into a sports fund, and get money. *(John Heath)*

We turned a full team out of North Yorks & South Durham League cricketers one year. Everybody had played in NYSD League. Harry Thompson who played for Norton and Durham. Gus Williamson played for Norton and Northants. Dickie Spooner played for Norton, Thornaby and Warwickshire. Alan Townsend played for Thornaby and Warwickshire. George Lannon, Synthonia. Myself, Thornaby, Billy Robson, Stockton, John Hunter, Stockton. Tommy Reece was the only one that hadn't played in the league and he was Synthonia centre-half. The departmental was a farce. It was just a matter of turning up. *(Norman Toulson)*

We had our own club at Head Wrightson's and sports facilities. Football fields and tennis courts, which Davy duly sold off, which theoretically in my opinion they had no right to. I think it's Stockton Football Club now. Because we all contributed to it, only pence a week out of your salary but at least in my book you had a shareholding in it and theoretically they had no right to sell it. But they did and got away with it. *(Barry Preece)*

I was always involved in the sports. I'd play anything from football, cricket, whatever came up I'd have a go. Bowls, old man's marbles if you want to call it that. I used to get involved with anything that was going, sports wise. In every department, from being in the Apprentice School to going to the Bridge Yard,

Head Wrightson cricket team circa 1950s. L-R Back row: unknown, Norman Treeby, unknown, Arnold Wells, unknown. Front row: Alf Watson, unknown, Arthur Herron, Harry Wilson and Les Wilson. (Photograph courtesy Les Wilson)

every department that you went to all had a team of whatever the case may be, and you represented that department that you were in at the time. I used to enjoy the different bits of fun we used to have with the sports or a bit of competitiveness and stuff like that. There was a fishing club I think, which you can call a sport I suppose. There used to be a lot of lads into angling. There was the Head Wrightson Club, a social club where they used to go and play darts or whatever and have a drink, socializing. *(Dennis Longstaff)*

I played football in Head Wrightson's. I was very keen on football as a youngster, and when I went in I was playing football for Billingham Synthonia and I continued with that when I worked for Head Wrightson. The only time I played football for Head Wrightson was in the inter-departmental competitions each year. But I owe Head Wrightson's an awful lot in relationship to what's happened after I left. I worked for Head Wrightson, played football for the department but, as I was saying, I was playing football for Billingham Synthonia. When I was sixteen or seventeen I damaged the tendons in my ankles and I was going to Stockton and Thornaby Hospital twice a week to have electric treatment or some form of electronic treatment on my ankles. The surgeon said to me one day, he said, 'Can I give you some advice young man? I would stop playing football now if I were you. Because whilst they're okay, in a couple of years' time you're going to find yourself riddled with arthritis or something of this nature, so take heed of what I'm saying.' So once again I decided to stop playing football when I was eighteen. The company had a former Football League referee on the place called Alec Brown, another prominent referee called Harry Bage, and we had two or three other referees in there. And when I saw Alec Brown he was always saying, 'Take up refereeing, take up refereeing.' I said, 'No, I'm not interested, I'm quite happy to go and watch Middlesbrough play or watch Billingham Synthonia play.' Anyway, this went on for two years and I finally succumbed and I said, 'Okay to get you off my back I'll take this referee's course, I'll take the exam and I'll prove to you that I can't do it,' and for fifty odd years I've proved that I couldn't do it. Head

Wrightson were the instigators of me starting out in refereeing. If it hadn't have been for Head Wrightson, whether or not I'd have been in the position that I've found myself in, I don't honestly know. But I owe them an awful lot. *(Pat Partridge)*

We had the tennis courts and the initial tennis courts were next to the bowling green and some years ago somebody said, 'Oh have you been to Head's? They've got a sports ground.' And it was luxurious, equivalent to what they've got at Rockliffe Hall, by comparison. It had wonderful bowling greens. I mean they used to play county matches and everything. We had county players and England players at bowls. The football field was alongside. It was the guy who laid Ayresome Park in those days also did the one for Head Wrightson's. If you could play football that was the place to be. Anyway, they decided that we would have a new pavilion, a brick one. Up to then we'd had a wooden one, like a hen-house shed which did for the football and did for the cricketers but they decided no, we would have a new one. *(Bob Close)*

Pensions

It was a good firm but it was poorly paid. When I first started down there do you know how much a week I got? Ten bob in old money. Four pence off for a stamp. Nine and eight pence. When I got turned twenty-one, of course, it was a condition of employment that you joined the Superannuation Scheme. You couldn't contract yourself out, you had to join. February 1947 I went in, anyhow. I finished in fifty-six so it will tell you how many years I was in it. But after a while they started paying for overtime. *(Fred Watson)*

There was a pension scheme. One for the works and a better one for the staff. The works scheme was an improvement on the State Additional Pension Scheme but not really a good one. It was proportional to what we paid. Pensions never seemed to be a high priority in the works. *(Albert Roxborough)*

There was a works scheme, a staff scheme and an executive. The works scheme was not very good. The staff scheme, was in those days. I mean, decent occupational pension schemes didn't come into being until the late Fifties anyway, so they hadn't been going all that long. But an interesting observation I made in Pensions was that when we used to set up pensions for staff, the people that appreciated what we did for them more than anybody else were the workmen and they used to bring things like chocolates to the girls. None of the big guys did, *(Peter French)*

At first at Head Wrightson, the pension scheme was a money purchase scheme. You paid so much a week and that earned you so much pension. But then it was changed to a final-salary scheme, in present day parlance. But they were both fairly good schemes. At one stage we were proposing to introduce a final-salary scheme for the hourly-paid people. And it's amazing that their reaction to that is they were dead against it; they thought we were going to have the worst pensions. Now in today's world, you'd never believe that, because things were different. The trouble with these pension schemes is when you looked at the money purchase amount it looked absolutely wonderful, for working for forty years you got all that money. But of course, in forty years, inflation would have been roaring away and I don't think there was any index-linking on the amounts you'd be paid. You just got a sum of money. The money went up from year to year, of course, but it didn't compensate for the previous years such as a final-salary scheme would do. It was a very good scheme. Nowadays, employers are stopping these schemes because they can't afford them. *(Joe Doran)*

Long Service Awards

We had a do for our twenty-five years' service. I got a watch for that. And for forty years' I got that.

A table?

I had to go and pick it. I got it at Debenhams in Stockton.

So you could choose what you wanted?

Israel 'Tutty' Smith upon his retirement after working an astounding 73 years at Head's. Richard Miles presents him with a clock. Others present include Col. Francis, Mr. Hickman, Frank Shepherd and Peter Wrightson. (Wright Ahead)

Yes. Up to a certain figure. If it was any extra you had to put it in. But everybody got a watch for twenty-five years'. We had a good do and the chappie who presented us with the watches, John Eccles, came down to Head Wrightson's and he was one of the top lads. He presented the watches at that do. *(Fred Watson)*

How long were you at Heads?
Thirty-three years.
Did you get anything for that?
Got a watch at twenty-five years. I've still got it. It's an automatic watch. They had reduced the qualification from forty years to twenty-five and there was a mass presentation because there were a lot of people got it all at once. Not sure whether I was in the first batch or the second. Previously the awards were for forty or fifty years' service.
Where was that?
The Marton Country Club. I think that's where it was. Yes, I'm sure it was Marton Country Club we went to. We had a dinner dance and a presentation. *(Jim Heward)*

Did you qualify for any long-term service award?
Yes. I've a watch upstairs which I'm still wearing. It was a twenty-five years' service award but I got that when I'd done about thirty-seven years. Then, of course, they had a forty-year service award. For the twenty-five years everybody got a watch. For the forty years they gave you a voucher which you could spend in about two places, one of them was H Samuel's. The sum wasn't that great. I can't quite remember how much they gave us for the forty years. It was something like an eighty-pound voucher. You had to spend it at H Samuel's. We got wine glasses and a decanter. We've still got them. *(Wilf Bradley)*

They'd always given out forty-year watches and fifty-year clocks for long-service employees.
Well you had to be old to get a watch, even older to get a clock. Then we managed to negotiate and get it down to twenty-five years for a watch. And it's strange, we were in this period of economic uncertainty and low orders and yet they agreed to recognise twenty-five years' service with a watch. They held a dinner for the recipients and the wives, where the watches were presented with a main-board Davy director present.
So before that did they have ceremonies?
Oh yes, they'd always held forty and fifty-year presentations but with much smaller ceremonies for a handful of people, the

awards being presented probably by Sir John Wrightson. There would be photos and a short report in the company magazine - *Wright Ahead*. *(Albert Roxborough)*

Retirement

My dad got a twenty five-year presentation. He was erecting out on a job with a big derrick crane. Well, the chain snapped on the job. The chain flew and took the top of his head off. He had a steel plate put in his head. Well, they gave him a job for life. Looking at his papers after he died I think he got a hundred pounds but they give him a job for life. But in the meantime, the war had started and he joined the Army again because he'd been in the Army when he was a young lad. Of course, when they found out about his steel plate after six months they threw him out. So Head Wrightson's took him straight back on. Into his job again. He never broke his service and they give him a twenty-five year watch. *(Rodney Crosbie)*

One thing about Head Wrightson you haven't mentioned, there was no compulsory retirement age at Head Wrightson. You could go on working as long as you wanted, as long as you were still able to do the job. You didn't have to retire and so we just had to persuade people to retire because they were too old. I remember the oldest one I came across was at the Head Wrightson Iron Foundry at seventy-seven, still working there every day and quite happily. But we managed to persuade him to retire. He thought it was about time he packed it in. *(Joe Doran)*

Social life

I remember a Christmas party and Major Miles came down to cut the cake and he brought his ceremonial sword with him and he cut the cake with the sword. He said, 'I wish you all a jolly happy Christmas. I hope you all have a very good time and behave yourselves.' And this voice from the back shouted out, 'Make your mind up,' which of course caused immense amusement, but I don't think he understood quite what he'd said. *(Gerald Morton)*

Head Wrightson Drama Group entertaining for Hungarian Relief, early 1957. L-R Eddie Dunne, Ian Griffiths, Edna Farriday, Barry Curson, Don Raper. (Wright Ahead)

They had their own drama group. Like the Court Players. They used to put plays on at Head Wrightson's. You know they had the canteen down at Head Wrightson's in Thornaby which was a massive place. They used to use it. They had a dance hall down there. Oh, and they had a dance hall up at where the sports field is. All Head Wrightson's works employed about 5,000 and a lot of them had been there all their lives. *(Fred Watson)*

We did have one celebration at the Forge, I can't remember what year it was. We were all apprentices and somebody got the idea of having a works party and they arranged it with the apprentices at St Luke's Hall. Well you know what it was like for rationing and so on. Mrs. Astle, the canteen manageress, and all the canteen lasses were all invited. She used to make cakes and things and she'd put a dozen or so to one side and then the next day she'd get them out and put two dozen on one side and she built up a stock. And that supplied us. We had quite a good show down there. *(Les Ellis)*

I think there was a very good social life. I don't know whether it was just for the Fitting Shop or which department it was but he did play bowls and he won a little silver cup of which he was very proud. They also had a swimming club based at Thornaby Baths. I think that started just after the war. They had dances every Christmas at the hall on Teesdale and every so often the Senior Staff Guild used to gather at Neasham Hall, home of their boss and have a nice garden party. *(Kath Riley)*

We used to go for a pint sometimes. After working Sunday mornings we might all go for a pint somewhere in the Telstar, the Billingham Social Club. You used to meet up with workmates and things like that. We used to have a little social, what we call 'smokers', every so often. If anyone retired or anything like that we'd all get together. And since our days at Head Wrightson's finished there's been one or two reunions where different people have organised a reunion at a venue. *(Tony Lodge)*

Even on a dinner-time I remember we used to go to the Collingwood and have a pie and peas and a pint, sometimes two pints. You shouldn't really be drinking and going back to work. But everybody did it and I think everybody knew it happened. *(Steve Featherstone)*

We had a good time. Anything we wanted we got. We decided to start up a dramatic society and straight away they gave us so much money to start it up. Just after the war we thought we'd have a young people's club so we decided we'd go to Whitley Bay for a day. All the young people from Teesdale. So of course, Frank Shepherd told Mr. Miles about it, 'Oh,' he said, 'we'll pay for the buses and we'll pay for them a lunch.' And there were ever so many bus loads of us and they paid for us a lunch. It was just after the war because you know there used to be canteens in each town for people to go in, I forget what they called them now, and that's where we had our lunch at Whitley Bay. Even when some of the men wanted to start the work's band Frank Shepherd went and told Mr. Miles and he said, 'If they get sufficient men to form a band we'll buy them a uniform each,' which they did. That was not long after the war that the work's band started up, and they used to play at all the functions. It was quite a successful band. *(Enid Thurlwell)*

Frank Shepherd was the Personnel Manager. He was very much a doer. But he enjoyed doing things and he got this drama group and once upon a time I was stage manager for it. It was quite a good group and we used to meet in what became known as Shepherd's Hall, which was the new canteen block that was built in Trafalgar Street. *(Bob Waller)*

We collected so much a week, and this was on top of what we paid for Head Wrightson's grounds. I think you had a penny stopped out of your wages and that paid for the grounds. There was a very good bowling green. There was the cricket pitch, there was a football pitch and that all helped to pay for that and a groundsman. And on top of that we used to all put away just a little bit ourselves and every so often we would have a trip away. I know one particular year we saved up and we went to York races. For some unknown reason we got into a rhythm and we always went to Blackpool for the lights. So we went Friday night. As soon as you finished work everybody shot out, went home, got bathed. We went to Blackpool on the Friday night and you had Saturday and Sunday morning. Then you were back home again on Sunday afternoon. We made it so that we put a bit extra in and then you could take your wives or your girlfriends or whatever it was at that time. *(Trevor Briggs)*

They used to have some good dances and social events like that in Head Wrightson's canteen. They used to have a big hall there. It was a good hall as well, with a bar and canteen facilities so you could have a full dinner or whatever. There was some very good catering done there, some very good catering. In fact I had my wedding reception there. But we've had some very good nights in the Head's hall. Very good nights. So yes, there was a good social life. We used to have Christmas parties and things like that. *(Barry Preece)*

After the war finished the firm held a dinner dance every year around Christmas time at the Palais Ballroom in Skinner Street and this was attended by Sir John and Mr. Peter with their wives, also Mr. Rodney and Mr. Oliver. They mixed well with the staff and these dances were really enjoyable and always well attended. *(Norma Pelmear)*

I was only in the motor club side of things. This was something that started up in the 1960s. We went on car rallies and met through social events and committee meetings. We had a badge to stick on the front of the car. We had probably twenty or thirty members and we would combine with some of the other local motor clubs to organise an event. *(David Auld)*

We had a staff dance which was for the whole Teesdale staff. It was a dinner I think, at the Kirklevington Club. I remember we went up and they had a gambling room, roulette and what have you, and they went in there and played the roulette. It was for wives and partners as well. There were spot prizes, late transport and a late bar. Dancing was eight till one. There was a live band and it was probably a Christmas event as it was on the twentieth of December. There were quite a few of these staff dances, some at the Kirk, and I think we went to the Swan in Billingham. I have a photograph somewhere of the children's party. It was in the canteen and I've got a photograph somewhere of all the kids and they must have had a magician or somebody because they're all sitting, looking at the stage. We used to have pantomimes as well and my bairns went. They're in their fifties now. We could sit anywhere, the earliest there got the best seats. I think the last one they had was at Billingham Forum. *(Norman Metcalfe)*

That was when Head Wrightson's used to go to the pantomimes. They used to book the whole theatre for one afternoon performance and all employees were entitled to free tickets for their children and mothers. The people who ran the welfare, they were asked to go down just to make sure everything was okay. *(Trevor Briggs)*

Transport

Kelly's Ferry brought many people to work. They used to come across to work in a boat and he used to row it. But he worked with us. He was injured in the Battle of the Somme. He used to talk to me and tell me all his experiences and it was great. *(Rodney Crosbie)*

I used to bike until I had a car. In 1976 I passed my test and I got myself a car but up till then I used to get either the bus there or I used to get a lift with people, or pushbike or whatever. Sometimes I used to walk it if was a decent day. *(Tony Lodge)*

Seaton Carew was quite a difficult place to get to. On a Monday morning you got the 69 bus to the Transporter, which was the United, and then from there you got the Hartlepool Corporation bus to work. After that there was a work's bus on. Took you home at five o'clock and picked you up on the following Tuesday, Wednesday, Thursday, Friday mornings. *(Fred Britton)*

Due to living in Stockton and with the wages office being at the bottom of Trafalgar Street, I used Jimmy Kelly's ferry to get to work instead of getting a bus to Thornaby railway station and then walking the whole length of Trafalgar Street. There was a set of staithes at the bottom of Thistle Green leading to the river's edge from where you got onto his row boat and after alighting from the boat on the Thornaby side it was just a very short walk to our office. Jimmy was from a well-known Portrack family and used to come into our office for a drink of tea. At the end of the week I used to give him Woodbines in lieu of my ferry fare. He did a lot of work on the river, being retained by many businesses along the river, and he also knew the best side of the river to bring ashore any dead bodies he found! One day my boss Mr. Vickers, looking out of the window, said, 'Look here, Jimmy's towing a tanker.' In fact it was a tanker which was being brought to the Shipping & Salvage Company's wharf and it had a tow line from its bow attached to Jimmy's row boat, but in fact whilst it seemed he was towing the tanker, the tide was bringing the boat up and he was merely keeping the bow pointing in the right direction. *(Don Raper)*

I rode to Thornaby all the time on my bike. I couldn't afford bus fares. Bikes weren't dear like they are now of course. But my mam bought me a bike. We could take them into the Fitting Shop. We'd take it inside. But there was a bike shed outside, at the back of the offices actually. You could put your bike there but we used to take ours in. A lot of us used to keep them on the landing at the top end near the door. *(Thomas Wilson)*

Kelly's Ferry ran from the bottom of Trafalgar Street across the River Tees to Thistle Green, as it was called, in Stockton. My recollection of this was that men used to use Kelly's Ferry to go home and sometimes for lunchtime but certainly morning and night. They got a pass for a week for a few coppers less than it would cost for the whole of the week going single journeys. On a Saturday morning Mrs. Kelly and somebody helping her, one of her boys, had to stop fellows walking over those days to get back. They were dodging paying for the week. They were the true British working men. If there was room you sat, and if it was full you stood up. Kelly rowed you across. He wouldn't make a great deal of money but he was a hard working fellow was Kelly. *(Bob Waller)*

I mean in those days there was not many people had cars. A few had motorbikes but it was mainly push bikes. When I used to leave work you'd get to the end of Bridge Road and there was a policeman on point duty and it

Jimmy Kelly with his boat. (Photograph courtesy Evening Gazette Media Company (GMC) Middlesbrough)

was like the mass start of the French Tour de France. He was very melodramatic about it, he would hold his hand up to stop the traffic coming over the bridge, stop it coming out of Thornaby Road, and then he'd point at the bikes, and then he'd wave us all out. It was just a mass going out, right to go over the bridge, straight across to go up Thornaby Road. *(Jim Heward)*

I can tell you about Jimmy Kelly. He was self-employed on the river and he used to get retainers from different people who had premises that went down to the riverside, which was Head Wrightson's, the Malleable and others, and his main retainer was the river authority. They kept falling off and at the finish I think the river authority weren't bothered with him any more because what he used to do was to keep the river clean of anything that was floating, because it was tidal and the ships used to come up. Head Wrightson's needed him so they employed him as a boatman at the beginning but he finished up in the Erection Yard, where they used to send the stuff on to sites. At the end of Trafalgar Street he used to pick up there when you were leaving or dropping off when you were going into work. There was like a board, a thing that you walked on. You didn't get your feet wet. But about Jimmy Kelly, he used to pull the people out of the river when they'd drowned. If they weren't found straight away he'd know the day that they would come up and the place that they would come up in, because he knew how the currents ran in the river. He never took them over to the Stockton side. He always brought them to the Thornaby side because at the Thornaby side he used to get seven and six per body. At the Stockton side he used to get five shillings. I can remember once one of his tales was he went up to Yarm and it was high tide, and this person who'd committed suicide was left in a tree. So he rowed up and made sure that his boat was underneath the body, he cut him down to land in the boat. And of course, when he landed in the boat he burst wide open. But the thing was we said to him afterwards, 'Jimmy why did you go so far up there?' He says, 'Well, I knew he was in his pyjamas and I was going on holiday and I wanted a pair.' He was a character, you know. *(Bob Irwin)*

One memory of Head Wrightson's at Ironworks was everybody, but everybody, used to go to work on a bike. They used to have the RAF rucksacks with a pump in and they would take the pump off the bike, everything valuable was taken off the bike and all the bikes were in racks. It's all changed now; everybody goes to work with cars now. So I used to cycle from Stokesley in the summer, and in the winter I would go on the bus because it was inclement weather *(Michael Waring)*

Trafalgar Street at coming out time was an eye-opener. In the early Fifties and Sixties at four o'clock the whistle blew, that was your finishing time, everybody clocked off. And then, well you've seen anthills where the ants just parade, well that was Head Wrightson's at clocking-off time. You had to keep on the pavement because you'd get run over by the bicycles on the road, because there were hardly any cars, they all rode bicycles. If you could have seen that at four o'clock, that really was an eye-opener. *(Harry Foster)*

We had Jimmy Kelly, the ferry man, and we used to borrow his boat to go over to Stockton at lunch time for shopping or whatever. He didn't charge us. If anybody wanted to go over we'd row over. But there was a lad one day from R&D, Research and Development, which was at the back of the engineers. He got in the boat one day, pushed off and the ebb tide was going down and he was off. We couldn't get him back and there were blokes standing alongside the river throwing hand lines to him. They had to get Jimmy Kelly and Jimmy knew what was going to happen and where it was going to land. He got it and we had to tow it back up to the site. It was quite a strong tide. Jimmy used to find bodies regular in the Tees. He got ten shillings if it was the Thornaby side and five shillings if it was the Stockton side, and he used to tow them over to Thornaby to pull them out to get the extra bob or two. Possibly every six months they would find a body in the Tees. Jimmy Kelly came to work with us in Erection. He used to help with the loading up and offloading. This was after he stopped running the ferry but he still had the boats there. In fact they're probably still down there. They'll be rotten now because they were getting a bit passed it then. *(Norman Metcalfe)*

Sickness

If you were really ill and you needed an operation there was a hospital down in London, Manor House. Some lads used to go down for operations and we used to pay a shilling a week into it. For recuperating and everything. It was good. We paid a shilling a week into it. Everybody paid. Didn't have an option, it was taken out of your money. It was a good thing. Alright, people might think, 'Well, why should I pay, I'll never use it?' But you don't know when you'll want to use it. They had families as well. It included them, yes. It was a good thing. But you don't know when it's going to happen. *(Dennis Johnson)*

There was so much a week taken out of your pay for the welfare committee and that money accumulated so that if anybody was off on sick for a length of time, if they needed any help they could give them a little. The shop stewards really looked after it. You know they did a lot of work. But you see they were very amiable people, they weren't troublemakers like you hear about today. Everybody seemed to get on well together. *(Enid Thurlwell)*

Eventually, the company introduced a sickness scheme. And all employees paid so much a week into the Works Welfare Fund which was set up and overseen by the Works Councils but administered by the company. So much of that went to Manor House Hospital in London where employees could go for medical treatment. And some employees went to Manor House for an operation which was quicker than waiting for an NHS bed. Also part of the contributions went to the Ropner Convalescent Home in Middleton-one-Row where employees could apply to go for convalescence after an illness. And part of the money helped to pay for Teesdale Park. Then there was also a scheme where if you were off work for a month you could get paid four pounds. Individual shop stewards used to look after that. I did it for the Machine Shop, by going to the cashier with a chit saying so and so's been off for a month and claims his four pounds. The cashier would give you the four pounds and then you'd pass it on to them. I mean four pounds was nothing compared to the money lost by being on the sick but some people thought it was their entitlement. They'd have a month off so they'd get the four pounds out of the system. *(Albert Roxborough)*

Housing

They opened up a small section of Neasham Hall as a guesthouse for important visitors. I went up there to have a look round. Then they had a staff hostel on Yarm Road that they started up. When we were starting up research and development in nuclear power they decided it would be a good idea to have this hostel where people could stay until they got into the area. That was right next to the golf course, it's a hotel now at Stockton. Head Wrightson's bought that and turned it into a hostel for senior staff people. *(Enid Thurlwell)*

But the other thing you could have if you were buying a house, Head Wrightson's would loan you two hundred pounds as your deposit for your mortgage, and indeed we took advantage of that and bought our first little middle-terraced house in Acklam. It was interest-free, and I can't remember how long we had to pay it back. I think it must have been quite a decent time because we never felt pressured that it was a huge amount of money we had to pay back. Now whether that offer of two hundred pounds went to men and women I can't really remember that. But I know that was taken out of Don's salary but it must have been over a period of time. *(Wendy Heald)*

They arranged for anybody that was interested to come down on a day visit with their wives and girlfriends, whatever the case may be, and that's what happened. I think they had a full coach load of people coming down. We all came down by train to Darlington and they met us at Darlington and the coach took us to Teesside Airport. They gave us our lunch and then took us round the area and showed what the area was like and then took us into the factory and showed us what the factory was like. Then they took us back to Darlington to get on the train.
Did they provide you with any housing when you got down here?
Yes. This house here. I think they must have applied to the Council that they were bringing down qualified people and we were allocated houses through the Council. We were allocated this as a council-house and then later on I took out a mortgage and paid the mortgage off and the house is my own now. *(Jack Hare)*

There was a time that I went to a place at Eaglescliffe, near the golf course. The Claireville? That's before it was the hotel. Head Wrightson's bought it and at that time they were bringing people in from all over the place to work there in Research and Development. They made that into a lodging house for them. *(Bob Irwin)*

Chapter 9

'I felt as if I was doing something for the war effort': Head Wrightson at war

Engineering companies clearly had an important role to play in the government's armaments programme in the Second World War. Head Wrightson's war-time products included munitions such as bomb castings made in the steel foundry.

The iron foundry made tunnel segments used in the production of deep air-raid shelters. In line with the spirit of cooperation engendered by the war, Head Wrightson also collaborated with other companies. For example, they joined with Ashmore, Benson and Pease to build the Mulberry Harbour floating bridge, an important technological advance which aided the Normandy landings. A consortium of four local companies combined to manufacture and assemble landing craft for the D-day landings at the Richardson Duck slipways, part of the HW Thornaby site. They also joined with other firms to produce ships and submarine mines. A subsidiary company in South Africa produced tanks and armoured cars. In addition, Head Wrightson was involved in the engineering for Operation Pluto (Pipeline Under The Ocean), designed to supply fuel to the Allied Army from England to France.

It's not surprising then that the Nazis targeted industries around Teesside and made regular bombing raids on the Head Wrightson's sites. Fortunately, there were only a handful of the raids which hit their target. There was a little damage done to the infrastructure but thankfully no evidence of any harm to the 5,500 men and women employed during this period.

To help keep damage to a minimum, the company encouraged the formation of a home guard and fire brigade at Thornaby. Some of our older contributors worked during the war and were able to recall their experiences clearly.

In the following extracts, they recall their unique perspectives on this significant period in the history of Head Wrightson.

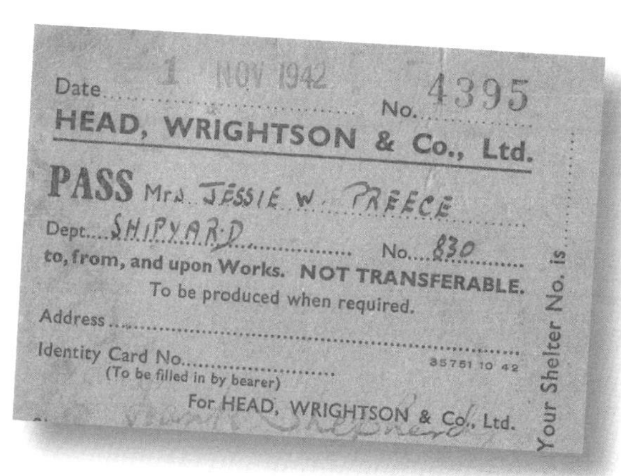
Date 1 NOV 1942 No. 4395
HEAD, WRIGHTSON & Co., Ltd.
PASS Mrs. JESSIE W. PREECE
Dept. SHIPYARD No. 830
to, from, and upon Works. NOT TRANSFERABLE.
To be produced when required.
Address
Identity Card No.
(To be filled in by bearer)
35751 10 42
For HEAD, WRIGHTSON & Co., Ltd.
Your Shelter No. is

War-time pass to gain entry to works. (Supplied by B. Preece)

Head Wrightson's Home Guard unit - includes Maynard & Les Wilson. (Wright Ahead)

Head Wrightson's war work

I wasn't there during the war but they did a lot for the war effort. There's an article in one of the papers about Pluto, which was Pipeline Under The Ocean. It was a big reel put on a ship. There was a pipe which was rolled down the reel and that ship went from England to France and laid this cable underneath. It was the petrol for the convoys and all the tanks and everything. They made Mulberry Harbours for D-day. When they floated the harbours out there was a storm at night and two of the things broke free and they sent welders down from Head Wrightson's to weld them back up again. They did invasion barges. When I first became an apprentice we had to strip all the jigs down they used to build the invasion barges. They had special jigs for doing them. *(Jim Smiles)*

It was wartime so we were on wartime production. I mean the Foundry actually was producing bombs at that time and there was a foundry at Stockton Forge. It was an iron foundry. So we were working more or less for our own foundry at that time but I say they were making bombs and wartime stuff. We did have a session in the Pattern Shop where we made what were called transoms and they were wooden sleepers like railway sleepers about nine inches by three inches but they were soaked in creosote. They were made for the forces for boggy land, like in the jungle. They were rolled up like a carpet and dropped off at the front and the tanks went over them. We made quite a lot of them. Not a very nice job. Because they were coated in, say, creosote, you had an apron on. And, of course, with the sun coming through it burned you. You had creams on. We did quite a lot of them. *(John Heighly)*

It was 1930. There was a recession worse than now, much worse than now. In fact Head Wrightson's fabrication shops were empty, there wasn't a job in. All the men were finished. One foreman, one yard manager were kept on and the apprentices were kept on, week on and week off. At sixteen year old I was drawing dole, little bit it was, it wasn't much, but that's how it was. We went like that until 1935 when Major Miles joined the company and then from 1935 things began to get a little bit better. And of course, came the war years and that did change things completely and for the first two or three months we weren't doing anything at all, we were changing over from peacetime to wartime production. We got so fed up, five of us, that we went to join up. We got down to the Labour Exchange and they took our names. When we got back to work we had the biggest trouncing of our careers, 'Don't you realise that you're in reserved occupations? You're more valuable at home than you are at the front.' The Managing Director was there, the General Manager, everybody was there waiting for us to come back – five of us – and we got really and truly trounced, but we deserved it I suppose because we hadn't really realised just how valuable our efforts were going to be. Because during the war we built mines, sinkers, bombs, aircraft hangers - we built four of five of those – and we built landing craft, we built twelve a month of those. We also built Pluto, around which they wrapped a copper pipe, which took the petrol, or the fuel from England to France for when our lads got there and they wanted fuelling up. Pluto had great big wheels. It was a Ferris wheel, terrific size. We built that in the works and then took the sections down to wherever it was they took the petrol from. And that copper pipe was wrapped round this thing to get the petrol across the Channel for our lads on the other side, so that we built that thing Pluto which was very big. There was loads of stuff as well besides that but I think the biggest success were the aeroplane hangars. They were very big. The tank-landing craft and bombs, mines and things built in the Machine Shop there. *(Maynard Wilson)*

We made the tank-landing craft. Then every time they got up to a hundred, because they made a lot, they used to have a celebration and invite the Navy. They used to have it in a decontamination hut they called it. They'd have drinks and they used to have a celebration when they got up to a hundred and then perhaps another hundred. You know that they made the Pluto do you? It was the pipeline laid over to Normandy for the petrol for the war. You see it was so handy having the river near. The tank-landing craft were all just launched into the river. It's such a pity that we've lost it all. When you think that all the tunnel linings in the Underground in London were made by Head Wrightson's. *(Enid Thurlwell)*

At the beginning of the war when I first started, Stockton Forge concentrated a lot on the mining industry, particularly coal. But also for overseas and the metals mining of gold, copper, tin, zinc, you name it. We were doing process plants for the mining industry. The first site visits I ever had were to collieries in the County of Durham. For example, things like the head frame. I remember Boldon Colliery was starting to corrode and we were asked to go and do a survey, replace all the members supporting this tower, this head frame. I remember going there with one of the cricketers that we had, Harry Thompson, he was from Template Shop. I was only maybe seventeen or eighteen and he was about ten years older than me and he virtually took over when we got measuring up. They were swab angles, where the angle had been opened up or closed. When you've got this big building with all these swab angles how the hell were we going to make it to fit? Harry was a template maker by trade and he kept me right. He was brilliant. So that was in the colliery. I learnt a lot about the geography of Durham because at the Drawing Office we used to have to go to site visits to measure up and things of that sort. *(Ray Shaw)*

As the war started your bread-and-butter job was mines and sinkies. You know I can remember starting work and they were making them then, and of course, we were doing blast-furnace work as the war started. And that just all mothballed in a week, you never saw anything of it. Just shoved away, out of the way, and we started doing war work then, which included Bailey bridges, aeroplane hangars and we did wagons for carrying tanks. I remember one time we made this catapult thing they were going to put on the merchant ships. For a reconnaissance plane to go off and look round, but how he got that back on board I don't know. So from then

An example of the landing craft manufactured by HW for D-day. In a consortium of Cleveland Bridge, Cargo Fleet, Whessoe and HW, two hundred and thirty-eight ships, at the rate of eight per month were manufactured, four times the number shown. (HW Company brochure)

on we started building the landing craft that took the lads over. I think before that we were building what they called tank-landing craft as well. *(Les Wilson)*

I went into the Drawing Office but it was for the Admiralty you see. They took over the bottom half of what used to be Richardson Duck Shipyard and they started building landing craft then. Now my job was to go and see that the landing craft were as they should be. You had a drawing showing the pipe work and one thing and another, and guns. Well, my first job was to see that the welds were alright. Now that was a terrible flipping thing that. You won't know what a cofferdam is, but at the bottom of the ship there's a cofferdam and they have a hole in it about fifteen inches. I had to crawl through them. Now there's cofferdams and there must have been about ten cofferdams between each compartment and I had to crawl underneath them and examine the welds. Not actually check them because we checked them in another way, I just had to see that the welds were done. It was claustrophobic in there because you couldn't turn round. You had to come back the same way as you went in. But it was good actually. I felt as if I was doing something for the war effort. We were making landing craft then so it just shows that somebody higher up realised that one day we'd need these things to invade Europe. *(Frank Stephenson)*

You made patterns for shells and bombs. Big bombs and shells and armour plating. Sometimes we made armour plating with tank turrets. You made gear wheels, you cut teeth out in wood. In wood in them days when it was not as sophisticated as the world is now. It was sort of primitive work. People ordered gear wheels, you made lots of gear wheels and they ordered them with the teeth on so you had to make a wheel with all the teeth carved on and then it went to the Foundry and moulded off that. *(Ron Nichol)*

We also built Bailey-bridge transoms. Now that's an interesting story because the Bailey-bridge transoms in mild steel had to weigh

Stockton Forge employees pictured the in 1940s. Included in the picture are Mrs. Kirton, Madge Hornby, Anne Husband, A. Gollogoly, Nurse Riley, Bill Heron, Joe Gill, W. Sowerby and Rhona Caldicott. (Picture courtesy Bill Hornby)

no more than 640 pounds so they could be carried by four men. And, of course, you had to remember that when they're building these they were under fire. When they got the new Cromwell tank it was too wide for the old girder bridge so I had to find something that weighed no more than 640 pounds but was wide enough to take the new tank, so they hit on aluminium alloy. Four firms applied to do the job and when they saw the tolerances that were required they dropped out one by one, but Head Wrightson's didn't, we kept on and we built the lot, two hundred and forty-eight we built. Sir John sent for me one morning and he said, 'I've had a call from Chichester, Ministry of Works, will we build their last twelve Bailey-bridge transoms because they got into trouble with theirs?' So I said, 'Well providing...' He said, 'The material's all done ready.' I said, 'Well providing it's done ready, okay Sir John, we'll do it but they better send it all up here first.' So they sent it up to us and none of it was any good, it was all out of tolerance so I had to tell Sir John we couldn't use that material. So they ordered new material and we built the last twelve, so in effect we built the whole lot. They were a big success. *(Maynard Wilson)*

Cold isn't the word because there were no roofs on the shops for a time you know. When I first started there in thirty-six there was no roof. Well, some were on but some weren't and they were just putting them up and had to paint them all black. You know, keep all the electric lights out for the war. When it rained and you worked outside you had to go home. You couldn't work on, you had to go home. I was in the Template Shop. I wasn't so bad, but I did have to work outside a bit, marking off. The angle chopper and the guillotine and all those things were outside. *(Les Wilson)*

Women workers

Mr. Bob Iddison knew the family and I really think that with them all working there that's why I got the job really, with them all being family. It was him who said to me, 'Right, you're a girl that can look after herself because I know you.' He said, 'We'll send you up to Egglescliffe.' There was a foundry and these two machines and a crane. I really enjoyed it there. I was there about six months I should imagine. *(Connie Wass)*

We had an iron foundry at Thornaby when I started, which was situated at the end of the main offices along Trafalgar Street. I know if you went to the Ambulance Room, you had to pass one of the entrances to the iron foundry and I wondered what kind of a place it was when I first started. Because they used to have big piles of horse manure with steam coming off it and that was used when they had poured the metal into the moulds. They used to put this horse manure on the top to get the gases out. But, of course, then after the war with all different things coming out they got a chemical that used to be sprayed on, the same as the steel foundry. *(Enid Thurlwell)*

The machine was in the middle of the room where there were the two men there and us three women were there. In the big Machine Shop there was a lad. They were about that long, the bars, but a big head on the end. Now he drilled the hole through that head. It was carried by a labourer to my machine in the Tool Room and I would fix it in the machine and just press a button and the broach would go along. It was like teeth, you know, going through. Milling the hole. Making a square hole. It was always fantastic. They all used to come and have a look and all that. *(Connie Wass)*

We had like a cap. It's a very funny thing. When I was doing the square holes I had very short curly hair and one of the men used to say, 'I'll borrow your hair to clean the chimney.' It was really short and curly. There's always one complained that I wasn't wearing anything on my head. It was just a straight machine, there was no belts or anything like that. So they decided to go on strike to suit them and the machine women in Machine Shop. About six of them. So he said to me, 'Oh Connie.' I said, 'Look, I'm not doing what they want me to do. I know I'm okay, I want my cards tonight.' He says, 'You do what?' I said, 'I mean it.' I was sent for, and the manager said, 'Connie you're not leaving this place through them, tie something round your head.' I said, 'Oh I'll find something.' So I found this scarf and a great big bow. *(Connie Wass)*

My wife-to-be worked as a clerk but there were some women in the Bridge Yard. They were called drilling helpers. I don't know exactly what helping they were doing because it was heavy work. I started at Head's in nineteen forty-four and there were women working during the war. Apparently my wife's mother worked in what they called the mine shop at Head Wrightson where they made mines for the war. That was before I got there and I can't remember her mother being there. I think she

These three photographs depict the blast damage to HW Bridge Yard from a landmine which fell on land near to Crosthwaite's Foundry. The Bridge Yard roof, previously open to the elements, had been roofed just prior to the war. The blast blew all the glass out, scattering it across work benches, floor, machines and work in progress. The mess was soon cleared allowing vital war work including the manufacture of bombs and sinkers to continue. (Remembering Thornaby Group)

worked there just in wartime. They only made mines in wartime. It was a hard job. *(Ron Baker)*

Another time something cut me in the eye, we didn't wear glasses, and I burned my eye and I had to go into hospital. I was on two till ten. This is true. I went to the Parliament Street *(Ed - Stockton & Thornaby Hospital, which was demolished many years ago, stood opposite the top of Parliament Street)*, she put a patch on. A couple of minutes later I took the patch off, went in two till ten, clocked in and the big boss of Head Wrightson said, 'What's she doing coming in this time?' They said, 'She's just come from the hospital.' I didn't get paid. *(Connie Wass)*

Bombing

It came down on Whitwell's, old Whitwell's Ironworks tip. It was a landmine in actual fact because I well remember being on Home Guard duty that night where we were billeted in the Whitwell's Ironworks offices which had become unused, the ironworks having closed down. *(Bob Waller)*

We were responsible for the blackout. There weren't curtains. They were a frame with blackened material fastened to it. Every piece of shuttering was tailor-made to the windows and of which there were an awful lot. So the apprentices used to have to carry these things and put them up every night. During the summer we'd put them up at five o'clock before we finished work but in the winter you did it at dusk. That was quite a task when there were maybe probably a hundred odd shutters to put up. They were a bit of a nuisance but that was one of the things about the war. Also, there were a lot of the windows that had sticky tape across them. The idea of that, of course, was if there was a blast the glass wouldn't shatter all over. It would break but hopefully it wouldn't cause any damage. *(Ray Shaw)*

It was a holiday time. We'd heard that Head Wrightson's had been bombed. I said, 'Oh I'm on two till ten today, thank God I'm not going.' A knock on the door, 'You're working today.' She says, 'You're two till ten today.' Blocked all the windows up, shut them up with wood in Lennie Allen's shop. *(Connie Wass)*

Can you remember there was a bomb dropped at Head Wrightson's or near Head Wrightson's?

Oh there was one near it and, of course, all the windows were all smashed in. When they dropped that one, all the windows in Stockton High Street were all blown out. But I remember going to work that morning and where I had my bench in the Template Shop it was all just covered with glass and everything. But the funny thing was, they sent all the labouring lads home and they kept the tradesmen there to get the job cleaned up and get back onto work again. But I think it was a parachute bomb. I think it was a heavy thing, because all these roofs we'd had put in were all out. *(Les Wilson)*

I was on night shift when they dropped a bomb one night and it blew the windows out.
I walked home from Thornaby to Billingham in the middle of the night. All the electricity had gone and you couldn't work because there were no lights. It blew the windows out. This one hit the Electricity Board's power station. That was on the Sunday night. We went to work the next day. It had blown the windows out. But we still went to work the next day. I was never laid off. Even the time when I was on six till two and they bombed Middlesbrough railway station. *(Stan Hume)*

During the war, as far as I can remember, there was no difference to the work one had to do and I do not think there were any daytime bombing raids although one night a landmine was dropped on the Welding Shop causing considerable damage. There was also once a large fire in the Tool Room resulting in a lot of damage but not due to enemy raids. There was a fire-fighting team stationed in the works and the Stockton and Thornaby Fire Services would also be in attendance if required. Our work involved the repair and maintenance of various machinery which included overhead cranes, steam cranes, steam locomotives, moulding machines, sand mills, sand-blasting machinery, air compressors, large grinding machines used in the fettling yard, and installing new machinery. *(Kenneth Pelmear)*

Home Guard

Now as soon as the war started my father was an air-raid warden so I joined him in that but when you got to eighteen then you could join the Home Guard, which I did. There were two Home Guards. There's one for Thornaby which was run by our VC – Major Edward Cooper. But we had our own. And that was more or less run by Major Miles. I used to put a night in every week. Where you used to go down and turn to the right where the offices were and down in there round towards Crosthwaite's Foundry. Well, we had a place there. We used to do a two-hour stint walking round the works once a week to guard them *(sic)*. There used to be a barrage balloon around near where the Clevo flour mill was. I had a rifle but no bullets. Only when you had to go on these exercises. We had a rifle, and then we also had what are they called, Sten guns? these machine-gun things. But they come over from America, I think. Very cheaply made, but never mind they did the trick. Our sergeant was a fellow called Danny Thurston and he had been a regular sergeant in the Army but he was invalided out. So then he took over Head Wrightson's. We used to have a pit we built, we had an anti-aircraft gun in there. And if the sirens went we used to go and man this gun. But, actually speaking, if ever they'd dropped anything we hadn't a chance at all. *(Les Wilson)*

Nationally, I think it was Anthony Eden made an appeal to the country for people to volunteer for what was called the Local Defence Volunteers. I applied for this and it eventually solved itself by way of Head Wrightson forming their own company, Third North Riding Battalion. Three NRE it was called, and Richard Miles, the Managing Director of Head Wrightson, took over command of the Home Guard. His assistant was Dan Thurston who became a captain in the Home Guard, Danny Thurston.

How many Head Wrightson's men were in that division?

Well there were at least twenty on every night so that's a hundred and forty a week. There must have been more than a hundred. I can't remember how many.

And what were your duties on your night on?

Parading with broomsticks round the river bank with clubs and things until they got some rifles, shotguns, and then you were allowed to go out on your watch, sent out on your two-hour spell with a shotgun. You went out in pairs and you had one shotgun between two chaps. They were good days. Very, very, serious days but very enthusiastic people. The man who took over and did the weekly parades was Bill Papworth, who was a draughtsman but he'd been in the First World War. But it had a very similar style to the realistic *Dad's Army*.

Very similar sort of thing.

And they also had a fire brigade?

They had. Harry Soppett was the boss of the fire brigade. And I don't know why but Frank Shepherd, who was the Personnel Manager, he was keenly interested in the fire brigade. Stockton Forge, it was halfway between Stockton and Norton, but how they'd got the name of Stockton Forge nobody seems to know. It had been there since the 1890s I think. It was a complete engineering works with foundries, welding shops, machine shops and plating, and of course, the big drawing office, and that's where I was a young man, joined in 1941. The war was on and they were recruiting women into the works at that time as welders, and some of whom were very rude. We were young drawing office boys of the age of fifteen and sixteen years of age, were very innocent and as we used to walk round the works these girls used to make quite lewd and crude comments. I remember that well. But it was strange that they could train women to be welders in about six weeks when the normal apprenticeship for a welder was the usual five years. They did a good job welding, particularly on tank-landing craft I remember, and Bailey bridges. We did a lot of Bailey bridges to the designs of the Military. *(Bob Waller)*

We accepted a Home Guard duty round Head Wrightson's at night once a week, training at weekends and then you were working overtime to build all that we were building. So really, we got half a day a week off if you like, it was hard work, really hard work. So we really did feel involved. Not only that but when we got back home from work we were on duty at home, fire watching and things of that sort. There was a great communal spirit among people in those days. Everybody was helping everybody. If your next door neighbour was in trouble you saw they got out of trouble or tried to get them out of trouble. I used to write letters to the Forces. The Church of England Men's Society asked the people to give their names in to us and we would write to the lads, to the husbands if they wanted to, and we did quite a lot of that. We got many, many replies back from the lads saying how much they appreciated the fact that we were thinking about them. They were very, very difficult days, they really were. And we were bombed, of course. Head Wrightson's was hit. Crosthwaite's, who were next to Head Wrightson's were hit, the bomb fell in there actually but it damaged one of Head Wrightson's shops. But it didn't stop production, within hours it was cleaned up and we were back at work. But the spirit in those days among people generally was fantastic. I've never seen anything like it since, and I'd love to because that's what's missing today. *(Maynard Wilson)*

Head, Wrightson & Co., Ld.

'Victory' War Loan

In order to assist their regular Employees to subscribe to the above

National War Loan,

the Directors are prepared to

Purchase War Loan Stock,

in Multiples of £5, on behalf of their regular Employees, to be paid for by the Applicants in Weekly Deductions from Wages due, extending over a period not exceeding one year.

No charge will be made to the Employees and the Interest received on the War Loan Stock purchased, will be paid to the Applicants.

Applicants are requested to give their names, with the amount they wish to Invest to the Timekeeper.

FEBRUARY 9th, 1917.

Reproduction of actual poster

By courtesy of Miss Jocelyn Wrightson

'Victory' War Loan poster. (Wright Ahead)

Entertainment

We had Stockton Forge Male-Voice Choir, and that was good fun, run by one of our senior draughtsmen, Bertie Brewis. He was a member of St. Michael's Church at Norton. I'm not sure if I told you but during the war they had these ENSA concerts in the canteen. They were budding entertainers - singers, comedians, musicians - and they were supposed to keep the workers happy during the war and so they would tour round the country. It was a government-sponsored organisation and we had it. I can't remember now whether it was once a week or once a month, but we had ENSA in the canteen. We were a bit naughty because if they were poor we would let them know they were not very good. But we had this male-voice choir. Also at that time the BBC ran this *Workers' Playtime* and we were invited to sing. We actually went to Head Wrightson's Thornaby, and we gave quite a nice choral programme on the BBC, and that was quite a memorable day. Again, they were all chaps from Stockton Forge – Drawing Office, Welding Shop, Machine Shop. I remember particularly a very good tenor, he was part of the Gilbert and Sullivan Choir, but he was our leading tenor in our choir, and once you got one or two really good singers it helps the whole. Still, they were happy days at the choir. *(Ray Shaw)*

Chapter 10

'It came as shock': closure

In September 1997, Margaret Thatcher was photographed on the derelict Teesdale site with the old abandoned Head Wrightson Heavy Plate Shop in the background. The media headlines labelled the image as the 'walk in the wilderness' and, indeed, it did graphically symbolise the decline of heavy industry on Teesside. But Head Wrightson's decline had begun many years before. From the late 1960s, the company was facing increased international competition and falling demand at home, prompting a programme of rationalisation. For instance, Stockton Forge was closed in 1969 and Head Wrightson Machine Company in Middlesbrough was shut in a shock decision in 1979. Following both closures some of their work, machines and personnel were transferred to Head Wrightson Teesdale (HWT).

In 1976 Head Wrightson merged with Davy Corporation although much of the workforce felt that it was effectively a takeover. It quickly became clear that Davy was no longer interested in manufacturing and wanted to concentrate on design and contract management. This was also in line with the recommendations of Lazard, an influential global firm which provided advice on corporate mergers and finance. They proposed that some foundries should close as part of a national restructuring scheme of the heavy engineering industry and Head Wrightson agreed to close all their foundries thus ending a foundry tradition at Thornaby which had started in 1859. The continued contraction of production facilities and shortage of orders culminated eventually in the closure of the Teesdale site in 1984. At the last minute it was bought by ITM (Offshore) Limited, a locally-owned company specialising in offshore exploration. ITM closed in 1986 when it was declared bankrupt, sadly bringing to an end the area's long association with the manufacture of quality engineering products.

The only remaining part of the company is Stampings at Seaton Carew who now trade as Caparo Forgings. Following the closure of HWT in 1984 some enterprising HWT engineers bought the drawings and copyright to the HWT products and still supply spare parts for these products worldwide.

The following extracts illustrate the impact of the decline and closure of Head Wrightson on the workforce.

Closure of Stockton Forge in 1969

I don't think it was at that time a conscious effort to close Stockton Forge but there was certainly a running down of it. The company got in management consultants, Urwick Orr & Partners. They came into Stockton Forge for planning. We hadn't planners before but the foreman would plan his own work routes. I, as Chief Draughtsman, planned what we were doing. I don't want somebody else saying so many weeks for this and so many weeks for that. They created quite an empire. Eccles was not very keen on it so I had a sympathetic ear when I used to criticise Urwick Orr. For example, I remember him saying to Urwick Orr, 'If you could change anything in the Drawing Office what would you do?' I said, 'Well, the biggest change is if I could get a workload that was consistent, instead we get too much work and then nothing.' And then I said, 'You get these fluctuations all the time. So if you could change anything you'd change the world if you like and you had a steady, steady workload all the time then I can plan ahead who's doing what.' They weren't a great success, Urwick Orr. We'd never had redundancies before. Before that there was a time, when I was first in the Drawing Office as manager, if a guy came for an interview and he could hold a pencil, I almost employed him. I was so short of draughtsmen. But then, as the years went by and Eccles said, 'Reduce by more than...' I think it was fifteen odd per cent so there were about a dozen people I had to get rid of. It was a surprise to me when they closed Stockton. Leading up to the closure, I should have seen the clues. So I had a year at Teesdale, a very unhappy year in the sense that I didn't feel as though I had a job. I felt I had been fitted in. But it was then John Eccles again, now part of the parent board, he got me down to what we called Head Wrightson PEL, Process Engineering Limited. Their offices were right down beside the river. They were a separate company to Teesdale, who were manufacturing and this Process Engineering was purely contracting. Stockton Forge site was sold off and do you know to this day it's still an engineering works. *(Ray Shaw)*

While I was there they got Urwick & Orr in, the management consultants. And, to my mind, I don't think they did a very good job. The Forge never seemed the same after they came. For example, they took the best turner on the big lathe, took him off the machine and put him in the Planning Department. So your best lathe operator now he's in the Planning Department. And the same in the Template Shop, and so on. We formed a Planning Department which increased the overheads, and so on. But Stockton Forge still had plenty of work. I think they'd obviously decided to close it down and move us over to Teesdale. I think they all went from the Drawing Office. And, of course, I was Engineering Sales, and all of us on Engineering Sales, all my team, went to Teesdale. The workforce, I didn't know really. My father went over. He went over not in his capacity as manager but on procurement. I forget what they called it, but it was basically chasing round firms who were doing sub-contract work for Head Wrightson's, and checking on the work and so on. *(Alan Sowerby)*

We were such a close-knit family that when it was announced, and I can't remember to this day how we actually heard of it officially, people literally were in tears. They really were so despondent. It came as a shock, it came totally out of the blue, and I would say that the help we got from the union at that particular time was probably non-existent. Whether it was a world market or whether somebody at the top had thought that this sort of business was now over. *(Trevor Briggs)*

Closure of foundries under Lazard's Scheme

About seventy-five I left the foundries. It was like everything else, it was running down. At the time I actually met this fellow Leon Brittan because I was a steward at the foundry. He came round and explained to us all that all the foundries were running on half power and it would be better if we all ran on full power. Close half of them down and keep the other half open so they would get all their work and have a foundry running on full power. And of course, the famous words, 'But you won't be affected.' We agreed to it and the next thing you're getting the chop, do you know what I mean? So they closed Billingham down. In fact all Head Wrightson's foundries closed down in one go. They took all the work away from them in one go. Part of the job was I went and burned it all up for scrap. I got a job for this company dismantling all the foundry and I burnt it all down.

So Leon Brittan came round. Was he addressing a shop steward's meeting?

Leon Brittan came round the works and he had all the shop stewards. We closed ten weeks after that. Well, they were basically shutting down as he was telling us. They wanted us to agree to it. I think he was something to do with Lazard's bankers because it was known as the Lazard's Scheme. There was him and the bloke who done the railways, Beeching. They were all part of this American Lazard company. They were supplying the money. We hadn't expected to close under Lazard, not when he said we're a good foundry and everything's running smashing. But apparently Head Wrightson's got a lump sum to close the foundries and not to open another one for at least ten years. Now I know this by being one of the stewards. The men didn't get any of the money, we just got what we're entitled in our pay offs. We got no extra, just standard redundancy and so much a week for every week you'd been there and you got two years then you got your redundancy money. A lot of people were put out of work. Stockton Steel had closed prior to that. That's how I got transferred from Stockton Steel to Billingham. Then they closed Billingham and Thornaby together. I was at Billingham when they closed. *(Robert Chaney)*

Can you tell me what the Lazard Scheme was all about?

Well, a lot of us couldn't understand what it was. The company got money for shutting places down and somebody said they were transferring a lot of work abroad and this was what it was all about. Getting work transferred abroad rather than be made over in this country.

In effect, they were paid to close the foundry?

Yes. *(Eddie Peacock)*

A group called Lazard came over and they wanted to shut half our foundries down. Then it was Davy's after that, wasn't it? And all they wanted to do was keep the fabrication shops open, they wanted rid of the foundries. So that's what happened. They sold out. But we all had big orders in. Billingham had just had a new big furnace put in, a brand-new big furnace and they just shut it down. They shut it all down.

What was this Lazard incentive to Head Wrightson's for shutting it down?

They must have got a big payout, must have got big money for it all.

What was the reaction of the people to that?

Oh everybody was against it. Head Wrightson's was massive in Thornaby. We went to see the MP and everything but he said nothing could be done.

So what about your redundancy?

We did what we could do but they were just determined to shut it down. We didn't have much choice really. We all got paid off in eighty-three, but it all shut down eighty-four. They sold most of the equipment but they couldn't build on there for ten years, apparently. Once it all got demolished you couldn't build on it because they had money for it.

Did they continue at Steelcast then or did Steelcast at Billingham close as well?

I think they all shut down. I don't know whether they were after us or not but I know they had brand-new furnaces and theirs went down as well. I think the Iron Foundry at Eaglescliffe went on a bit longer after we went. *(Michael Nichol)*

They were paid to close it. As far as I was concerned those people that were laid off went up the road with no job and no chance of it reopening it again. Because under the Lazard Scheme what was happening in some places in the country, they were claiming the money and shutting the foundry, and some were buying the furnaces and opening up another foundry. So the ruling came that the furnaces had to be chopped up, burnt up so they could never be used. And that was very sad because they knew there was no hope. It was finished. *(Les Ellis)*

Out of the Lazard's money, did any of that filter down to the men in the form of enhanced redundancy payments?
No, I don't think so. I don't really know as I wasn't there at the time. I think the worst part about it was that Head Wrightson's Billingham had just put in a new fifty-ton arc furnace and it never poured an ounce of steel. They just burnt it up. It was never used. It was just burnt up on the spot. It must have cost a few million quid. It just became a nothing place didn't it? *(Colin Waugh)*

Whilst the Stockton Steel Foundry had already been closed, the plan I put forward meant that we would have retained one foundry. This involved consolidating the Thornaby and Billingham foundries over at Billingham. Unfortunately, the Davy Board didn't see it that way. I think that their view was based on the premise that they were hell-bent on concentrating on engineering and contracting and on exiting from all forms of manufacture, with the exception of Davy Roll & Davy McKee, Sheffield. Prior to this they had already closed the HW Machine Company in Middlesbrough.
So this was in the Eighties now?
Yes. Teesdale was fighting for its life and subsequently got sold. Grosvenor's order book had been moved into Teesdale to try to improve Teesdale's prospects and Massey had been relocated to Davy McKee, Sheffield, into the Hydraulic Press Division. It was quite tragic really. All the good profitable parts of companies were moved elsewhere within Davy and the other bits were either sold or were closed. And so, in addition to running the Forge, I was then given the unenviable task of, unfortunately, both running and shutting down Steelcast at Billingham and Thornaby. I hate to say it but it went extremely well, with all the employees being very co-operative, very helpful and we actually shut the company down one million pounds less than budget. The Steelcast employees were very professional and they made a very difficult and sad task almost easy.
How do you feel about the Lazard Scheme, you know, the closure of steel foundries?
At the time I felt I wasn't happy with it as I genuinely believed that we might have been able to successfully consolidate the two sites into one viable business. Sitting here today, however, I think the business probably got paid to close something that ultimately it would have had to have paid to close itself.
So there was money there for closing?
Well the theory was, that if you decided to stay open you put money into the pot which was topped up by the government and, if you decided to close, then that fund contributed very significantly to your closure costs. The real downside was that in the process, all of a foundry's melting capabilities, namely the furnaces, had to be destroyed.
Can you recall the year that was, when some of the foundries went?
I think it was at eighty-one. It was a pretty traumatic time for all concerned. The only plus that came out of that period as far as I was concerned was, as I've said, I'd acquired two forging presses, I'd got the investment programme that was so essential for the future of the forge and its entry into the niche aerospace and defence-market sectors. Out of the closure, in crude terms, I was able to 'borrow' an awful lot of the Steelcast infrastructure and transfer it to Hartlepool. For example, we even moved an electricity sub-station. So a lot of Head Wrightson Steelcast is still, even to this day, in Hartlepool. The forge benefited very considerably from that exercise. *(Ian Ford)*

Davy merger in 1978

From 1969 when Davy had a serious loss and they tried to sell everything they could to us –

the company plane, the directors' house in Eaglescliffe where they had a senior resident, guests and all that et cetera, et cetera. But other things were sold, we acquired their foundries, they acquired certain of our types of contract work and it was only therefore in seventy-six when it was finally agreed with Davy that the two companies would merge as the Stock Exchange were told. In fact, Davy took Head Wrightson over and it happened at the beginning of seventy-seven. I continued to report to John Eccles, a nephew of Sir John Wrightson and a former premium apprentice who had spent time moving around the company's various workshops and offices. He was the Chief Executive, or Managing Director of Head Wrightson prior to the merger and he became the head of the Foundries and Forges Division of Davy. So he was responsible for the Head Wrightson foundries, such foundries as Davy still had, principally relating to roll foundries because Davy's big business originally had been building rolling mills. John Eccles was the boss of that and I effectively became, I'm not sure what my title was, but I was the equivalent of the Commercial Manager in other parts of Davy. We used to have meetings of all the commercial managers and we would discuss contract conditions and one thing and another. They were not legally qualified - the others. This was the interesting thing about Head Wrightson who had all these lawyers dealing with its contracts. They had commercial people that might have had an engineering background or an accounts background or whatever but I don't think any of them were legally qualified. So I was a Commercial Manager in Davy and I continued in that role until John Eccles became a non-executive director. Obviously, I couldn't report to a non-executive director and Davy's Company Secretary suggested I should be in London and I declined and left Head Wrightson. That was in 1981. *(David Jowett)*

Well it was depressing actually but you have to do it. It was surprising how cheerful the chaps were themselves because they'd mostly known about this. They knew it was going to happen and they were quite resigned to it and many of them had already got better jobs outside. But some of them hadn't and it was a bit depressing having to talk to them. I didn't like being taken over by Davy, I'll tell you, but the people I met at Davy's seemed perfectly reasonable people. But I suppose Head Wrightson probably could not have stood on its own the way things were going in those days. *(Joe Doran)*

I suppose the start of feeling that Thornaby might be under threat was towards maybe the last couple of years when I was there after Davy United took over in 1978. So that's when you maybe started worrying a bit. If you looked at Davy, and they had this big plant Davy Loewy at Sheffield. I'd seen pictures of their machine shop and facilities and it was much larger than ours. Yes, so you felt maybe the writing was on the wall then. You thought, 'Why have two facilities when they had bigger and better equipment down there?' *(Ken Peacock)*

Davy and Head Wrightson's merged, contrary to popular belief that it was a takeover. It finished up as a takeover by Davy but in the original concept was a merger, but the Davy management was much stronger than the Head Wrightson top management and they eventually ruled what was going on everywhere. But Davy to a degree, and also Head Wrightson, weren't that interested in manufacturing any more. It was easier to make money in project managing and contracting, as they call it, than actually physically making things. We had a succession of managing directors who were very poor if the truth were known and put onto us by Davy, and in the end Davy decided that they would sell Head Wrightson's Teesdale off. And they sold Head Wrightson's Teesdale to ITM. *(Barry Preece)*

I think everybody thought it's an amalgamation. But I don't think it was. I don't know to this day what it was really. But we always used to say, 'Well, they took it over because they wanted the McKee.' Now that was the blast furnace section. *(Les Wilson)*

And Davy gradually asset-stripped the company. One example was sinter machines. We would get an order for a sinter machine through the drawing office and we would manufacture everything, machining, the fitting and everything like that would all be done in-house. And then Head Wrightson Processes got the contract to do the sinter machines and they sub-let all of the bread-and-butter work to these small machine companies and left the heavy and non-profitable bit for Teesdale to build. So we lost the bread-and-butter, and then of course, we were making a loss on the sinter machines. The work dwindled away. And then Davy Corporation said they were going to close the place down – 1984, something like that. It was taken over by a company called ITM and we were involved mainly with oil-rig work. *(Jim Heward)*

Davy's moved the roll side up to Gateshead, and all the lathes that were used to machine turn they all got taken away and moved up to Gateshead. But they did utilise that Machine Shop, with other work. Well, there'd be turners, there'd be machinists, there'd be different sorts. There'd be fitters and the tool personnel. You would have the lads who were labouring and doing the crane driving. A few guys went up to Gateshead but in the main a lot of the lads changed their jobs because moulders, turners and things like that was a dying trade. Core makers, moulders, pattern-makers.

What did they put in the Machine Shop?

Well, they used a lot of it for storage. Motors. Crane gear and things like that. But they employed a few more metal dressers. They used that as an alternative to taking all the stuff down to the top site. They used to have a couple of metal dressers in the old Machine Shop where they could shift the casting if they wanted to. *(Tony Lodge)*

I think what Davy's got out of it was obviously the removal of a competitor. I mean what would Davy's get out of it? They'd get quite a lot of engineering people who they would know. They got some manufacturing, they would get some manufacturing capability but they didn't want it because they'd already closed their own manufacturing down and the style of the day was very much to buy at arm's length, worldwide if you could. Don't tie yourself to your own manufacturing. They weren't at all interested in the iron foundry and steel foundry business. I think they really wanted the Process Engineering, engineering capability and technologies which I was part of. They had their own blast furnace but we had things like sinter plants, which is a preparation process for the blast furnace, preparing the ore. We had that technology which they didn't have. There was the Head Wrightson Machine Company down in Middlesbrough that had some process lines, you know, annealing, pickling and that sort of thing for the finished steel, that they didn't have. So I think that they were probably getting a fairly limited amount out of the bargain is my own reflection. But eliminating a competitor is never to be sneezed at, and Head Wrightson, I think, were never negotiating from a position of strength. We hadn't got the financial muscle that Davy had. When I kept in touch with my friends in the Friarage and I saw them leaving or been given non-jobs in London, it looked like a favourite tactic of the Davy people to get people to move to London. They'd put them in a little office in their corporate headquarters and give them nothing to do and of course, you can only do that for a certain period of time before you get fed up and say, 'Well, that's it, I'm going to resign.' That happened to James Iveson, the Company Secretary of Head Wrightson. Other colleagues went into private practice. So it became pretty clear that the Friarage had got no future. Indeed it didn't, it was closed down reasonably quickly. Iron foundries were closed and we've all seen what eventually became of the Thornaby site with the famous Mrs. Thatcher walking across it. *(Robin Millman)*

Head Wrightson was a traditional family business and when Sir John retired that was the end of the family line and I think, when Davy came in and took over, it was quite definitely

the end of an era. The family business was definitely no more and we were being subsumed into quite a different animal. So I think there was always quite a lot of concern about the motives of Davy. But that's the art of a takeover, you have to sell it to people. I suspect they were not exactly professional about doing that. I think it became increasingly clear that Davy did not like manufacturing, it was something they were not overly keen on retaining. The foundries went. We had the Lazard Scheme for the foundries where you were given so much money to get out of the system that, in ten years of their best ever profits, the foundry would never have made that much money. In the current parlance it was a no-brainer, take the money and run.
So I think Davy was always regarded with some sort of scepticism. *(Barrie Hope)*

Davy didn't know how to cope because they didn't know how to run a manufacturing company. They didn't in my opinion work with us, in the sense that they didn't feed us. They still went out to open competition, and a lot of work they had which should have come our way, which would have benefited us all, went elsewhere. I never understood because eventually it ended up with us all going to the wall. I wouldn't describe it as a merger because I think Davy were more of an anchor to Head Wrightson's than anything else, pulling and helping to pull us down. Because they didn't really know how to manage Head Wrightson. They didn't know how to cope with a fabrication company, and they could have fed us better and worked with us better. There was still a lot of mistrust between the two companies even when they were supposed to be as one.
The divisionalisation, was that good or bad?
I always thought that it was a fancy name for something that could have been achieved without that. I think it caused a degree of duplication which was unnecessary. From my point of view it was an enormous success but I'm less convinced that overall for the company it was such a success. Because divisions were competing with each other for what was available in the works, because the works were serving all the divisions. You almost got the situation where the Pressure Vessel Division was competing with Mechanical Engineering Division for space in the shops, for performance in the shops, for delivery in the shops. In that sense divisionalisation was divisive. In other respects, I'd say purely from a selfish point of view, for me it worked extremely well. We were given a lot more autonomy than we used to have i.e. we used to manage the work without having to keep referring to inept managing directors all the time. Well, we were lucky in that we had a very sound chap running us, in Bob Wright, who was head of the Mechanical Engineering Division. He was an engineer and he knew Head Wrightson inside out, he knew the products inside out and he was a very easy guy to work for and with. And from that point of view I think that was one of the reasons why that grouping was, beyond any shadow of doubt, a storming success. Others less so. *(Ken Pattison)*

Closure of Middlesbrough Works in 1979

But we'd had a very busy period in seventy-eight leading up to Christmas and we'd taken on some work from Sheffield, which was the Davy's office, which was for Russia. I always remember it because the lads were loving it because they were getting stacks of overtime because it was very important that this stuff was finished round about the Christmas time. It had to be shipped over to Russia and they wanted to beat the Russian winter to get it across there and onto the site before the winter set in. They must have had contract deadlines. Albert Snaith, who was the new director, we were told, 'the axeman cometh' because he'd been at the forge. But I got along with him alright and he said, 'No, no, I'm not here to do that. I know I've got this reputation but I've come here to continue running this thriving company.' But I felt sorry for him really because I do think he was crapped on from above to a certain extent. But anyway he said to me,

'There's a guy coming down from Sheffield, we need to be all in the canteen, everyone.' I said, 'Everyone?' You see, normally we used to have a Works Council. He said, 'Oh I think it's a big thank you for what we've done on the Russian job.' So we all were there on that particular morning and the canteen was full and this guy come up with a briefcase, and he's stood at the desk, opened his desk up. 'My name is Mr. Ashcroft', he says, 'I've got some sad news but nevertheless it has to be said. Unfortunately, Head Wrightson's Machine Company, as we know it, will be closing as from April.' *(Stuart Thompson)*

Closure of Teesdale in 1984

I knew just how hard it was to get a job. You knew that if you did get made redundant you were going to be trying to compete for jobs where there were blokes with ten, fifteen years' experience. So it did seem very daunting. You were beginning to think, 'Oh well, if I did get finished from here I probably wouldn't get another job in the trade.' Hence, when ITM took over and you had the option to stay, me and a lot of the younger lads just jumped at the chance.

So it would come as quite a shock to you when it was announced that Head Wrightson's was actually closing or being sold, rather?

Oh yes, yes. Quite devastating to be honest, devastating. Luckily, I got the chance to stay on with ITM and I think it was finally 1987, when ITM shut the doors.

And did you stay with ITM right through?

I was one of the last. They called us 'the twelve disciples'. I was one of the final twelve there. It was mainly two machinists and a couple of slinger labourers and half a dozen fitters. We were finishing work off for Clyde Dynamics. It was a big crane ship that was getting built. That was basically the last job that we done there. *(John Stainthorpe)*

How did you feel about the future for Head Wrightson, Teesdale?

Well, it was always in the balance, but what saved it I think in many ways were the oil rigs, getting orders to make shells. Then they were transferred down to the yards where they put them together. It was a lot of work. But finally, you could see the end coming, there was nothing coming in except these oil rigs. I remember one night in the Planning Department, our boss in there said, 'Look, you're all working this weekend whether you like it or not.' He said, 'If we don't get this order for these rigs, we're closing.' We never got it but we didn't close then. *(Les Wilson)*

Eventually Head Wrightson's, Middlesbrough, closed down and some of the machines came up to Head Wrightson's, Thornaby. Their deputation came and said, 'You'll be next, Thornaby.' Well, Head Wrightson's *was* Thornaby. 'Right, no, it won't happen here, we won't close down.' 'It's to die, you wait.' I think that was about seventy-eight or seventy-nine I think - Head Wrightson's, Middlesbrough. Then all of a sudden Davy's bought us out, Davy Corporation, I think that was about seventy-nine and then they sold out to ITM in 1984. *(Dennis Johnson)*

But Davy became part of Jardine Matheson I think. It was owned principally by Jardines, they didn't own the whole company but they owned enough to put all their people in. Then it went to Trafalgar House. I think there was Jardine Matheson and then there was Kvaerner. I stayed basically with the same organisation doing the same job although I went off to South Africa for four years with the company in Davy South Africa. Then I came back again, but the notepaper kept changing. Head Wrightson had been where it was for a hundred and fifty years or something and then suddenly in the next fifteen years you've got six changes of notepaper. Eventually, my part of Stockton was sold to an Austrian company, the iron-and-steel making side, and so I was asked to head up that operation by the Austrians and we moved out of Bowesfield Lane and took on a new office on the river on the Teesdale site. It's where they used to load the dock gates into the river, because we had a launching pad for the dock gates. I was in an office right on the river by the slipway where we used to load these things out. So a full circle really. *(Robin Millman)*

I think we lost out to Ashmore's because they bought us. So we knew then, like me at the time, there was going to be two sales managers, there was going to be two chief engineers, stuff like that, and eventually we were closed down. So they took the mantle. Everybody was given a job over there but the ultimate was the axe for quite a lot of the Head Wrightson people. Me, included. So we knew then that they were only favouring their own people, obviously. They still had good talent to draw from, with Head Wrightson people as well. But I don't know what happened further above but there was a financial agreement and I think most of the work was transferred from Head Wrightson to Davy.

But you were taken on by Davy?

Every year we were given a bottle of Bell's whisky in the sales team, and hung round the neck of the Bell's whisky, I don't know whether you know, it says, 'Afore Ye Go'. Little did I realise it was afore *you* go. Blown out come the following Christmas. So that was it and I'd no idea who sold me down the river or what happened. I was just given notice together with redundancy and thanks very much for your services. *(Max Clark)*

I left Head's when I was made redundant in 1983. I was there eleven years. All the work had run out and times were getting hard for Head's. It didn't take long after that that they had to sell up and pack up. It all fell apart after that just through lack of work. Then another company came along called Davy International and they took over and they had it for a time. Actually, when they took over I went back. I got a start back shortly after, and I went back and I worked for them about four or five years. Then ITM took over and then we worked for them for a short period of time and then that was it more or less. *(Dennis Longstaff)*

The main site was acquired by Teesside Development Corporation and, curiously, the site is known now officially as Teesdale. I think following Davy's acquisition when they didn't really need it they submitted a plan for its development to Stockton Borough Council and, of course, the plan was for the development of the Teesdale site. That's what *we* called it - the Teesdale site.

When did The Teesside Development Corporation finally take it over?

They took over the half of the site where the steel foundries had been in 1984. The other half of the site was sold in 1984 to ITM headed by Alf Duffield who was also chairman of Middlesbrough Football Club. *(David Jowett)*

The work dwindled away. Then Davy Corporation said they were going to close the place down.

What year are we talking about now?

Oh 1984, something like that. It was taken over by a company called ITM. It had two managing directors, Brian Pearson and John Wilson and the chairman was Alf Duffield who was chairman of Middlesbrough Football Club for a while. Brian Pearson had been one of the draughtsmen in our heat exchanger drawing office. Taken over by ITM and we were involved mainly with oil-rig work and things like. *(Jim Heward)*

How did you feel in 1984 when the closure was finally announced?

Bloody awful. But those who wanted still had a job, you see, because Alf Duffield took them over. There were some people still had the opportunity for a job. Some people stayed and some people left. I fought to try and keep all the jobs in. *(Thomas Wilson)*

So were you there when it finally closed down then?

Yes I was. I'd gone through all that trauma, and the drama. We were dealing with largely

Davy managers who had a different mindset to the managers of Head's. Full-time union officials seemed to be in and out and it didn't seem to make all that much progress because I don't think that attitude was there for them to change. We had to change, we had changed but we still had to take what was given to us. When the closure was announced, to be quite honest, I wasn't surprised and I was glad in that it ended the uncertainty and worry we had endured for so long. I'd seen the way things were going and I had actually gone back to night school. In the early Eighties I did about three years at night school at Billingham Tech. I don't know what for but I just knew that HW was not going to last. I thought, 'Get yourself a little bit of something behind your name.' Then they announced it was going to be sold to ITM, but you could either have your redundancy or stay and work for ITM. We'd met with these ITM people in the Works Council and asked the question, 'What about the Works Councils, are you going to continue with work?' They said, 'We most certainly will not be continuing with Works Councils like this.' That sort of made my mind up that somewhere outside of Head Wrightson's there was another life. So I just took my redundancy. Left on the twenty-ninth of June 1984. That was our last shift. I was on two till ten at the time. I came home and I thought, 'What have you done?' *(Albert Roxborough)*

Reasons for closure

There was a downturn in the demand for products, but at the same time the Germans in particular were doing research into high-output equipment that we found difficulty competing against. The German company Lurgi was a formidable competitor on sinter plants and won major contracts that a few years earlier would have been taken by us. *(Eric Brown)*

We had an iron foundry at Eaglescliffe. It was a one-product casting operation, made the segments for the London Underground tunnels. Just made one product! Should we have kept it just as a one-product or should we have ever made it as a one-product company? You see what I mean? Inevitably we're going to run out of places to build tube stations and tunnels. The last one was the Jubilee Line. When was that built? And there's not been another one since. I think that aspect of it is very sad and I can only suggest that the blame for that lies at the top and not thinking these things through. *(Ted Sinnot)*

It was always hard in the selling business because we were in depression. We had redundancies at Head Wrightson's Stockton Forge in 1968. I think I counted up once, I lived through twenty-six redundancy programmes. So times were hard. Work got tighter and tighter internationally. The Japanese, the Koreans, became very, very aggressive and they got a lot more state backing than we did. We didn't get any state backing at all, no government money. It was a bit discouraging when you went to a meeting and you put in a bid you thought was a good bid and they turned round and said, 'Well, you're out on your shipping costs.' And you said, 'Well, shipping costs are pretty standard', and they said, 'not if you're Japanese, because they own the shipping line, so they don't put any in.' That was the sort of thing you were up against. It was very, very hard, very hard and very political. So it got harder and harder in heavy engineering, it became unfashionable, really, in a way. *(Barry Preece)*

It started to contract. They stopped using induction furnaces first, and I was still at Stockton Steel Foundry then, but we'd heard that they were shutting the induction furnaces down. They'd started to lay people off but I think that a lot of people had started to see the signs, some of them just got out of it and went to other foundries or other places. The company got money for shutting places down and somebody said they were transferring a lot of work abroad and this was what it was all about. Getting work transferred abroad rather than be made over in this country. *(Eddie Peacock)*

It was developing from what originally was a small family company and growing and becoming a large company of international standing. Of course, that has its own problems because the engineering industry was very, very competitive and it was very difficult for a small firm to remain in business. But they managed that for quite a long time, then they were taken over by Davy, and Davy was taken over in turn by Kvaerner and so it goes on. *(Joe Doran)*

I think Head Wrightson suffered from top management, Board level in certain areas. I don't think they were politically astute enough or well connected enough, because that's always very important. But, you know, even the mighty Davy fell in the end. *(Barry Preece)*

I think they tried to move with the times but I think they were an old-fashioned company trying to work in a modern environment, and they weren't used to this. What had happened in the past was if things went wrong on a contract our Managing Director would possibly go and see their Managing Director and say, 'Look things aren't right,' and it would be sorted. All of a sudden the accountants moved in and the accountants started to run the business rather than the engineers running the business. And our people weren't as sharp as the other people. We got ourselves into a lot of trouble through the naivety of some of the people in certain positions who really weren't up to the mark. *(John Heath)*

A major thing that came through in seventy-three, as well, was suddenly something called inflation. Now inflation had been with us a long time, but we were suddenly facing seventeen, twenty per cent inflation. Now in an industrial context, pricing and contract prices you'd just throw out of the window. We used to have things called escalation formulae and you always tried to write it as cleverly as you possibly could in the contract but it couldn't cope. There was no way it could cope with these sorts of price increases so the company was losing money on these contracts. I remember one year the whole profit from Head Wrightson Group was eight hundred thousand pounds, paid to Barclay's Bank in interest. Eight hundred thousand pounds. The whole of the profit had gone in trying to fund the business. So the company was struggling to make a go of it. *(Robin Millman)*

A lot of people were working under a lot of pressure to try and get jobs done, perhaps trying to get too many jobs done, and so people didn't have these arguments for the sake of it, it was because they were passionate about succeeding in really what were very difficult circumstances. The time that I was moving into Teesdale the writing was on the wall for British manufacturing and it was an agonising decline whatever we tried to do. I suppose when you think about it, the whole of the company, we were the architects of our own downfall because we were selling technology abroad. But if we hadn't done that then the company would have failed earlier. So it prolonged the inevitable. Whatever people say about the government, and this has been going on for thirty or forty years, the government has not supported industry and manufacturing. You can't compete with countries where the proverbial bowl of rice is a weekly wage. It might not be quite that in China now but it's still very cheap, and it's easy to buy the technology and run the plant with relatively unskilled labour force. In the Seventies or the early Eighties I was buying steel from Brazil and Poland because we'd built the blast furnaces there, steel-making plant. Which of course, reduces the need for domestic supply of the same. *(Barrie Hope)*

But one of the things that the management of the company got wrong is that they did not know how to change the emphasis. There were a lot of damned good foremen in the workshops but when Head Wrightson were going down the 'Swanee' what was noticeable, you were not getting the younger end in. Nearly all the foremen were probably late fifties, going into their sixties and they were retiring. There was nobody coming through who had the knowledge to do something about it. The management was remiss in that. At Head Wrightson you had a lot of local engineers, they'd been brought up in the area, they'd been brought into Head Wrightson and they knew Head Wrightson products pretty well, and in a normal sort of world, where competition wasn't quite so fierce, they would have done okay. They knew what they were doing but they had a certain pace about them and I think they were lacking technology. Because in those days it was starting to be the end of the Raj. Late Sixties, 1970s, this country could no longer just expect to be handed work on a plate, as we used to be, contracts from India, from Australia, from Africa. You had to go out there and you had to start fighting the Japanese, you had to start fighting the Koreans, you had to start fighting all the Far Eastern companies and it was hard work and the management failed miserably. Senior management I'm talking about, failed miserably to recognise that what they had to do was completely change the character. Not so much of the workshops, because that would have happened eventually, but the character of the front end in the engineering knowledge and engineering expertise, and bringing and keeping us up to date. We used to produce a lot of vessels for companies that went out there and did specific tasks. What we never did, which we should have done, and I advocated this so many times, we should have gone out to those sites where those vessels were working and we should have talked to the guys who were running those vessels and finding out what problems they'd had, what problems our manufacturing and our designs had caused them and how we could develop them better. There was no sense of development design in there. *(Ken Pattison)*

Essentially, Head Wrightson's worked a lot for the nationalised industries which slowly contracted. Stockton Forge closed. They specialised in mining. We got some of their work. Middlesbrough Works, who supplied specialised equipment to the steel industry, closed and their work was concentrated at Teesdale. But there was a declining order book, because the collieries were shutting right, left and centre, steel plants were shutting right, left and centre. We were building steel plants for abroad and showing them how to build them. I can remember, when I was in my early days as an apprentice, the company was involved in the construction of the steel plant at Durgapur, and we sent people out there to show them how to put it together and run it. Well it's only going to go one way, that. Export abroad and they take it to bits and find how it was put together. So we were in a contracting industry. If you look around Teesside, Ashmore's shut well before we did. Metrovick's, who made railway carriages, they also closed well before we did. So Head's seemed to hang on, although the satellite plants were closed. *(Albert Roxborough)*

When the aluminium section folded, people could buy greenhouses at knock-down prices and there were all sorts of things. Pots and pans that were made of aluminium were available to the employees at discount prices.

So why do you think the aluminium failed?

Because of the market, we just couldn't compete against the others because Head Wrightson's were a universal engineer, and if anything needed doing, and if somebody placed an order, they would bid for it. They were too much of an all-rounder. They had the capability to do any sort of thing. If you had an apprenticeship at Head Wrightson's they generally reckoned that you could work anywhere, because the way you were instructed, the way you were, and the type of work that was available to you, there was great variety. *(Allan Ayre)*

They were classic good old days where everybody had a reserved car parking space, apart from the works' employees, and many other status-related perks. For example, chauffeurs took you to, and met you, at the airport. It was quite common for chauffeurs to travel to Heathrow, London, to meet someone who didn't want to kick their heels for a few hours until the teatime flight to Teesside. The sad thing was that too many people, in their heart of hearts, really wanted those days back regardless of the cost and consequences. They would have their own rules about what time they would charge a furnace. In other words, they wouldn't charge a furnace until the shift started. Ideally, and logically, a small team could have come in early before the shift started to charge the furnace. This would have meant that a hammer crew could immediately start production at the beginning of the shift. There were also similar complex arrangements involving the time allowances to change press tools. All these complexities came at a very expensive cost. The result was that management didn't manage the men and the business, and the net result was total chaos and very big losses. The housekeeping and the disciplines required for success just didn't exist in the business. It was, inherently, at one time a very profitable business and it had just drifted obliviously onwards when, at the same time, many of its competitors had made very sound investments in equipment, skills and marketing. It's only when you wake up one morning that you suddenly realise that the world has become a totally different place and that you have to accept the fact that you are into deep losses and serious trouble. *(Ian Ford)*

It was the front end where the problems were. Because you had to maintain specialists in wagon design, you had to maintain specialists in heat exchangers, pressure vessels, rotary dryers. Now that was not necessarily a bad thing but they were too diverse, they were too split. They needed pulling together. You needed younger blood in who had been trained. You needed computerisation and you needed to keep up to date. At the front end you had a massive overhead which the works had to support and at the end of the day that in part helped to pull the company down. *(Ken Pattison)*

Thoughts about Head Wrightson closure

We thought there'd always be a Head Wrightson because of its history and the way it had gone, and it was really a very well respected company that had done work all over the world, bridges and goodness only knows what. When the Forge closed I think people were disappointed but I think they really knew that things had to change. We didn't want to be a dinosaur, and that these things had got to happen if we were going to be successful in the modern world. *(Eric Brown)*

I was bitter. I was bitter at the way it was done. I realise that people a lot better educated than me could have done something about it. For a long time Head Wrightson's had been making stuff to sell abroad into the big wide-world open market but at the same time they were doing this they were cutting their own throats and someone should have realised. Because eventually they were selling blast furnaces. They were selling top-class machinery that would last for a lifetime and making tin cans and pellets and Concast. You've probably heard of Concast, it's continuous-casting plant that was built at Middlesbrough Works over thirty years ago and it's still turning out. But you sell that to somewhere in Brazil or to India, they don't need to come back to this country any more to buy. I always remember reading an article about we built a tin line for Ebbw Vale in Wales, and it was called the Rolls-Royce of tin lines where you actually rolled your mild steel and you covered it in tin, and it went through this marvellous machine - the classifier - and I helped build that. They said it was unbelievably fast and quick and it was a testament to the industry. And I always remember someone said at the time Head Wrightson's were the Rolls-Royce of engineering. *(Stuart Thompson)*

I joined them in 1958 and stayed until 1982. I was just sixty and things had changed. I didn't have the freedom I had earlier on. Everything had to have a meeting once it was taken over. A meeting with twenty people attending of which two were taking part but all the costs were being added up to the job. I kept being asked why is it just so man-hour expensive. Because with having meetings and there's nobody doing anything apart from myself and somebody else. So yes, I was fed up at the end. But in the early days I had enjoyed it. *(Ron Hughes)*

We got an idea it was closing when Margaret Thatcher came on the scene, and then there were little rumours going round the works, 'Head Wrightson's closing', but nobody believed it. Then our shop stewards got wind of it and they said it could be closing, and still nobody would believe it till the crunch came. Believe me, once the government says, 'It's closing,' nothing on this earth will save it. There was nothing wrong with the conditions and the equipment. The equipment was marvellous, it was always being updated, and wherever it could be updated it was updated. For instance, we had a train that would pull various pieces or equipment to different places where it needed to be delivered. Then we had a tractor which we used with a trailer for quickness to deliver plates, beams, joists, channels, whatever, to different parts of the works. So yes, it was constantly being upgraded. The technology was good. *(Harry Foster)*

When I joined Teesdale in seventy-three I think I seem to recall we were about 1,200 people – big, which was probably less than half of what it had been not many years earlier. By the time we got to something like 1980 I think we were about 600. You know, the writing was on the wall for the reasons I've said before. So this passion or this shouting, however you want to describe it, I think came about for two reasons. They were passionate about the company because some of them had been there for years. It was the only employment they'd ever known. Because people were not as concerned to move as they are now. So they were fighting their corner with passion but there was also frustration. So it was easy to sit there at the time and say, 'For God's sake stop shouting, let's conduct ourselves calmly.' That's with the benefit of hindsight. But it was frustration and passion. *(Barrie Hope)*

There were, of course, no more coal mines. So collectively whether somebody had come to that conclusion, but who it was I would have thought it certainly was not somebody from the Forge. I think you would have to go back and at that time the only other person that I knew who was top of the tree was John Eccles. We certainly weren't called into a meeting by any management or anything like that, and to this day I'm still baffled. I don't think it sank in until I was going home and I bought the *Evening Gazette*. And it was big headlines in the *Gazette*, 'Stockton Forge To Close'. It was only at that particular time I think that it sank in to say we were closing. *(Trevor Briggs)*

Campaigns against closure

You could have heard a pin drop. People were looking at each other and people were looking at me and saying, 'How long have you known?' And we were declared redundant in April of that year. But in between time we set a big campaign up and if people go in the archives they'll see in the *Gazette* it was running 'Joe Jobless' and they would have backed us to the hilt, us and Haverton Hill (Steelcast) because they were closing. I went down to London and I was on a TV documentary, *World In Action*, manufacturing being sliced in the North East, jobs cut at a frightening rate and all this sort of thing. Anyway, we went to all the powers that be and met all these MPs, did everything we could. In the end it closed and that was it. I was there till the end. There was lots of work to do. We had a lock-in, we took the keys and we said, 'Nothing, nothing's going out', and there was nothing left the factory from that day. We had a big campaign, people were putting money in because we had a fighting fund to pay for our expenses and we were doing leaflets. And Davy's at Sheffield, we went down to see the shop stewards there. They gave us about a thousand pounds towards our fighting fund, that's the workforce not the

The Head Wrightson Machine Company action committee outside their workshops. This committee, comprised of employees from all sections of the works, led by Stuart Thompson (in front of the picture) fought a vigorous, robust fight against closure. Their efforts, involving collecting a fighting fund levy from all employees and meeting with MPs and trade union officials from other companies, sadly came to nought as the company's determination to close the works went ahead. (Picture courtesy The Northern Echo)

management, because they were disgusted. *(Stuart Thompson)*

We started off and everybody's idea was, 'Right, we're not going to let it close, there's no question of its going to close, we are going to fight to keep it open.' And on reflection, the management and everybody else were of the same mind. But it was obvious they were so determined to close it, and we were so busy trying to fight to keep it open we never left enough time to negotiate to try to get a better deal. I think everybody who left got what they were entitled to. But it was absolutely just the total bare minimum, nothing extra whatsoever, after people had put in thirty, forty years' service. *(Trevor Briggs)*

The other lads were allowed to go for job interviews without loss of earnings. They were encouraged to, people were coming on site. Smith's Dock had got a lot of work on so they came down and gave a bit of a presentation and said that they wanted fitters to work at Smith's Dock. There were a lot of small machine shops. There was the Middlesbrough Machine Shop, mass of machine companies, they'd all set up over the years and they were picking up work off the big people like Head Wrightson's. Anything that we had too much work going on, we'd subcontract out to these people. So once they knew, I mean if you worked at Head Wrightson's, you'd get a job anywhere. At the time we didn't have a redundancy scheme. The government had just introduced this sort of half-hearted redundancy payment so we said, 'Well, what about the company putting in something?' So in the end after a lot of argy-bargy the company addressed it and paid the same as this government redundancy scheme, which wasn't a lot but it gave a bit of comfort to someone's pockets. Those that didn't get fixed up straight away, it gave them something. *(Stuart Thompson)*

Final days

We had gone in and were collecting all our bits and pieces up and the tools that we'd had over the years. I remember us all trooping out and, as I say, there were more tears and one thing and another, and then they told us to go back in a week's time where we were given our last pay. It was very emotional and we even decided very quickly we would have a big concert with everybody from the Forge. We went to a club in Stockton actually. We hired the room and even Albert Snaith came over and spoke and said how he was sorry and that there was a lot of people with a lot of very fantastic skills, and one thing and another. He put it across very well, but deep down everybody was upset. I would say that some people came out of it very well because they probably wouldn't have gone to other companies had it not closed down. So to my knowledge, I did know one or two people who did very well. *(Trevor Briggs)*

The last day we had to come into work but not to work. We had to come into work to pick our last cheques up. That was done in alphabetical order. But that night we had a knees-up in the Golden Eagle at Thornaby. The balance of our fighting fund was given to the hospital, for at that time I think it was saving up for cancer research, or was it an iron lung or something? Our meal was classed as 'The Last Supper'. There was a big spread in the *Gazette*. There were thirteen of us on this fighting committee and it said, 'The Last Supper' and the *Gazette* reporters came down and took photographs and did other things. It was good. *(Stuart Thompson)*

At the redundant employees 'Last Supper' in the Golden Eagle at Thornaby on 27th April 1979, a donation from their fighting fund was made to the Cleveland Scanner Campaign. Committee chairman Stuart Thompson said, 'We wanted to leave with dignity but to enjoy ourselves at this social event.'

Chapter 11

'I loved it': final thoughts

I enjoyed it. It was an enjoyable place to work. The people were good, characters were good, particularly the staff people. We used to go out socially. So it was just a nice place to work for. Never the best of pay for us but you just enjoyed it. It also helps that you're close to home. I didn't have a lot of travelling to do. But, as I said earlier, it's a place I think that you either love or hate. *(Barry Davison)*

I remember when I was a very young child he used to come home and he was talking about the shop and, 'So and so came into the shop.' Or, 'I did so and so in the shop.' I thought it was like a grocer's shop or something like that. I don't know how old I was when I realised that the shop wasn't a shop as I knew it. I remember once, my parents were out at a dance and one of the workmen came and told me this machine had broken down. I think it was a machine called a little shaper, but I got it wrong and when my dad came in I said, 'The big sifter's broken down.' He said, 'I don't know what that is.' It was a little shaper, probably, but I got it wrong. So for years afterwards he used to tease me about this big sifter that I'd invented. *(Kath Riley)*

I liked horizontal boring. I loved it. It's great when you get a job and it all wants machining out. Then when it's all finished, 'Oh it's great that, it looks great.' I took pride in my job. Every job I have done. Well, we all did. You had to because it had to be right. You couldn't say, 'Oh that'll do.' Had to take pride in it. *(Dennis Johnson)*

There were a lot of long-serving people with Head Wrightson's, certainly. They seemed to be a loyal lot of people. I don't think Head's were the greatest. I don't think they paid the greatest wages of any company around but the people seemed to like working for Head's. *(Peter French)*

Everybody knew each other at Head Wrightson. It was a big family community and everybody knew one another and it was Thornaby through and through. Everybody knew everybody and there were the sons and fathers and grandfathers right through, and in every family. You always thought you'd go to somebody and say, 'Well when did you start?' 'Oh so and so.' 'Who got you in, who gave you the job? Who's your dad?' or, 'who's your granddad?' or, 'who's your uncle?' It was just like that at Head Wrightson. But it was all fun as well. *(Dennis Longstaff)*

I enjoyed working at Head Wrightson's. I was really taught and learnt a lot through them. What not to do, and how to do something properly. It was just a regret the way things have happened to them. It meant that they're not here nowadays. *(Eddie Peacock)*

The firm seemed to be almost a family, that you were well thought of, you were well looked after. Everybody seemed to be kind to you and encouraging and helpful, so it was really a happy place to work. *(Alan Sowerby)*

It is a great pity that such companies as Head's have not survived. Head Wrightson had a fantastic manufacturing base and were involved in such a huge variety of engineering projects all over the world, not forgetting all the skilled people working for them. We now have a situation in this country that very few companies exist that offer the training and opportunities that Head Wrightson did, and I feel that it is today's youngsters that have been let down. *(Ken Lee)*

I was content. They were a very nice group of people you were working with, and it was very much a family firm, family atmosphere. They looked after you well. *(Michael Waring)*

If you had an apprenticeship from Head Wrightson you could go anywhere, anywhere you liked. If you served your time at Head Wrightson's you could go to any firm in the country or any firm in the world and you'd get a start because you were skilled. That's why I can't understand why it shut down. There are no apprenticeships like it now. Where's the skill? Nothing can beat doing your time and learning from people with skills. *(Harry Foster)*

I enjoyed Head's. I enjoyed the people there, I enjoyed the job. It suited me down to the ground and I still grieve when I go past there now and I see all those bloody stupid houses there instead of what used to be there. Mrs. Thatcher said, 'The phoenix will rise.' What a load of crap. I mean it rose, and it was bloody houses for students. *(Ken Pattison)*

What did it do for me? It made me ambitious. And it made me a perfectionist in what I was doing because you were in a crowd of people, of scientists, who were perfectionists. They did fantastic work. They were top of the game, and there's no way I wasn't going to be the same. Everybody was so helpful. *(Alan Simpson)*

I was looking at something on the Internet the other day and I recognised the old office building, which was taken from above Teesside, and then all the plants and the forges around. I can remember the noise that it was frenetic. The heat, the sounds, the smells. It was 'boom', and I was very, very young but it struck me as being a kind of powerhouse. It was very busy, very active, very productive. It was the core of engineering on Teesside. The powerhouse of the North East of England, and it was a great pleasure and a privilege to see it all. I enjoyed it. *(Simon Wrightson)*

My dad worked there, I worked there, my husband worked there and my brother did an apprenticeship there until that was cut short. It was just the feeling of everybody's family. Lots of families had a connection with Head Wrightson. There was a community spirit. I used to love it. *(Barbara Mifrej)*

Definitely the best job I've ever had. Whether it's because it was my first job, I don't know. But I can honestly put my hand on heart and say, if it was open tomorrow and I had a chance to go back, I would have been there like a flash. *(John Stainthorpe)*

I enjoyed it while I was there; it's a pleasant thing to look back on. A lot of good friends, a lot of nice memories. *(Albert Roxborough)*

Friday June 29th 1984. The Machine Shop's 2-10pm final shift. Photograph taken by P. McGann (deceased), seen far left.

Contributors

Our contributors have been drawn from across the company's works and offices on Teesside and represent a good mix of trades, skills and professions within the group encompassing a wide age range. Sadly four contributors have died since being interviewed – Max Clark, John Fuller, Jim Smiles and Maynard Wilson.

David Auld (1949-79)
M'Bro Works Sales Engineer

Allan Ayre (1947-81)
Forge and HWT Erection Engineer

Ron Baker (1944-78)
HWT Maintenance Electrician

Wilf Bradley (1937-84)
Commercial

Trevor Briggs (1950-84)
Forge Fitting Shop / Stampings

Fred Britton (1945-63)
HW & Stampings Purchasing

Eric Brown (1953-84)
HWISWEL Project Director

Ted Burridge (1947-84)
HWT Fitting Shop

Robert Chaney (1958-75)
Stockton Steel Foundry

Keith Chapman (1959-78)
M'Bro Works Turner & Planning

Max Clark (1956-80)
HWISWEL Sales & Marketing Manager (Deceased)

Bob Close (1948-83)
HWT Fitter / Inspector

Rodney Crosbie (1960-79)
HWT Erection Stores

Ken Davies (1955-61)
HWT Bridge Yard Plater

Ken Davies (1964-84)
HWT Bridge Yard Slinger

Barry Davison (1977-87)
Stampings Inspection

Derek Delahaye (1945-51)
HW Thornaby Stampings

Joe Doran (1965-78)
Group Personnel Manager

Les Ellis (1940-84)
Stockton Forge Fitting Shop & Training School

John Everett (1969-84)
Stampings Hammer Operator

Steve Featherstone (1974-84)
HWT Bridge Yard Plater

Colin Fletcher (1954-75)
Steel Foundry Shipping Office

Ian Ford (1979-84)
Stampings Managing Director

Harry Foster (1947-84)
HWT Bridge Yard Plater

Peter French (1972-84)
HW & Co Pensions

John Fuller (1965-78)
MD Eaglescliffe Iron Foundry
(Deceased)

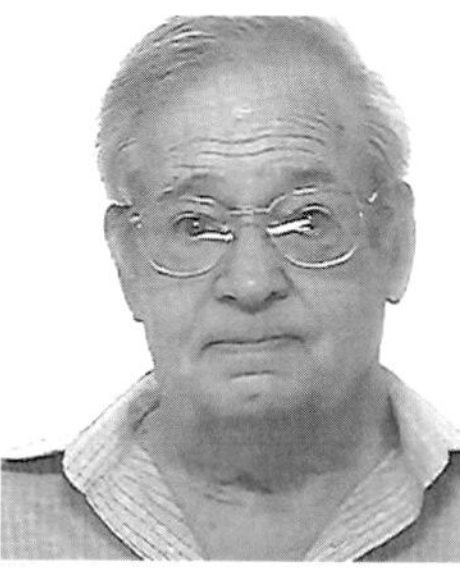
John Glasper (1945-48)
HWT Draughtsman

John Harding (1962-72)
Thornaby Steel Foundry Welder

Jack Hare (1970-80)
M'Bro Works Turner

Cath Harrison (1952-56)
HW Bridge Yard, Thornaby,
Windy Driller's Mate

Doug Hauxwell (1969-79)
Steel Foundry Pattern-Maker

Ian Hayley (1966-84)
HWISWEL, Draughtsman

Wendy Heald (1957-62)
HWT Secretary

John Heath (1953-84)
HWT Template Shop & Drawing Office

John Heighly (1943-80)
Steel Foundry Pattern-Maker

Mrs. Irene Henderson (1953-64)
HWT Tracer

Jim Heward (1951-84)
HWT Fitting Shop and Planning

Barrie Hope (1966-84)
R&D Physicist

Margaret Hope (1956-64)
HWT Secretary

Billy Hornby (1953-60)
Stockton Forge Plater

Ron Hughes (1958-82)
HW Nuclear Division Engineer

Stan Hume (1940-79)
HWT Heavy Machine Shop & Rate Fixer

Bob Irwin (1953-63)
HWT Joiner

Dennis Johnson (1949-84)
HWT Heavy Machine Shop

David Jowett (1966-81)
Company Secretary

John Kirk (1956-66)
HWT Bridge Yard Plater

Ken Lee (1961-73)
HW Nuclear Dept.
Draughtsman / Site Engineer

Tony Lodge (1964-81)
Steelcast Maintenance Electrician

Dennis Longstaff (1971-83)
HWT Plater

Jim Matthews (1975-84)
Stampings Metallurgist

Norman Metcalfe (1962-77)
Teesdale Erection Dept

Barbara Mifrej
Eaglescliffe & Thornaby Canteen

Robin Millman (1974-84)
HWISWEL

Gerald Morton (1958-64)
HWISWEL Civil Engineer

Michael Nichol (1966-80)
Steel Foundry Moulder

Ron Nichol (1942-83)
Steel Foundry Pattern-Maker

Margaret Partridge (1955-84)
HWT & HWISWEL Secretary

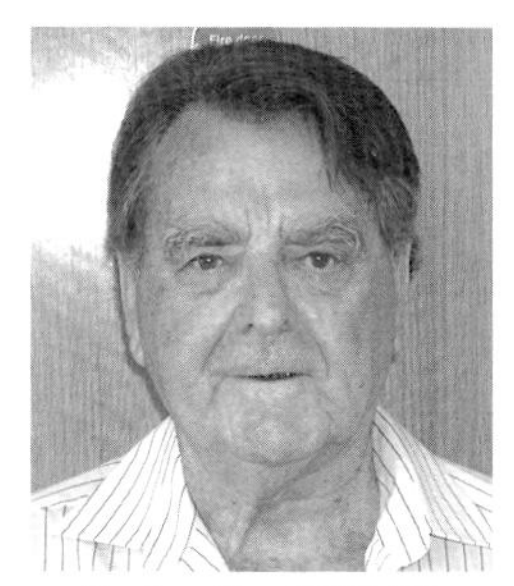
Pat Partridge (1949-68)
HWT Maintenance Electrician

Ken Pattison (1973-84)
HWT Project Engineer

Eddie Peacock (1958-80)
Steel Foundry Moulder

Ken Peacock (1962-75)
Stockton Forge Fitting Shop & HWT Planning

Ken Pelmear (1939-51)
HW Maintenance

Mrs. Norma Pelmear (1942-51)
HW Secretarial

Jack Picken (1945-61)
HWT Draughtsman

Barry Preece (1950-84)
Stockton Forge Template Shop & HWT Sales Manager

Derek Proctor (1963-84)
HWT Maintenance Fitter

Don Raper (1950-57)
HW Wages Department Forge & HWT

John Reeve (1952-62)
Stockton Steel Foundry Electrician

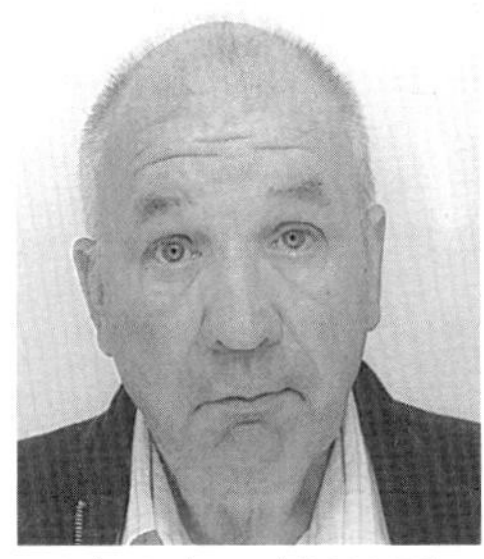
John Richmond (1964-74)
M'Bro Works Fitting Shop

Kath Riley
Memories of father, Ted Dalgliesh, Forge Fitting Shop

Richard Robinson (1953-78)
M'Bro Works Maintenance Fitter

Albert Roxborough (1955-84)
HWT Tool Room Fitter

Bill Sharp (1962-84)
HWT Fitter / Inspector

Ray Shaw (1941-84)
Stockton Forge Chief Draughtsman

Alan Simpson (1958-81)
Company Photographer

Anne Simpson (1959-69)
Company Photographer

Ted Sinnot (1962-84)
Forge & HWISWEL Planning Engineer

Jim Smiles (1946-68)
HWT Template Maker & Training School (Deceased)

Alan Sowerby (1934-73)
Stockton Forge & HWT Draughtsman

John Stainthorpe (1980-84)
HWT Machine Shop

Frank Stephenson (1942-71)
Bridge Yard & Drawing Office

Chris Stoddart (1970-78)
HWISWEL Engineer

Noel Thompson (1959-69)
M'Bro Works Turner

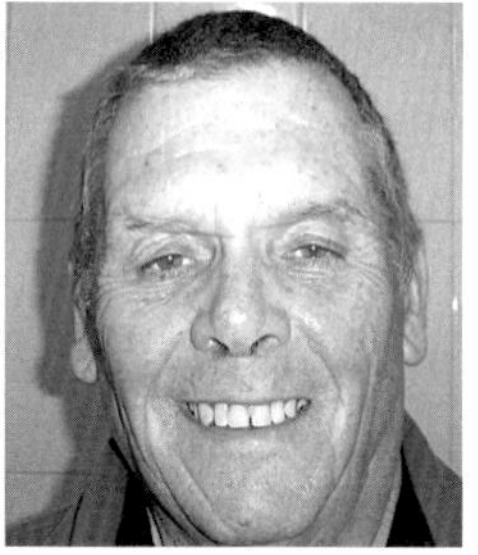
Stuart Thompson (1965-80)
M'Bro Works Fitting shop

Enid Thurlwell (1942-84)
HW Personnel, Steel Foundry & Pensions Secretary

Charlie Tighe (1962-78)
HWT Welder & Welding Engineer

Norman Toulson (1948-56)
Stockton Forge Plater

Bob Waller (1937-61)
HW & Co Buyer

Michael Waring (1959-68)
M'Bro Works, Design Engineer

Connie Wass (1941-48)
HW Thornaby Machine Operator

Fred Watson (1939-81)
HWT Paint and Despatch

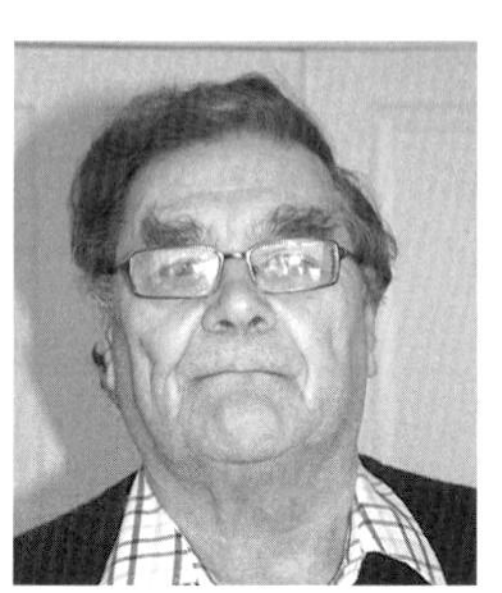
Colin Waugh (1957-78)
Assistant Foundry Manager

Les Wilson (1936-84)
HWT Template Maker & Planner

Maynard Wilson (1928-78)
HWT Bridge Yard Manager (Deceased)

Tom Wilson (1946-84)
HWT Fitting Shop

Bob Wright (1947-84)
Forge Engineer,
HWT Engineering Director

Simon Wrightson
Memories of father,
Mr. Peter Wrightson Joint MD

Photographic Archives

Launch of a Bradwell boiler circa 1950s. (Remembering Thornaby Group)

HWT Template Shop circa 1970s. (HW Photographic Section)

Teesdale Maintenance Inter-departmental football finalists June 1978. Back row (L-R) G. Parkin, C. McArthur, B. Cross, F. Jopling, R. Barron, D. Proctor, P. Moor. Front row (L-R) D. Laverick, D. White, D. Nolan, E. Kilvington, D. Wright. (Wright Ahead)

HW Angling Association arriving at Eryholme to compete for the Sir John Wrightson Shield. (Wright Ahead October 1978)

After work away from it all. HW Thornaby employees enjoying walking on the North York Moors circa 1970s. (Photograph courtesy E. Burridge)

HW Works Band. (Remembering Thornaby Group)

Stockton Forge trip away circa 1960s. (Photograph courtesy Bill Hornby)

To mark the occasion of the election of HW Stockton Forge employee John Scott to be Mayor of Thornaby in 1953, HW donated the Mayor's robe and hat. (Another HW employee, Walter Wood, was elected Mayor in 1964.) (Photograph courtesy of The Northern Echo)

Senior Staff Guild Chairman's regalia. (Wright Ahead)

Thornaby Town library, endowed by Thomas Wrightson. (Photograph by D. Proctor)

Redcar Pier built in 1872/3 with a total length of 1,300 feet. (Head Wrightson Album of Manufactures 1903 edition)

Plate girders for the Pretoria-Pietersburg Railway. HW supplied fifteen bridges for the 200 mile railway. (Head Wrightson Album of Manufactures 1903 edition)

Bridge for the Natal Government Railway designed to carry a single railway line. The bridge is shown under test. (Head Wrightson Album of Manufactures 1903 edition)

Hydraulic casting crane for Steel Melting Shop. Capable of lifting 15 tons of molten metal on a carriage travelling 3 feet at a radius of 20 feet. (Head Wrightson Album of Manufactures 1903 edition)

Cast-iron tunnel lining for the City & South London Electric Railway. (Head Wrightson Album of Manufactures 1903 edition)

Floating-head-type heat exchanger. (Company brochure 1952)

One of six caissons for the Kotri Bridge over the river Indus, India. (Head Wrightson Album of Manufactures 1903 edition)

Seventy-two inch by twenty inch Windbox Sintering machine. (Company brochure 1952)

Twelve cubic capacity clay gun. (Company brochure 1952)

Upcut shear manufactured by Middlesbrough Machine Company. (Company brochure 1952)

In the 1950/60s the HW House Magazine *Wright Ahead* produced profiles of long serving personalities from around the various Teesside sites accompanied by a pencil sketch. Here are a few examples from *Wright Ahead* supplied by D. Longstaff.

T. Dea. (November 1957)
53 years' total service

Retired as a crane driver in the Thornaby Bridge Yard in 1957. Previously he had been a labourer, driller, slinger before crane driving for 35 years. He recalled belt-driven machines, the manufacture of many bridges, unpaid holidays, working a 53 hour week and the improvement in working conditions.

R. Higgin (March 1956)
53 years' service

A lifetime Thornaby resident who started work in the Thornaby Iron Foundry pouring and slinging hot metal in the ingot shop. He moved to Egglescliffe Iron Foundry as an ordinary slinger as 'he doesn't stand the heat so well nowadays'. He preferred working at Thornaby as there was less travelling.

T.E. Smith (June 1952)
53 years' service

Still working at 69 years old. He followed his father who worked as a coachman and later horse keeper for HW from 1898. Mr. Smith started in the Bridge Yard and later worked in the old factory. For a while he drove the work's horse and cart but when it was sold in 1932 he worked in the Machine Shop as a labourer.

I. (Tutty) Smith (March 1952)
73 years' total service

Joined in 1885 as a skimmer boy, aged 12 years, in the Iron Foundry at Teesdale and recalled the Steel Foundry site being green fields. Remembers Sir John and Mr. Peter working near him during their apprentice training. He transferred to Stampings. He worked for seven foremen and said at the interview he is not planning retirement.

J.W. Wardle (April 1958)
48 years' split service

Started at the Forge as an apprentice draughtsman in 1903. Appointed Chief Draughtsman in 1925 and later General Manager. When the Forge became a subsidiary company he was appointed Managing Director. A keen amateur historian who wrote a 'History of Yarm' and a 'History of Head Wrightson'.

J. Franklin (June 1956)
44 years' service

Commenced work at the Forge in 1912 on a drilling machine and worked his way through various machines ending up on the big lathe. After a spell in the RAF he worked as a journey-man fitter then in 1939 transferred to Thornaby as assistant foreman later taking overall responsibility of the Machine and Fitting shops.

Colour Archives

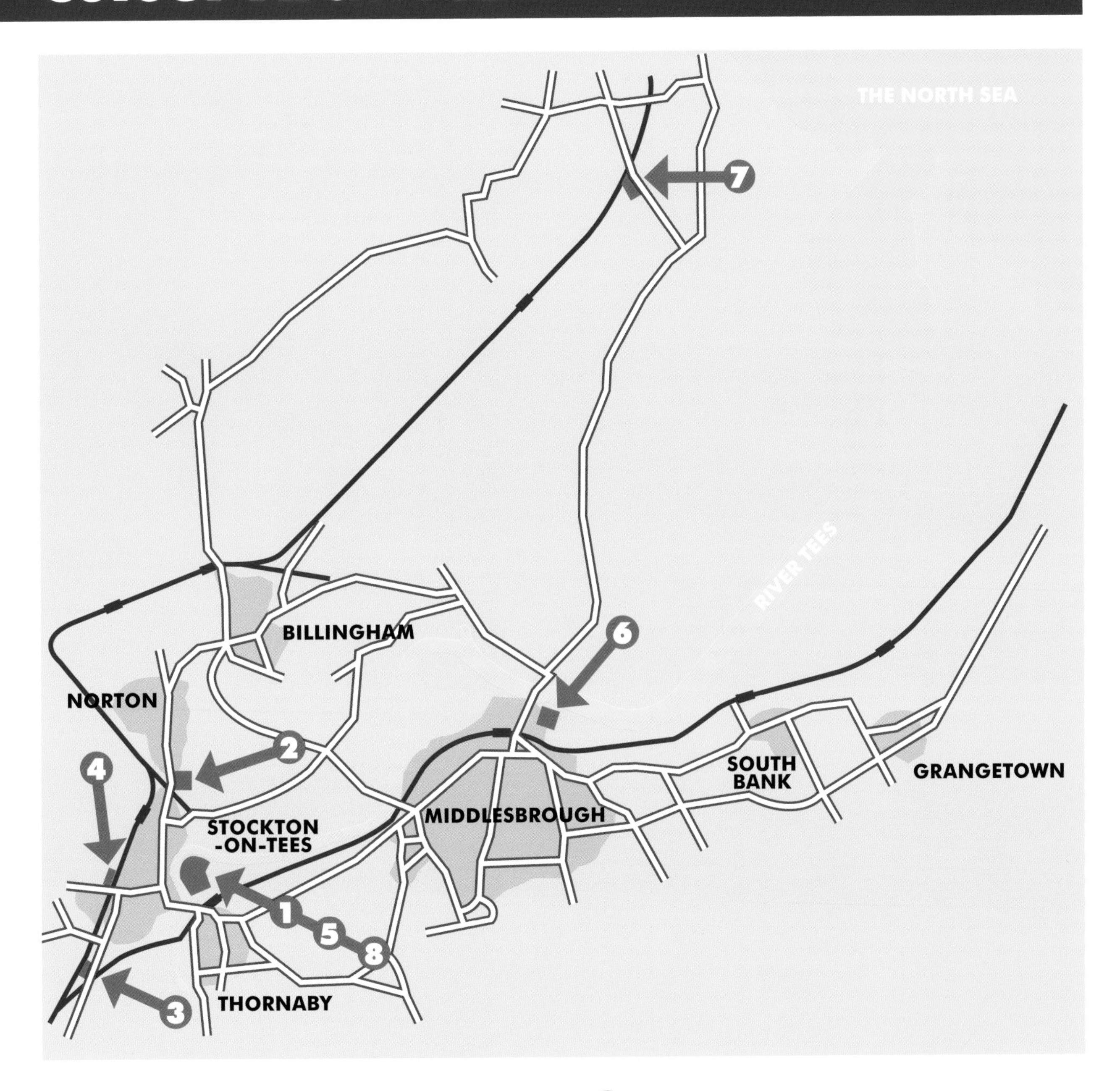

1. Head Wrightson Teesdale Iron Works

   Head Wrightson Steel Foundries

   Head Wrightson Process Engineering Limited

   Head Wrightson Iron and Steel Works Engineering Limited

   Head Wrightson Teesdale

   Head Wrightson Research & Development (R&D)

2. Head Wrightson Stockton Forge
3. Head Wrightson Egglescliffe Iron Foundry
4. Head Wrightson Stockton Steel Foundries Limited
5. Head Wrightson Alloy Steel Foundry
6. Head Wrightson Machine Co. Limited
7. Head Wrightson Stampings Limited
8. Head Wrightson Aluminium Limited

Thornaby steel stockyard circa 1940s. It stocked plates for fabrication and billets for the stamping operation. The Bridge Yard is straight ahead, the Stampings operation behind the camera man. The man in the foreground is Mr. Preece, a metallurgist. It must be lunch time as two boys can be seen running. (Photograph courtesy B. Preece)

A view of the Thornaby stamping operation. (Photograph courtesy B. Preece)

Foreman and manager discuss a machining operation at Middlesbrough Works. Horizontal borer in background. (Company brochure)

Horizontal boring machine at Middlesbrough Works. Inspector checking machining work. (Company brochure)

Innocenti horizontal boring machine in the Heavy Plate Shop at HWT Thornaby. This machine was previously at Middlesbrough Works. (Company brochure)

A stack of completed pallet frames awaiting shipment. (Photograph courtesy A. Simpson)

Ball mill nearing completion at the Forge. (Company brochure)

Completed heat exchangers ready for shipment to Mexico. (Photograph courtesy A. Simpson)

Three ethanol columns leaving the works. (Photograph courtesy A. Simpson)

Pegson Company body casting (25 tons) coming out of the annealing furnace at Billingham Steelcast. (Photograph courtesy A. Simpson)

Completed ball mill in the Heavy Plate Shop at HWT. (HW Photographic Section)

Craven lathe sited in the Heavy Plate Shop at HWT which could accommodate work 45 feet between centres with a maximum swing of 27¼ feet. (HW Photographic Section)

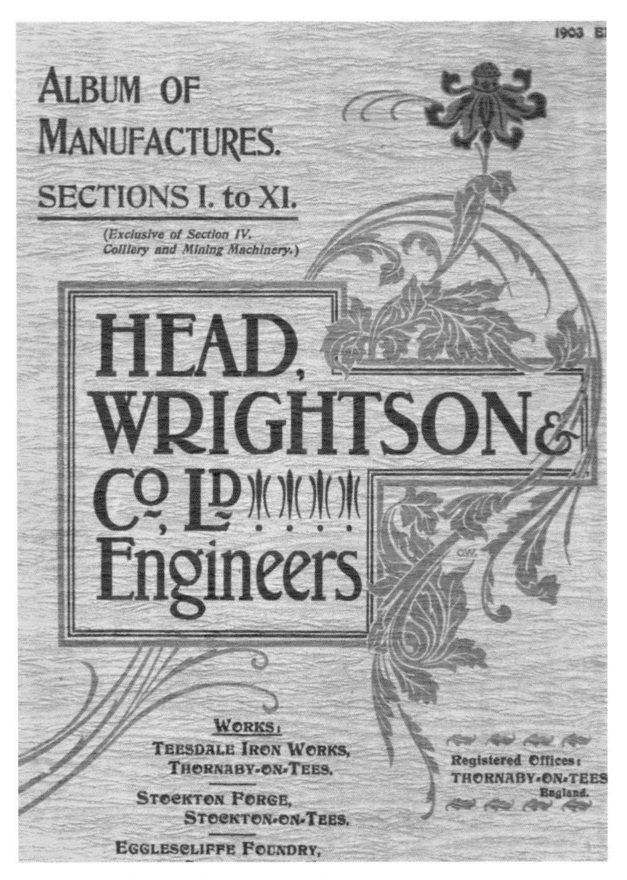

Cover of the 1903 'Album of Manufactures' company products brochure. (Courtesy of G. Eggett)

ICI column construction in the Heavy Plate Shop at HWT. (Northern Photographic Services)

These rolls, installed in Teesdale Bridge Yard in the mid seventies, were one of the largest four-roll hydraulic-operated machines in Europe. The foundations for this machine, weighing two hundred tons, were jokingly referred to as a 'swimming pool' for employees, as a pit around 18m square by 10m deep was excavated across bays 3 and 4 at the south end of the Bridge Yard, allowing for a five-metre-thick concrete base foundation. Four Italian engineers sent to install the machine were on site for many weeks, assisted by HW maintenance staff. Hydraulic power, from eight huge pumps drawing on 1,000 gallons of hydraulic oil, enabled cold rolling of 75mm-thick plate and hot rolling of 100mm-thick plate 3m long. In the picture the operator, Jimmy Allsop (left), and his helper Jim McGregor check the finished diameter, around 3m, of a foundation plate rolled from 90mm-thick plate for the Hong Kong & Shanghai Bank. The rolls used to curve the plate were 1m in diameter and 3m long. (HW Photographic Section)